READER'S DIGEST

30 MINUTE
COOKBOOK

READER'S DIGEST

30 MINUTE
COOKBOOK

Sydney • Auckland

30 MINUTE COOKBOOK

First published in Australia in 1998 by Reader's Digest (Australia) Pty Limited
26–32 Waterloo Street, Surry Hills, NSW 2010

National Library of Australia Cataloguing-in-Publication data:

30 minute cookbook.

Includes index.
ISBN 0 86449 258 8.

1. Cookery. I. Reader's Digest (Australia). II. Title: Thirty minute cookbook.

641.5

CONSULTANT
Pat Alburey

WRITERS
Pat Alburey, Val Barrett, Claire Clifton, Christine France, Carole Handslip, Katie Highfield,
Sybil Kapoor, Patricia Lousada, Jenni Muir, Mary Skinner, Colin Spencer,
Rosemary Stark, Berit Vinegrad

RECIPE TESTERS
Helen Alsop, Terry Farris

PHOTOGRAPHERS
Martin Brigdale, Gus Filgate, John Hollingshead, James Murphy, Peter Myers, Jon Stewart

HOME ECONOMISTS
Louise Pickford, Janet Smith, Linda Tubby, Berit Vinegrad

STYLISTS
Antonia Gaunt, Suzanne Gibbs, Katie Highfield, Penny Markham, Janet Mitchell, Helen Trent

ILLUSTRATORS
Diane Broadley, Stan North

PHOTOGRAPHS: SWIFT FRUITY STARTERS (*page 2*);
CHAR-GRILLED BABY OCTOPUS WITH ROASTED CAPSICUM (*page 3*); WARM DUCK BREAST SALAD
WITH RED WINE AND APPLE (*right*); BAKED APPLE WITH BRIOCHE (*page 6*);
RACK OF VEAL ROASTED WITH GARLIC (*page 7*).

- CONTENTS -

GREAT FOOD IN MINUTES

*T*he skill of creative cookery is not only reserved
for those who have plenty of time to spend in
the kitchen. All of the recipes collected here can be
prepared and cooked within half an hour, with an
emphasis on fresh, healthy ingredients and a little
help from a well-stocked food cupboard.

*Fast-cooked food not only leaves you with more
time to spend on other things, it also carries a health
bonus, as the most valuable nutritional components
of food are best conserved by reducing the amount of
time they are exposed to heat.*

*Best of all, these dishes taste especially delicious,
because when good-quality ingredients are cooked for
the minimum amount of time, they retain all their
fresh, intense flavours.*

THREE STEPS TO SUCCESS

HEAT When you don't want to waste any time in
the kitchen, the first important ingredient is heat:
before you even wash your hands, turn on the oven
or the griller to preheat, or put a kettle or a saucepan
of water on to boil.

Domestic ovens vary a great deal in how long
they take to come to the required temperature. In
general, about 10–15 minutes have been allowed for
preheating the oven. An electric fan oven usually
does not need to be preheated. But if you know that
your oven is slow to heat up, be careful to preset it to
the required temperature for the recipe as long in
advance as you need to, before you start to assemble
the ingredients.

Grillers must also be properly preheated before
use. For fast, even cooking, it is best to have the
griller on high in order to avoid any cool patches,
and to keep an eye on the food. If any tender items
such as fish cutlets seem in danger of burning, drop
the griller rack a few centimetres away from the heat
source, or take the food off the rack and sit it on the
base of the griller tray.

For best results – and quicker cooking – charcoal
barbecues should be lit well in advance so that you
are cooking on coals, not flames. Light a gas
barbecue at least 5 minutes before cooking to allow
the hotplate or grill to heat thoroughly.

ORGANISATION After heat, the next secret of
successful fast cooking is good organisation. Make
sure you have all the ingredients you need at hand –
a dish can easily be ruined if you have to spend time
hunting for the sesame oil, for example, while the
contents of the wok are seconds away from burning.

Before you begin to prepare a recipe, read it
through to familiarise yourself with the method, so
you won't have to waste time stopping to read each
step. Then take a few minutes to assemble the
ingredients, dishes and tools so that everything you
need is within easy reach. This is especially
important when the recipe demands items that you
don't use every day. The hand blender, lemon zester
and nutmeg grater are invaluable aids, but not if they
are in the back of the cupboard.

Clear an adequate working space with plenty of
elbow room. Remove utensils from your working
area after use – clutter will slow you down.

SIZE The third weapon in the hands of the busy
cook is size: the smaller the ingredients, the quicker
they will cook. Chopping, dicing, slicing and grating
food into fast-cooking morsels saves time – and this
preparation is included in the timing of each recipe.

BASIC INGREDIENTS

SALT The amount of salt to add in these recipes has
been left to personal taste. But doctors advise that it
is healthier to reduce salt consumption, so try to add
as little as possible when you cook, and consider
whether you could leave it out altogether if the recipe
includes other salty items such as bacon, capers,
olives, smoked foods or soy sauce.

PEPPER Freshly ground whole black peppercorns
taste much better than ready-ground pepper, and
they last much longer. When pepper is included in a
recipe, it should always be freshly ground.

HERBS When there is no time to develop flavours
through slow cooking, fresh herbs can add a boost of
flavour, and have been specified in most recipes. If
you cannot find a fresh herb, you can substitute a
dried one. The drying process concentrates the
flavour so in general use 1–1½ teaspoons of dried
herb to replace 1 tablespoon of fresh.

USING THE RECIPES

Ingredients are measured in metric cups and spoons: 1 teaspoon equals 5 ml, 1 tablespoon equals 20 ml, 1 cup equals 250 ml. All measures are level.

The recipes serve four people, unless otherwise indicated, but they can be halved to serve two, and this will cut down on the preparation time.

When cooking more than one dish for a meal, choose recipes where the preparation and cooking work together. If a starter or soup has to be prepared and cooked just before serving, select a main course recipe that can be cooked unattended. If a main dish needs last-minute attention, serve it with a make-ahead vegetable or a side salad.

HEALTHY EATING Use fresh ingredients and oils that are high in monounsaturated fatty acids for the best nutritional value and use fresh herbs and natural seasonings to enhance their flavours.

THE NUTRITIONAL BALANCE

Fast food can also be healthy food – all these recipes are designed to offer a good nutritional balance as well as minimum cooking. To help you plan a healthy diet, each recipe includes an analysis which shows how many kilojoules and how much protein, carbohydrate (including sugar) and fat (including saturated fat) there are in one serving.

Vitamins and minerals are also essential to a healthy diet. Most, such as vitamin A, are single substances, but vitamin B is a group of vitamins, which includes niacin, folate, pantothenic acid and biotin. Where the analysis states that the dish is a good source of a vitamin or mineral, it means one serving contains at least 30 per cent of the Recommended Dietary Intake – the amount that the experts agree we should consume every day.

Fast techniques

There are many time-saving methods that can speed up the cooking process. And the smoother and more methodical your preparation, the quicker the finished dish will come together. Follow these tried-and-tested techniques to achieve fast results without any last-minute hassles.

OFF TO A QUICK START

When you are peeling, trimming, topping and tailing, slicing or chopping ingredients, it is best to form an assembly line. Stand a colander nearby for rinsing the items, where necessary, and place paper towels or a spare basin by the chopping board to hold anything you are discarding.

If several chopped ingredients are to be added during cooking, put them into bowls or saucers and line them up in the order in which they will be used, or put very small amounts on one large plate. Then place them close to the stove within easy reach.

Have the salt and pepper alongside. If a number of flavouring ingredients are to be added at the same time, assemble them all on one saucer so that everything can be added in an instant.

CUTTING It is often quicker to cut up ingredients using a pair of kitchen scissors rather than a knife; for example, to snip the fat off bacon and ham, to chop herbs or cut up anchovy fillets, sun-dried tomatoes, stoned olives or spring onions. You can often snip the item directly into the pan.

It is easier to use your hands to tear up salad leaves than to use a knife. Tearing also causes less damage to the tender leaves, retaining more vitamins and minerals. Clean hands are also the fastest tool for flaking cooked fish, tearing up cooked chicken and crumbling cheese.

FLOURING To dust pieces of meat or fish quickly, put into a polythene bag with the flour and any seasoning and shake it, or toss with the flour in a mixing bowl. To dust slices of meat, sift flour over them with a small sieve or tea strainer.

PEELING You may not need to waste time peeling vegetables – many taste better and retain more goodness when cooked in their skins. The thick skins of older vegetables should be removed, but young, thin-skinned vegetables such as eggplants,

zucchini, new potatoes, chokos, carrots or parsnips will need no more than a scrub. And old potatoes and boiled pumpkin can be peeled quickly after cooking.

If you are removing the flesh from an avocado to be mashed or blended, don't bother peeling it: just cut the avocado in half, remove the stone (use it to stop the purée from browning) and scoop out the flesh using a large spoon.

Onions for chopping or slicing are quicker to peel if you cut them in half first, trim off the top and bottom and then peel off the skin.

Instead of topping and tailing snow peas and stringless green beans one at a time, take a handful and quickly cut off each end with kitchen scissors.

To peel garlic in a flash, press down on the clove with the flat blade of a large knife and the peel will split and slip off easily. Use a small sharp knife for garlic slices, but you'll find it's quicker to use a garlic crusher rather than a knife if you need to chop and purée garlic.

SKINNING To remove the skins easily from fruit and vegetables such as peaches, tomatoes and small whole onions, pour over enough boiling water to cover them then leave to stand for a minute or two. The skin will peel off easily

To skin capsicums quickly, spear with a long barbecue fork and hold over a gas flame, turning gently, until blackened. Peel off the skin as soon as it is cool enough to handle. With an electric stove, cut the capsicums in half and char under the griller.

To skin a fish fillet, place it skin side down on a chopping board. Insert a knife at the tail end with the blade held at an angle between the skin and the flesh, resting on the board. Pull the skin with one hand and use a gentle sawing action with the blade, folding the flesh over and out of the way as it comes clear.

FASTER COOKING

BOILING Root vegetables will cook much faster if they are arranged in a shallow layer in a large saucepan rather than a deep layer in a small one. Add just enough water to cover and use a pan with a tight-fitting lid to hold in the steam.

If the recipe calls for stock to be added to a dish, put it in a saucepan to start warming up before you do anything else; that way it will come to the boil much faster when eventually needed.

FRYING AND GRILLING If you slice meat, poultry or fish, make all the slices or escalopes the same size and thickness so they cook at the same rate, or cut the flesh into strips which will cook quickly.

Pat burgers, rissoles, patties and vegetable or meat fritters gently with your hands until they are a little flatter than you would usually make them, so the heat can penetrate easily and they will cook considerably faster.

MADE IN MINUTES!

PASTA SOUP

Make an elegant soup by simmering a handful of pasta soup shapes in some good stock – fresh stock in a carton would be very suitable. Garnish with a few slices of thinly sliced lemon, some finely chopped coriander or parsley and a few sliced mushrooms or snipped sun-dried tomatoes.

BUTTER-GLAZED FRUIT

For a frying pan dessert to serve four people, melt 1 tablespoon unsalted butter and 1 tablespoon caster sugar in a nonstick frying pan, then add 500 g sliced fresh fruit and 1 tablespoon fruit liqueur. Cook over moderate heat, basting with the sauce, until the fruit is just warmed through.

When stir-frying, the trick is to get the pan or wok as hot as possible using a high heat, then add the fat or oil, and only add the ingredients when the fat is sizzling so that they cook very quickly. Be sure to move the food around constantly, so that it does not have time to steam.

STEAMING Cooking food in vapour rather than water or fat reduces the loss of vitamins. If you have two or three steamer baskets, you can pile them up and cook a variety of vegetables at once.

TIME-SAVING EQUIPMENT

Y*ou can speed up your preparation and cooking considerably by choosing the right equipment. Here is a guide to the most suitable tools for fast cooking, and how to put them to the best use.*

POTS AND PANS

Use pots and pans which are the right size for the ingredients. It is a waste of time to boil up a large saucepan of water to cook a small quantity of vegetables, or to heat up a large frying pan for a small piece of meat or fish.

There are some exceptions: always use a large saucepan when you are cooking pasta: it will cook quicker with plenty of water to swim in. And it is better to use a large frying pan with plenty of space

when you are browning meat, as in a small pan the pieces of meat will be too close together and will steam rather than fry.

It is also important not to overcrowd the pan when stir-frying. The ingredients in a stir-fry cook most rapidly when they touch the surface of the hot pan, so choose a large wok which gives you plenty of room. It will take a little longer to heat up, but the cooking time will be shorter.

Frying over a high heat often means that you need to shake the pan vigorously to keep the food moving around: a pan with a single, heat-proof handle is ideal for this job. And a two-handled iron frying pan or shallow flameproof casserole that will fit underneath the griller or go into the oven is

another time-saver because you don't have to transfer the food from pan to oven dish when you are making dishes like gratins or casseroles.

A ridged, cast-iron grill plate will cook fish, steaks and chops very quickly and works even faster if you preheat it under the griller and then place the food between the grill plate and the griller, cooking from both sides. Cast-iron grills with fold-down handles are easiest to store.

A wok can double as a large saucepan and can be used for steaming, as well as for stir-frying, so make sure you buy one with a lid.

Not all pots and pans are equal when it comes to heat conduction. Heat makes food stick to the surface of a pan; to avoid this, nonstick surfaces are designed to be relatively poor heat conductors, and are not the best choice if you want to cook quickly. Copper pans which are lined with tin, or copper-based stainless steel pans and saucepans, are ideal heat conductors for fast cooking.

Cast-iron saucepans with a strong enamel coating also conduct heat well, though they are heavy to use. Stainless steel saucepans are much lighter, virtually indestructible, and they perform very well. Always scour the underside of pans thoroughly when you wash them to prevent any build-up of grease, which would impede the even distribution of heat.

A pasta pan that comes with a separate strainer basket, which you just lift out, makes draining pasta quick and easy. There is also less danger of fragile stuffed pastas breaking up, as they can if they are tipped into a colander.

And whatever you are cooking, be sure to put the pan on the right size burner, so that the heat is evenly distributed.

For oven-baking when time is limited, metal gratin dishes are better than porcelain, earthenware or glass, because they conduct heat better and help to reduce the cooking time.

GADGETS AND TOOLS

BRUSHES Invest in a small stiff brush for cleaning vegetables, and don't use it for anything else. Natural

fibre or plastic bristles are both equally efficient, but natural bristles must be left to dry out completely after each use.

A pastry brush is the quickest way to baste food under the griller with oil or a marinade – choose natural bristles, as plastic bristles will melt if they touch a hot surface. A pastry brush is also useful for cleaning rind out of the tiny holes in a hand grater.

CHERRY-STONER Using a single cherry-stoner is quicker than removing stones by hand; it can also remove olive pits.

CHOPPING BOARD Choose a large chopping board which sits firmly in place. It will make chopping easier, and nothing will fall over the edges.

ESSENTIALS A cast-iron grill lets you cook food fast, a pasta pan lets you drain pasta in an instant, and a wok makes stir-frying simple. Stainless steel tools are easy to use – and quick to clean.

COOKBOOK HOLDER Invest in a specially designed cookbook holder: you'll find it easier to keep the recipe book open in front of you.

GRATER A stainless-steel grater makes fast work of small items. If you need only one or two carrots, it is quicker to grate them by hand than in a food processor. Making pastry can also be quicker if you grate hard butter into the flour before rubbing in.

JAR OPENER A tool with large rings at the end that will grip firmly stuck jar and bottle tops and open them easily saves time and temper.

KNIFE SHARPENER Blunt knives slow you down. Use a knife sharpener and take a few seconds to hone the blades of knives and kitchen scissors to a fine, razor-sharp edge every time you use them. It will make short work of cutting and slicing.

LEMON SQUEEZER A cone-shaped hand-held squeezer will let you squeeze citrus juice straight into the salad bowl or saucepan.

POTATO MASHER A hand-held potato masher is an essential, as electric mixers and blenders turn potatoes (and potato-based soups) into a gluey mass.

SALAD SPINNER A simple plastic spinner is the most effective way to dry salad leaves. Put the washed leaves into the basket and rotate it to spin the water out.

STRAINER Wire mesh strainers strain off all the liquid better than a colander.

VEGETABLE PEELER A swivel-headed potato peeler makes a smooth job of peeling other vegetables, or cutting vegetables such as zucchini into ribbon shapes. It will remove strings from celery and shave chocolate and strips of Parmesan cheese. Learn to use it in smooth long strokes away from you.

ZESTER A zester makes swift work of removing rind from citrus fruit. Holes at the end of the blade shave off thin strips of rind without lifting the bitter pith beneath.

ELECTRICAL EQUIPMENT

BLENDERS You can purée a soup or sauce in a blender, or a liquidiser, in a fraction of the time it takes to push it through a sieve by hand, and the resulting mixture will be much smoother.

COFFEE GRINDER If you use a lot of spices, it is a good idea to invest in an extra coffee grinder for pulverising them into powder in seconds – a much faster and easier process than crushing them with a rolling pin or grinding with a pestle and mortar. You can also use a coffee grinder to make small quantities of breadcrumbs.

ELECTRIC BEATER It takes time and effort to whip cream or meringue mixtures using a balloon or mechanical whisk, whereas it takes only seconds with an electric hand beater.

FOOD PROCESSORS The chopping, grating and shredding blades of a food processor can make the business of preparing large amounts of raw food a matter of seconds rather than minutes. They are especially useful for chopping a succession of ingredients, for instance when you are making a vegetable soup or a salsa.

Processors make soft white breadcrumbs in seconds: cut the crusts off a few slices of thick white bread and process into crumbs. For dried brown

MADE IN MINUTES!

INSTANT SORBET

Use the food processor for an instant sorbet: tip a punnet of soft fruit, such as raspberries, into the food processor with 1–2 tablespoons icing sugar, process until smooth, then freeze.

breadcrumbs, dry some slices in a low oven at 150°C for about an hour until crisp and lightly toasted, then process. They will keep in an airtight container in the refrigerator for up to a month.

A processor can also make flavoured butters in seconds – if the recipe calls for only a small amount, you can make double the quantity and freeze half to save time another day.

If you want to chop only one item, it is often quicker to do so by hand, but new food processors often have an additional small bowl and cutting blade, useful for chopping herbs and other small items and for making mayonnaise. Keep extra processor discs and blades handy so you do not waste valuable time searching for them.

HAND-HELD FOOD MIXER This purées soup faster than a food processor or blender as you can use it in the saucepan. The result is not quite as smooth, but many cooks prefer the slightly thicker texture.

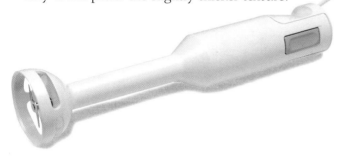

Hand-held mixers are also useful for making milkshakes and sauces, and for taking the lumps out of sauces that have gone wrong. They can also be used to mash pumpkin: it will smooth it quickly and remove any stringy bits – they wind themselves round the blades so they can be easily removed.

OVENS

CONVENTIONAL OVENS When you are using a conventional gas or electric oven, it is worth remembering that the heat produced inside the oven will be uneven – on average, one setting higher at the top than at the bottom. Always follow instructions for preheating, to make sure that the oven is up to temperature in time for cooking.

FAN-FORCED OVENS Because it preheats quicker than a conventional oven, a fan-forced oven saves time. It also provide faster cooking at lower temperatures, as the even heat circulation makes it hotter than a conventional oven. This should be taken into account when setting the temperature.

MICROWAVE SHORT CUTS
(based on a 650 watt oven)

Soften butter from the refrigerator
by warming on High for 20 seconds.

Warm lemons
for a few seconds on High and they
will yield more juice.

Make crispy bacon
by placing 3–4 rashers on a microwave rack over
a piece of folded paper towel; cook on High for
2 minutes, turn and cook for 1–2 minutes more.

Melt chocolate
by breaking small pieces into a bowl and leaving it
uncovered. It's best to melt all chocolate on Medium or
Low and to stir and check every 10 seconds or so during
the cooking time, as chocolate will hold its shape even
when it has melted. Keep checking, and expect to
stir the last few bits of chocolate in.
To melt chocolate for a quick decoration, place it
in one corner of a microwave roasting bag and melt it in
the microwave oven. Then snip off the tip of the corner
and drizzle a pattern over a dessert or cake.

Make fat-free pappadams
by cooking them, one at a time, on High for
40–60 seconds, and watch them puff up.

Toast nuts
such as cashew nuts; 30 g nuts, cooked on High for
5 minutes, will turn a golden, toasted colour.

MICROWAVE OVENS Though a microwave oven does nothing that cannot be done with other more basic equipment, it does speed up cooking time dramatically. Many foods cook in about a quarter of the time they take in a conventional oven. Those ovens with the clearest instructions and the fewest buttons are the most practical.

The foods that do best in a microwave are those cooked with moist heat: vegetables cooked in a few tablespoons of water, food in sauces, poached fish. And long thin pieces of food cook faster than short thick pieces of the same weight.

But unlike with a conventional stove top, if you double the quantity of the ingredients you cook in the microwave, the cooking time is nearly doubled too. And a microwave will not brown most food, nor produce a crisp crust.

THE CLEVER SHOPPER

Every good meal starts with clever shopping, and this is particularly important for the busy cook. Take care in choosing your ingredients and consider, too, whether it is worth the expense of buying ready-prepared ingredients when they are available – this can save you a lot of time.

FRESH MEAT, FISH, VEGETABLES AND FRUIT

Start by going to the best suppliers you can find – a reputable butcher and fish shop, and a supermarket that has a quick turnover of fresh produce.

For speedy meals, avoid joints and tough cuts of meat that need long slow cooking; use only tender pieces, cut into chops, steaks or thin slices.

Fish is a natural fast food. Ask your fishmonger to prepare it for you, or buy ready-cut fillets and cutlets. If the recipe calls for skinned fish, look for ready-skinned fillets.

Young vegetables require less preparation and shorter cooking time than tougher, older ones. Baby green beans, for example, don't need stringing, and new potatoes can be washed rather than peeled.

Although it is generally wise to avoid processed foods, some prewashed and ready-cut items are worth the extra money because of the time they save. Bags of ready-washed mixed salad leaves save preparation. Similarly, bags of pre-cut coleslaw need only a dressing to be ready to serve. Ready-peeled sliced pineapple or ready-made fresh fruit salad makes a delicious dessert – try draining off any syrup and using the fruit to fill a pancake.

Buying a packet of mixed mushrooms will save the time it takes to weigh out two or more separate varieties. If some of the mushrooms have been left whole to give the pack visual appeal, remember to cut them up into smaller pieces for faster cooking when you are preparing to use them.

Packs of ready-grated cheese, which can be melted over the top of a pizza or gratin, also save time and effort, with the exception of Parmesan, which should always be grated at the last minute.

NATURALLY FRESH Buy the freshest ingredients you can find for quicker cooking times and meals full of flavour.

THE ESSENTIAL STORE CUPBOARD

A busy cook needs to keep the cupboard stocked with a generous selection of flavouring ingredients and staples. Group ingredients that you tend to use together, such as Indian spices, side by side so you can find all of them at a glance.

CANS Anchovies, beans, olives, tomatoes and tuna can be combined into sauces for pasta and eggs, as well as used in pizza toppings and hearty soups.

Canned beans, such as white cannellini beans, kidney or haricot beans, butter and broad beans, borlotti beans and creamy chick peas, can be rinsed and tossed with a handful of chopped parsley, some finely sliced onion and a garlicky dressing for a filling main-dish salad, perhaps with some added canned tuna, or anchovy fillets, rinsed and chopped.

A can of drained tuna can be processed with half a dozen stoned black olives, 1 teaspoon capers, 3–4 tablespoons olive oil and 1 teaspoon brandy into a pâté to serve with toast.

Canned tomatoes, both whole and pieces, are especially versatile, and often have more taste than some fresh varieties, for which they can be substituted in almost all cooked recipes. Sun-dried tomatoes can be stirred into stews, risottos and scrambled eggs, or added to pasta sauces and pizzas.

OILS Besides a vegetable oil for frying and a good olive oil for cooking and making salad dressings, a nut oil – walnut, almond or hazel – is useful as it can provide a quick final touch drizzled over plainly cooked vegetables, or give instant flavour to salad dressings. Flavoured oils such as chilli or garlic can be drizzled over vegetables to add a final spicy note. Oils are best used up quickly, so buy small bottles.

DRIED FRUIT AND NUTS With little preparation, dried fruit and nuts give a lift to many savoury dishes and salads, particularly those made with grated raw vegetables such as carrot, cabbage and celery. Dried apricots, raisins or sultanas, soaked in a spirit such as brandy, Cointreau, fruit brandy (eau-de-vie) or rum for a few minutes, also make a great instant topping for ice cream.

MADE IN MINUTES!

CANNED BEAN MASH

Short of an accompaniment? Canned Bean Mash tastes great with sausages, pork chops or cold meat. For two people, fry 2 crushed cloves garlic and ½ teaspoon chilli flakes gently in 2 tablespoons olive oil, without letting the garlic colour. Stir in some chopped rosemary, sage or thyme leaves and 500 g can lima beans, including the liquid. Boil gently for 10 minutes until the liquid is thick and opaque, then mash roughly and season to taste with black pepper.

PEAR RICE PUDDING

In need of a quick family dessert? For four people, spoon 440 g can creamed rice into dishes and pour on a hot chocolate sauce made by melting 75 g dark chocolate gently in 3–4 tablespoons thick cream. Cover the top with slices of peeled fresh pear and sprinkle over some curls of chocolate shaved straight from the bar with a potato peeler.

PASTA Dried pasta is a great store cupboard favourite, but fresh pasta is three times faster to cook. Fresh pasta can also be frozen, and will take only a minute or two longer to cook straight from the freezer. In general, to serve four people you will need to cook 500 g fresh pasta, or 350 g if it is dried.

Small pasta shapes are very useful items to have in the cupboard: they can be used to thicken soups, as they cook much faster than rice used for the same purpose, and they are more filling. Vermicelli and fine Oriental egg noodles can also be used to thicken soup: crush the dry noodles between your hands to break them into tiny pieces, then stir the pieces into the soup 5 minutes before you serve it.

RICE Converted rice cooks faster than plain white or brown rice. Packets of pre-cooked natural rice are also available from the freezer section of your supermarket. If you are tired of rice and looking for a substitute, keep packets of 'instant' polenta and couscous on hand. And try using rice noodles: they cook quickly and work well with most Oriental dishes. Another alternative is to serve naan bread with curry instead of rice – it heats up in the oven in a few seconds.

SAUCES AND PURÉES Keep a bottle or two of your favourite sauces such as Worcestershire, hot Tabasco and soy sauce in the cupboard, and some good mayonnaise in the refrigerator. If you save time by buying mayonnaise ready-made, make sure you choose a good one.

A few small bottles of concentrated fruit purée, which can be found in most health food shops, are also a good idea for your store cupboard. They are very versatile and taste delicious, and can add a quick, colourful finishing touch to a wide variety of desserts.

SPICES Whole spices keep better than ground ones, but they take time to prepare. Buy small quantities of the ground spices you use most often and replace them as soon as they seem musty.

STOCK CUBES Though they are convenient, many stock cubes are aggressively salty: try using only half a cube to the given amount of water for a more delicate flavour. Or use one of the low-salt vegetable or chicken stock powders available in supermarkets.

VINEGAR Use red or white wine vinegar, either plain or flavoured with fruit or herbs – you'll find these very easy to make at home – to give interest to salad dressings. Balsamic vinegar, caramel coloured and slightly sweet, can be used not only to liven up salad dressings but also for deglazing the pan after frying meat or poultry.

FREEZER STANDBYS

BREAD Keep loaves of good, crusty half-cooked bread, or rolls, in the freezer, which can go straight into the oven without defrosting. They can be baked while you are making the rest of the meal.

ICE CREAM A good-quality ice cream can form the basis of many delicious desserts; for some great ideas, see pages 294–295.

PASTRY A frozen unbaked pastry case can be used to make a quick tart. Puff and filo pastry and ready-made pizza bases also save preparation time.

PRAWNS Green and peeled cooked prawns can be the basis of many quick starters or stir-fries.

STOCK Keep some high-quality stock in your freezer. You can make your own and store it in re-usable yoghurt cartons, or buy cartons of good, ready-made stock.

VEGETABLES Frozen broad beans, peas, spinach and corn cobs and kernels can be cooked straight from the freezer, and can be used to add both flavour and colour to many different dishes.

INGREDIENTS FROM AROUND THE WORLD

Many of the dishes in this book are inspired by the cuisines of India, the Middle East, Asia, Southeast Asia and Mexico, where powerfully flavoured local ingredients lend intense flavours to a wide variety of fast-cooked foods.

A long list of exotic ingredients can appear daunting if you are new to this type of cooking, and acquiring them may seem extravagant. But with a little experimentation, you will find that some new ingredients quickly become firm favourites and are used over and over again. On the other hand, if you try something and dislike it, get rid of it! You are cooking to please your own tastebuds, so you can add and discard flavourings to suit yourself.

INDIA

CURRY PASTE is much easier to use than curry powder, which can taste slightly raw and is best kept for giving a lift to Western dishes – as a flavouring for mayonnaise, for example. A wide variety of curry pastes are now available, and have been blended by experts to give an authentic flavour. If you like Indian food, keep one mild and one hotter curry paste in the cupboard. When you are choosing a brand, remember that spice mixtures manufactured in India are often hotter than those made locally.

SPICES are essential ingredients in Indian cooking. Popular spices which can give an authentic Indian flavour to a variety of dishes are black mustard or cumin seeds, dry roasted until they begin to pop, then stirred through a vegetable dish or a grated vegetable salad (if you are using raw carrot, add some lemon or lime juice). Favourite spices are cardamom, coriander seeds and cinnamon, which are usually added whole to the dish while cooking. Cardamom and coriander seeds should be crushed very lightly before use to gently release their aroma.

All ground spices go stale quickly and, like herbs, it is best to buy them regularly, in small quantities.

SAFFRON can be used to tint rice a rich golden colour. Whole saffron stamens should be steeped in a little hot liquid to draw out their flavour; powdered saffron can be added directly to the dish.

TURMERIC is a less extravagant way to flavour and colour rice and produces a darker yellow colour. It can also be cooked with leaf vegetables such as spinach.

ACCOMPANIMENTS are a very important part of Indian meals: you can add the finishing touches straight from the shelf. A handful of raisins, sultanas or chopped dried mango slices can be added to rice or vegetable dishes. Mango and other chutneys, and lime pickle, can add an intense flavour. And ready-made pappadams, or naan or some other Indian bread, quickly warmed through, are always welcome.

MADE IN MINUTES!

CUCUMBER RAITA

A cooling sauce to serve with curries can be quickly made in a food processor. Roughly grate a cucumber then drain it in a sieve for a minute or two to release some of its water. Put it into a food processor, add a small tub of natural yoghurt, salt and fresh mint, if you have any, or a pinch of ground cumin, process to the consistency of thick cream and serve.

CHINA

BEAN SAUCES are useful both as a dip and for cooking. Black beans, butter beans and yellow beans are often used to make cooking sauces. Hoisin sauce is made from fermented soya beans, and makes a particularly good dipping sauce – it is best known as the sauce served with Peking Duck. All Chinese sauces are very salty and should be used sparingly.

DRIED MUSHROOMS add flavour to many Chinese dishes, and many varieties are now available in large supermarkets and Asian food stores. Rinse before use to remove most of the grit, then soak in warm water

for as long as possible. Save the soaking water as it can be strained through muslin – or through a sieve lined with paper towel – to remove any grit, and added to the dish together with the sliced mushrooms.

GINGER is one of the key trio of Asian flavourings, along with garlic and spring onions. It keeps well peeled and stored in dry sherry in a screwtop jar in the refrigerator. If you find it difficult to obtain fresh ginger, buy it ready-minced in a jar: 1 teaspoon minced is equivalent to 2.5 cm fresh root ginger.

SOY SAUCE is the most basic flavour of Asia. It is very salty and is used instead of table salt. To make sure you get the best flavour, look for the words 'naturally fermented' on the label, which are most easily found on bottles of Japanese soy sauce.

SESAME SEED OIL is a powerful flavouring used in very small amounts. It is not used for frying as it burns easily; instead, it is added towards the end of cooking, or just before the dish is served.

JAPAN

MIRIN is a slightly sweet version of sake, or rice wine. It is a favourite flavouring agent and can be found in Asian food stores. If you cannot find a supply, sweet sherry can be used as a substitute.

RICE VINEGAR has a very delicate flavour, and adds interest to a dressing for salads or cold vegetables.

WASABI is sometimes called Japanese horseradish; it

has a clear, strong bite and goes superbly with grilled fish. It comes as either ready-mixed paste in tubes, or as a powder for mixing with water, similar to mustard powder.

SOUTHEAST ASIA

COCONUT MILK is made from coconut flesh, and in Southeast Asia it is often the only liquid used for cooking vegetable stews, curries and puddings, giving them a rich flavour and texture. It can be bought in dehydrated blocks or powdered, which have to be reconstituted with hot water, or as a ready-made liquid in cans. Coconut cream is sold in cartons and cans. The liquid forms are much quicker to use than the powders or blocks.

LEMONGRASS is a favourite flavouring in Thai cookery, adding a subtle citrus flavour and aroma to soups and curries. The tough upper part of the stem should be discarded and the lower half sliced into rounds. Dried lemon grass must be soaked in hot water until tender before use. Ground lemon grass is

also available, and cuts out the time spent in preparation: 1 teaspoon is the equivalent of 1 stalk.
TAMARIND is used as a souring flavour in some Southeast Asian and Indian dishes. It is dried in sticky blocks which need to be soaked, or comes as a concentrate; the concentrate is quicker to use because it can be spooned directly into dishes.
THAI FISH SAUCE called *nam pla* or *nuoc nam*, is used as a flavouring in cooked dishes or diluted with water to use as a dip. Choose a brand with a clear, sherry-like colour and check that the label lists 'fish' as the main ingredient.

THE MIDDLE EAST

BURGHUL AND COUSCOUS are as popular as rice in the Middle East and North Africa, and much faster to prepare; simply reconstitute in hot water.

To give rice dishes a Middle Eastern flavour, add cardamom pods, slightly cracked, a cinnamon stick and two or three whole cloves while cooking. You can discard whole spices before serving, if you wish.
ORANGE FLOWER WATER AND ROSEWATER evoke the Middle East more intensely than any other

flavouring. Sweetly perfumed, they are added to cream, or to nut and date fillings for sweet dishes, or added discreetly to vegetables such as spinach and carrots. They are available from Middle Eastern and Indian food shops and some larger supermarkets. Avoid flower 'essence', which has an unpalatable synthetic flavour.

HARISSA is a fiery chilli paste which is flavoured with coriander, cumin, garlic and mint, and is sold in tubes or cans. It is traditionally served with couscous. To store leftover canned harissa, transfer into a container, cover and keep in the refrigerator.
TAHINI is a nutty-flavoured, oily paste made from sesame seeds; it can be diluted with lemon juice, milk or water and seasoned to make a quick sauce or added to a salad dressing.

MEXICO

CHILLIES can be bought fresh, canned or bottled, and are readily available. They are used extensively to give flavour to Mexican dishes, along with fresh coriander and fresh lime juice. To save the time it takes to prepare fresh chillies, buy them flaked or crushed, or use some Tabasco, chilli sauce or cayenne pepper instead, to taste.
SALSAS can be found in many large supermarkets, either canned, bottled or fresh, and in a range of chilli heats from mild to red hot. You'll also find a good selection of accompaniments such as corn chips, taco shells and tortillas.

MADE IN MINUTES!

INSTANT HUMMOUS

If you have some canned chick peas and tahini in your kitchen cupboard you can make instant hummous. Put a can of drained chick peas in a processor or blender with 2 tablespoons tahini, 1 or 2 cloves garlic, the juice of a lemon and a generous pinch of salt. Thin to the consistency of thick cream with a little water while processing it. Serve with pita bread, bread sticks or sliced raw vegetables.

FAST FINISHING TOUCHES

Think about colour, texture and presentation when you are serving food. It need take only seconds to transform the simplest dish so that it appeals to the eye as well as the taste buds.

PRESENTATION

Soup can be garnished with chopped herbs or a sprinkling of the main ingredient, such as a few slivers of mushroom. Alternatively, spooning a little fresh or sour cream into each soup bowl just before serving and swirling it around with a teaspoon adds a decorative finishing touch.

Colour is as important in a sauce as flavour, and should provide a striking contrast to the main ingredient. Quickly snipped sun-dried tomatoes or finely chopped black olives can give an instant visual lift to many pale sauces. A little crumbled blue cheese or a handful of chopped walnuts can look pretty scattered over dark green salad leaves. You can also vary your method of presentation – sauces often look better if they are poured carefully on to the plate first and the meat, poultry or fish positioned on top of them.

Choose accompanying vegetables to contrast or complement the colours of the main course – try combining crisp green broccoli with bright red tomato-based dishes; vivid orange carrots with rich green spinach dishes; and jewel-bright capsicums with grain or meat dishes.

While you are cooking, reserve a few small whole ingredients that have visual appeal. Save a few prawns in their shells to garnish seafood, for instance, a few sprigs of fresh herbs to place beside grilled meat or fish, and a whole strawberry or a little sliced fresh fruit to decorate desserts.

A fine dusting of icing sugar or cocoa sifted gently through a tea strainer is an elegant way to decorate a dessert. Because so little sugar is used, it will not oversweeten the dish, but icing sugar does dissolve quickly, so make sure you add it just before serving. Fresh fruit, such as sliced mango with a squeeze of lime, looks appetising frosted lightly with icing sugar and dotted with some raspberries or thinly sliced strawberries and a few leaves of fresh mint.

GARNISHES

Biscuits, fruits, nuts and chocolate
all make attractive toppings for ice cream. Use crushed almond praline, peanut brittle, amaretti, macaroons or ratafias, raisins soaked in hot rum, chopped dried or glacé fruit, or toasted nuts. Curls of dark chocolate shaved off with a vegetable peeler are also very effective.

Breadcrumbs
can be quickly fried in very little oil or butter until golden, and used to top a vegetable or pasta dish, adding both flavour and colour. They are easily made in a food processor (see pages 14–15).

Croutons
can be made in minutes to add crunch to soups or salads. Cut slightly stale bread into small cubes and fry with a little olive oil and a few slivers of garlic for extra flavour.

Nuts and seeds
such as flaked almonds, pine nuts or sesame seeds, dry fried or toasted for a few seconds until golden, add a pretty touch and rich flavour to many dishes, and also provide a good helping of protein in vegetarian recipes.

Onions
can be sliced and quickly deep fried to add intense flavour as a garnish over the top of rice or egg dishes. And bacon, fried until crisp and dry, can be crumbled over salads, grain dishes and creamy soups.

Orange and lemon rind
finely grated or taken off with a zester, can add a splash of fast colour to grills and fried meat, and looks pretty on creamy desserts. If you like, blanch the shreds, or put in a sieve and pour boiling water over them, to make them less bitter.

Watercress
makes a bright, peppery garnish, and is more unusual than a sprig of parsley. A handful of watercress can take the place of a separate side salad, and tastes especially good with grilled meat as it blends with the juices on the plate but retains its crispness.

LAST-MINUTE SALADS

If you feel a dish needs a side salad but do not have any salad leaves, young green vegetables such as beans, zucchini or peas make a tasty substitute. Cook briefly so that the vegetable remains crunchy, then refresh under cold running water and serve with salad dressing or mayonnaise and a sprinkling of whole or chopped fresh herbs.

Alternatively, make a salad from raw vegetables such as carrots, turnips and white or red cabbage, grated and tossed with a strongly flavoured dressing, some caraway or mustard seeds and a pinch of curry powder or mixed spice.

If you need to make a few salad leaves go a long way, shred them finely and add other items such as chopped hard-boiled eggs, crumbled cheese and a handful of croutons or toasted flaked almonds, or maybe some walnuts quickly fried with a tiny pinch of cayenne pepper.

Any three canned beans – kidney, butter, haricot, borlotti or cannellini beans – will make a salad. Simply toss in a blue cheese or vinaigrette dressing with fresh herbs, crushed garlic and a little coarse mustard, blended to a creamy texture.

QUICK TRANSFORMATIONS A little creative flair can turn versatile vegetables, pulses and nuts into stunning salads.

MADE IN MINUTES!

FRUIT SALAD

You can make an attractive fruit salad without making sugar syrup. Pour a thin film of bottled concentrated fruit juice onto individual plates – pink juice is the most attractive – and arrange the sliced fruit on top. Sprinkle with icing sugar and decorate with fresh mint.

MAKING USE OF LEFTOVERS

A bowl of leftovers in the refrigerator can provide the basis for many wonderfully quick dishes. But be sure to chill leftover food as quickly as possible, and use it within two days. Cooked rice, in particular, must be cooled quickly, kept refrigerated, then reheated quickly and eaten immediately.

MEAT AND FISH

Leftover meat, game and poultry can be turned into crunchy croquettes (see recipe opposite), and fish into fish cakes. For extra colour and flavour, top these with a fried egg, or make a quick tomato sauce by simmering canned tomato pieces with some chopped chives and parsley for a few minutes until thickened. For a more formal dish, accompany the croquettes with sautéed mushrooms and cherry tomatoes or grilled tomato slices.

Slivers of leftover meat, game or poultry can be quickly and crisply fried and tossed with salads of vegetable, rice, pasta or mixed leaves to turn them into main course dishes.

And you can make a delicious pâté or spread by finely chopping or processing leftover cooked meat with a spoonful of mayonnaise and a couple of dill pickles or gherkins, and seasoning well with salt and black pepper. Serve the pâté on top of a few mixed salad leaves as a light starter.

PASTA

Leftover pasta can be used to make a chunky rustic soup. Use small shapes whole and roughly chop spaghetti or tagliatelli, or cut with a knife and fork into 5 cm lengths. Sauté a small sliced onion and a clove of garlic, then add the pasta, a can of broad, borlotti or kidney beans, or chick peas, or a can of tomato pieces, and enough stock, water or wine to cover. Cook very gently until the vegetables are tender, then serve with grated Parmesan cheese.

RICE

Extra cooked rice is always useful: it will make a substantial stuffing for capsicums or tomatoes, or can be combined with crunchy cooked vegetables and salad dressing to make a rice salad.

Leftover risotto rice can be combined with egg and cheese to make delicious Italian rice balls (see recipe opposite). Rice balls can be served with fresh tomato sauce as a starter, or with a salad or vegetable for a light lunch. They are also pleasantly filling as an accompaniment to grilled sausages and ham, or to smoked, grilled or fried fish.

Cooked rice can also be used for a fast stir-fry (see recipe opposite) using whatever fresh vegetables you have, such as baby corn cobs, carrots, cherry tomatoes, zucchini, mushrooms, capsicums or spring onions, finely sliced or grated.

And cooked rice is a must if you plan to make fried rice. In fact, it's worthwhile cooking extra so you always have some available in the refrigerator.

POTATOES

Leftover potatoes are particularly versatile, and their subtle flavour makes them a good accompaniment to a great variety of other foods. Potatoes can give substance to salads and add texture to soups, and they can be combined with other ingredients, then reshaped and reheated to accompany many different main course meals.

Surplus mashed potatoes can be shaped into croquettes or potato cakes, coated in flour and fried. Adding a well-beaten egg will help to hold the mixture together. If you have another leftover vegetable, mash that into the potato first to make a colourful patty, or mix in canned red or pink salmon to make instant fish cakes.

Leftover new potatoes can make a delicious salad: toss in a little olive oil while still warm enough to absorb the flavour, then cool and refrigerate. To complete the salad, add extra flavour by dressing the potatoes with a herb mayonnaise just before serving.

Cooked new potatoes can be turned into a fast and tasty accompaniment to hot or cold meat or poultry by frying in olive oil or butter and sprinkling with a little grated Parmesan cheese, to melt and turn crunchy as they cook.

Leftover boiled potatoes can be turned into hash browns (see recipe opposite), to make a tasty brunch or breakfast served with eggs and bacon.

MADE IN MINUTES!

MEAT CROQUETTES

For four people, mince 400 g cooked meat and combine with the same weight of mashed potato and some chopped spring onions, chives or parsley. Shape into patties, brush with egg, toss gently in dried breadcrumbs and fry until very crisp.

ITALIAN RICE BALLS

For two people, mix 1½ cups cooked risotto rice with a beaten egg, a little grated Parmesan, salt and pepper. Shape the rice mixture into balls, roll in flour and dried breadcrumbs, and shallow fry in a little olive oil until golden brown.

HASH BROWNS

For four people, fry a thinly sliced onion in a little oil in a nonstick pan until soft and golden. Slice or dice 500 g cooked potatoes, add to the onion and fry until brown and crunchy. Season well, add some chopped chives or parsley if available, and serve.

FIVE-MINUTE STIR-FRY

For two people as an accompaniment, fry a little chopped garlic and ginger until slightly coloured. Add 150 g mixed sliced vegetables and stir-fry until cooked but still crunchy. Add 1 cup cooked rice, stir well and heat through. Season with soy sauce and sesame oil.

OTHER VEGETABLES

Vegetables that have been cooked in a sauce, such as cauliflower cheese, can be turned into a pasta bake. Put the leftovers into a buttered ovenproof dish, stir in some cooked pasta shapes, top with dried breadcrumbs and extra grated cheese and bake.

Leftover baked vegetables can be chopped and fried in a little butter or oil. And almost any boiled or steamed vegetable can be turned into a delicious side salad with the addition of chopped onion, capers, olives or croutons, and some mayonnaise or vinaigrette dressing.

To turn a leftover vegetable into a hearty main course salad, try mixing it with some more substantial ingredients, such as drained canned beans, tuna and artichoke hearts, or fry some bacon until crisp, drain well on paper towels, and crumble; add to the vegetables then mix in a little dressing.

SOUP

Served chilled on the hottest of days, or steaming when the temperature drops and appetites soar, a good soup – on its own or with crusty bread – can start a meal, or make one.

COOL CUCUMBER SOUP

This is a great soup to make on a steamy summer's day since it requires no cooking at all.
Just assemble the ingredients and mix them together, then eat and enjoy.

TIME: 15 MINUTES SERVES: 4

| 1 large cucumber |
| 4 bushy sprigs mint |
| 500 g natural yoghurt |
| 150 ml cream |
| 1 tablespoon white wine vinegar |
| Salt and black pepper |
| Ice cubes, optional |
| *To garnish:* 4 small sprigs mint |

1 Chill four soup bowls in the refrigerator. Trim the cucumber then grate it coarsely, with its skin, into a large bowl.

2 Strip the mint leaves from the stalks and shred enough to give 4 tablespoons, or bundle the leaves together and cut diagonally into fine strips with kitchen scissors. Add the mint to the cucumber.

3 Stir the yoghurt, cream and vinegar into the bowl. Season well with salt and pepper and stir again.

4 Divide the soup among the four chilled soup bowls. Add one or two ice cubes to each one, if you like, to chill the mixture quickly. Garnish with the small sprigs of mint and serve immediately.

VARIATION
You can use sour cream instead of pure cream if you prefer a sharper taste, and use tarragon vinegar instead of the wine vinegar for a herbier overtone. For a pretty contrast of taste and colour, add a few peeled fresh prawns to each soup bowl before serving.

NUTRIENTS PER SERVING: kilojoules 984, protein 10 g, carbohydrate 6.5 g (sugar 6 g), fat 19 g (saturated fat 11 g), good source of vitamins A, B group and E, and calcium.

GAZPACHO

*This crunchy floating salad, one of many versions of the
celebrated Spanish soup, is incomparable on a hot day.*

TIME: 30 MINUTES SERVES: 4–6

1 thick slice dry-textured bread	1 medium red capsicum
4 tablespoons extra virgin olive oil	1 medium yellow capsicum
3 tablespoons red wine vinegar	1 medium green capsicum
Salt and black pepper	1 fresh or dried red chilli, or 1 fresh green chilli
1 tablespoon paprika	6 large basil and/or mint leaves
800 g canned tomato pieces, with their juice	300 ml iced water
1 red onion	12 ice cubes (if required)
4 large cloves garlic	
1 large cucumber	

To garnish: 1 clove garlic, peeled,
a little olive oil and
3 slices thick bread to make
croutons, optional

1 Discard the crusts from the
bread, then put into a food
processor and make into crumbs.
2 Put the olive oil into a large
serving bowl and whisk in the
vinegar and salt to make a creamy
emulsion. Add the paprika and the
breadcrumbs and stir until
thoroughly combined.
3 Stir the tomatoes and their juice
into the mixture then put aside.
4 Peel the onion, garlic and
cucumber. Halve and seed the
capsicums and the chilli, then cut
into quarters.
5 In a food processor, coarsely
chop the onion and garlic together
and add to the breadcrumb
mixture. One by one, coarsely chop
the cucumber, capsicums and chilli
and add to the soup.
6 Tear the basil or mint leaves
into small pieces and add to the
mixture. Stir well, taste and season
generously with salt and black
pepper. The flavour should be sharp
and refreshing, with plenty of bite.
7 Stir in enough iced water to give
the mixture a soup-like consistency,
but do not make it too thin: the
texture should be quite dense.
Leave to chill, or stir in the ice
cubes and serve immediately.
8 To make croutons, put the garlic
into a frying pan with a little oil.
Cut the bread into cubes and fry,
turning often, over moderate heat
until browned. Discard the garlic;
serve the croutons with the soup.

VARIATION
Put some vodka into the freezer
before making the gazpacho, then
add 1–2 tablespoons to each bowl
just before serving.

NUTRIENTS PER SERVING, WHEN SERVING 4:
*kilojoules 1013, protein 6 g, carbohydrate
21 g (sugar 13 g), fat 16 g (saturated
fat 3 g), good source of vitamins A, B group,
C, E and folate.*

COOK'S SUGGESTION

*Using a food processor makes
fast work of chopping the vegetables.
You can chop them by hand, but
it will take much longer.*

THAI COCONUT SOUP

The creaminess of coconut milk imparts its own special aroma while the Asian herbs and red curry paste give a zing to the subtle flavour of the straw mushrooms.

TIME: 20 MINUTES SERVES: 4

2 cups chicken or vegetable stock
3 cloves garlic
2 stalks lemon grass
6 spring onions, including green part
1 small red chilli
1 tablespoon vegetable oil
1 teaspoon red curry paste
400 ml coconut milk
4 pieces dried galangal
2 teaspoons brown sugar
½ lime
1 tablespoon fish sauce
4 kaffir lime leaves
300 g straw mushrooms

To garnish: lime leaves, lightly toasted shredded coconut, finely sliced red chilli, coriander sprigs

1 Put the stock on to heat in a small saucepan. Peel and finely chop the garlic and the lemon grass.

Finely chop the spring onions. Seed and finely chop the chilli.

2 Heat the oil in a large, heavy-based saucepan. Add the garlic, lemon grass, spring onions, chilli and curry paste. Cook, stirring, over moderately high heat for 1–2 minutes.

3 Stir in the stock, coconut milk, galangal and brown sugar. Bring to the boil, reduce heat and simmer gently for 5 minutes. Meanwhile, squeeze enough lime juice to give 1 tablespoon.

4 Add the lime juice, fish sauce, lime leaves and mushrooms to the pot. Simmer for a further 2–3 minutes.

5 If necessary, toast the coconut for the garnish in a small frying pan and slice some chilli. When the soup is ready, remove the galangal and pour into a warmed serving

bowl. Garnish with lime leaves, shredded coconut, chilli and coriander, and serve immediately.

VARIATION

If you have time, you could soak about 25 g cloud ear fungus in warm water for at least 30 minutes and use instead of the mushrooms.

NUTRIENTS PER SERVING: kilojoules 775, protein 5 g, carbohydrate 4 g (sugar 3 g), fat 16 g (saturated fat 10 g), good source of vitamins B group and C.

COOK'S SUGGESTION

Galangal is sometimes available fresh, but is usually sold powdered, or as slices in brine, or as dried slices, in Asian food stores. The dried slices are used here, as they are the best for simmering in soups and curries.

CAPSICUM AND ORANGE VELVET SOUP

A soup to delight the senses, this derives its stunning colour from red capsicums and its heady aroma and fruity flavour from orange flower water and freshly squeezed orange juice.

TIME: 30 MINUTES SERVES: 4

2 tablespoons olive oil
1 kg red capsicums
Salt
3 oranges
2 cups vegetable or chicken stock

To garnish: orange zest, chopped parsley or croutons, optional

1 Heat the oil in a large saucepan over a moderate heat. Seed and quarter the capsicums lengthways. Slice them fairly coarsely in a food processor and add to the oil. Alternatively, slice by hand, adding the first capsicum to the pan while you slice the next, stirring with each addition and keeping the pan covered while you slice. Add a little salt to taste.

2 Grate the rind from one of the oranges into the pan. Cover and increase the heat to high until steam starts to escape from under the lid. Lower the heat and simmer, covering the pan again, for 15–18 minutes, shaking the pan occasionally and allowing the capsicums to cook in their own juice. Meanwhile, squeeze the juice from all the oranges into a small measuring jug: you will need ¾ cup.

3 When the capsicums are soft, process or blend to a smooth purée. It does not matter if some of them seem to have caramelised – this just adds to the richness of the flavour. Add the orange juice mixture and the vegetable or chicken stock and process or blend again.

4 Reheat and garnish with orange zest, herbs or croutons, if using.

NUTRIENTS PER SERVING: kilojoules 649, protein 2 g, carbohydrate 18 g (sugar 16 g), fat 8 g (saturated fat 1 g), good source of vitamins A, B group, C and E.

COOK'S SUGGESTION

If you like a strong orange flavour, add 1–2 teaspoons orange flower water, from delicatessens and Middle Eastern food shops. Check that it can be used for cooking – orange flower water sold as a beauty product is not suitable.

TWO TASTY VEGETABLE SOUPS: *(top)* THAI COCONUT SOUP; *(bottom)* CAPSICUM AND ORANGE VELVET SOUP

MUSHROOM SOUP

The earthy flavour of the dark mushrooms in this soup is given a lift by garlic, parsley and mace.
It has a deep smoky colour and a rich taste that needs no cream to enhance it.

TIME: 30 MINUTES   SERVES: 4–6

5 cups vegetable stock
150 g country-style bread, without crust
½ small onion or 1 shallot
750 g large flat or field mushrooms
3 sprigs parsley
2 tablespoons olive oil
1 small clove garlic
A pinch of ground mace or freshly grated nutmeg
Salt and black pepper

1 Put the stock on to boil. Soak the bread in a little cold water.
2 Peel and chop the onion or shallot. Clean and roughly chop the mushrooms. Chop the parsley.
3 Heat the oil in a large pan. Fry the onion or shallot over moderate heat until lightly browned. Peel the garlic and crush it into the pan. Add the mushrooms and cook until they release their liquid, then add the chopped parsley.
4 Squeeze as much water as possible from the bread, then stir it into the mushrooms. Add the stock and mace or nutmeg. Return to the boil, half cover the pan and simmer for 15–20 minutes.
5 Purée or blend the soup until it is creamy but still slightly grainy, then reheat, season with salt and pepper and serve immediately.

NUTRIENTS PER SERVING, WHEN SERVING 4: kilojoules 795, protein 7 g, carbohydrate 21 g (sugar 2 g), fat 11 g (saturated fat 1 g), good source of vitamins B group, E and folate, and selenium.

THREE BEAN SOUP

A trio of beans – green, broad and lima, fresh, frozen and canned – come together to add their individual flavours to this delicate pale green soup, garnished with chives.

TIME: 30 MINUTES SERVES: 4–6

2 tablespoons olive oil
4 cups vegetable stock
1 medium onion
1 large clove garlic
250 g thin green beans
375 g frozen broad beans
445 g canned lima (butter) beans
Salt and black pepper
To garnish: a small bunch of chives

1 Heat the oil gently in a large saucepan and put the stock on to heat. Peel the onion, chop it and add to the oil. Peel the garlic, crush it into the onion and stir.

2 Top and tail the green beans, chop into 2.5-cm pieces and add them and the broad beans to the pan. Raise the heat and cook for a few minutes.

3 Add the stock to the pan and boil for 5 minutes, then lower the heat and simmer for 10 minutes.

4 Remove the saucepan from the heat and stir in the canned lima beans with their liquid. Stir well.

5 Process or blend half the soup to a purée, then return to the pan. Season to taste with salt and pepper and reheat. Snip the chives and any chive flowers over the soup just before serving.

VARIATION
Coriander, mint or parsley can be used as a garnish instead of chives.

NUTRIENTS PER SERVING, WHEN SERVING 4: kilojoules 1058, protein 13 g, carbohydrate 29 g (sugar 4 g), fat 10 g (saturated fat 1 g), good source of vitamins B group, C, E and folate.

33

SPICY CARROT SOUP

Carrots and ginger bring out the best in each other, and here they are boosted with fresh green chilli and Eastern spices in a thick vegetable soup to make a real winter warmer.

TIME: 30 MINUTES SERVES: 4–6

4 cups vegetable stock or water
1 medium potato
1 medium onion
500 g carrots
2 large cloves garlic
Salt and black pepper
1 green chilli
5-cm piece fresh root ginger
1 lemon or lime
2 tablespoons olive oil
1 teaspoon garam masala, Chinese five-spice powder or mixed spice
1 teaspoon sesame seed oil
To garnish: coriander leaves, lemon or lime zest, or croutons

1 Bring the stock or water to the boil in a large saucepan. Peel the potato, onion and carrots and cut into small chunks. Peel and quarter the garlic cloves.

2 When the stock is boiling, stir in the vegetables, garlic and some salt. Bring back to the boil, reduce the heat, partially cover and boil gently for 15–20 minutes.

3 Meanwhile, seed and finely chop the chilli, peel and finely chop the ginger, and squeeze the juice from the lemon or lime.

4 Heat the olive oil in a small pan and fry the chilli and ginger for about 1 minute, but do not let them burn. Stir in the garam masala, five-spice powder or mixed spice and the juice; cook for 1 minute.

5 Add the sesame seed oil and stir over the heat until the mixture thickens. Remove the pan from the heat and put aside.

6 When the vegetables are tender, stir in the ginger sauce, then process or blend the mixture into a smooth purée. Return the purée to the pan, season with black pepper to taste, then reheat and serve with the garnish of your choice.

NUTRIENTS PER SERVING, WHEN SERVING 4: kilojoules 707, protein 3 g, carbohydrate 19 g (sugar 9 g), fat 11g (saturated fat 1 g), good source of vitamins A, B group, C and E.

MINESTRONE

You can vary the ingredients in this robust classic soup to suit your own tastes by using any fresh seasonal vegetables, some small pasta shapes and your choice of canned beans.

TIME: 30 MINUTES SERVES: 4

1 small leek
2 tablespoons olive oil
1 clove garlic
2 medium stalks celery
2 medium zucchini
A sprig of parsley
375 g canned cannellini beans
425 g canned tomato pieces, with their juice
1 bay leaf
150 ml dry white wine
2 tablespoons soup-pasta shapes
1 lemon
125 g savoy or other green cabbage
⅓ cup grated Parmesan cheese
Salt and black pepper
To serve: loaf of crusty bread; 4 tablespoons pesto sauce, optional

1 Put a kettle of water on to boil. Trim, halve and slice the leek, rinse well, then drain in a colander.

2 Heat the oil in a large saucepan and fry the leek for 1 minute. Peel the garlic and crush it into the pan.

3 Rinse and finely slice the celery and stir into the pan. Trim the zucchini, cut in half lengthways and then cut into half-moon slices. Add to the pan and cook for a further 3 minutes.

4 Rinse the parsley and drain and rinse the beans, then add both to the pan with the tomatoes, bay leaf, white wine, pasta and 2 cups boiling water. Finely pare off a strip of rind from the lemon and add to the pan. Cover, bring back to the boil, then reduce the heat and simmer for 7 minutes.

5 Meanwhile, finely shred the cabbage. Add to the soup, along with half the grated cheese. Season to taste with salt and pepper, then simmer for another 5 minutes.

6 Remove the bay leaf, pour the minestrone into four bowls, and sprinkle the rest of the cheese over the top of each bowl. Serve the soup with crusty bread and, if liked, pass around a small separate bowl of pesto sauce.

NUTRIENTS PER SERVING: kilojoules 2030, protein 21 g, carbohydrate 65 g (sugar 8 g), fat 15 g (saturated fat 3 g), good source of vitamins A, B group, C, E and folate, and calcium and selenium.

COOK'S SUGGESTION

Instead of adding the grated cheese at the end, you can add a small piece of Parmesan rind to the soup along with the canned tomatoes to give a cheesy flavour throughout. Remove the rind just before serving.

PEA AND ASPARAGUS SOUP

This pretty spring soup makes the most of fresh asparagus. A garnish of crispy bacon pieces and crunchy croutons adds savour, while a swirl of crème fraîche provides a smooth touch.

TIME: 30 MINUTES SERVES: 4

2½ cups chicken or vegetable stock
8–9 spring onions
500 g frozen peas
150 g small asparagus spears
Salt and black pepper
3 rashers rindless bacon
1–2 tablespoons vegetable oil, if needed
2 slices day-old white bread
2 tablespoons crème fraîche

1 Put the stock on to heat. Trim and roughly chop the spring onions and add to the stock along with the frozen peas. Bring to the boil.

2 Remove the asparagus tips and put aside. Roughly chop the stems and add to the saucepan with a pinch of salt. Reduce the heat, cover and simmer for 10–15 minutes, or until the asparagus is tender.

3 Meanwhile, snip the bacon rashers directly into a frying pan and fry until crisp and golden. Transfer to a plate and put aside.

4 If there is not enough bacon fat left in the pan for frying, add 1–2 tablespoons vegetable oil and heat. Cut the bread into small dice and fry for 2–3 minutes over high heat, turning the croutons frequently, until golden, then drain on paper towels.

5 When the peas and asparagus are done, blend the soup to a purée.

6 Add all but 12 of the reserved asparagus tips to the soup and simmer for about 5 minutes, or until tender.

7 Pour the soup into four warmed serving bowls. Swirl 2 teaspoons crème fraîche into each and sprinkle with the reserved bacon pieces, the croutons and the remaining asparagus tips. Top with some freshly ground black pepper.

NUTRIENTS PER SERVING: kilojoules 1381, protein 13 g, carbohydrate 24 g (sugar 5 g), fat 21 g (saturated fat 9 g), good source of vitamins B group, C, E and folate.

TOMATO AND RED LENTIL SOUP

An unusual green-and-white garnish of cream cheese speckled with basil adds a fresh touch to this intensely flavoured, richly coloured soup of tomatoes, garlic and lentils.

TIME: 30 MINUTES SERVES: 4

2½ cups chicken or vegetable stock
2 tablespoons olive oil
3 shallots
2–3 cloves garlic
1 red chilli
A few sprigs of basil
⅔ cup split red lentils
425 g canned tomato pieces, with their juice
100 g soft cream cheese, optional
Salt and black pepper

1 Put the stock on to heat. Heat the oil in a large saucepan. Peel and chop the shallots, garlic and chilli. Fry gently for 5 minutes, until soft.
2 Meanwhile, reserve a few leaves of basil for a garnish, then shred enough to give 1 tablespoon.
3 Rinse and drain the lentils and add to the pan with the stock and the tomatoes. Bring to the boil, cover and simmer for about 15 minutes, adding half the shredded basil after 10 minutes.

4 Beat the cream cheese, if using, in a small bowl until softened. Stir in the remaining shredded basil.
5 Blend or process the soup to a purée and season to taste with salt and pepper. Serve with spoonfuls of the cream cheese mixture; garnish with basil leaves.

NUTRIENTS PER SERVING: kilojoules 1260, protein 10 g, carbohydrate 20 g (sugar 4 g), fat 20 g (saturated fat 8 g), good source of vitamins B group, C and E.

AROMATIC PARSNIP SOUP

This fragrant, warming winter soup has a yoghurt creaminess and subtle spicing, with a sweet undertone of apple.

TIME: 30 MINUTES SERVES: 4–6

3½ cups vegetable stock
1 large cooking apple
600 g parsnips
1 medium onion
1 tablespoon sunflower oil
1 clove garlic
2 teaspoons ground coriander
1 teaspoon ground cumin
1 teaspoon turmeric
Salt
300 ml milk

To garnish: a few sprigs of coriander; 4–6 tablespoons natural yoghurt, if desired

1 Warm the stock over low heat. Peel the apple and the parsnips. Quarter and core the apple, then chop the apple and parsnips into chunks and put aside.

2 Peel and chop the onion. Heat the oil in a large saucepan, add the onion and leave it to soften.

3 Peel and roughly chop the garlic, add to the pan, then add the ground coriander, cumin and turmeric and cook for 1 minute.

4 Pour the warmed stock into the pan and add the apple, parsnips and salt. Bring to the boil, then reduce the heat, cover and simmer for 15 minutes. Meanwhile, strip off the coriander leaves.

5 Remove the pan from the heat and stir in the milk. Process or blend the soup to a smooth purée, then reheat.

6 Ladle the soup into bowls, swirl with a little yoghurt, garnish with the coriander leaves and serve. Or offer a small dish of yoghurt for people to help themselves.

NUTRIENTS PER SERVING, WHEN SERVING 4:
kilojoules 966, protein 9 g, carbohydrate 30 g (sugar 21 g), fat 10 g (saturated fat 2 g), good source of vitamins B group, C, E and folate, and calcium.

COOK'S SUGGESTION

If you are using a food processor or blender that will not take boiling liquids, cooling the soup by adding cold milk means that you can purée it immediately.

ZUCCHINI AND WATERCRESS SOUP

The mellow smoothness of the zucchini in this intensely green vegetable soup provides a subtle counterbalance to the underlying sharp, peppery flavour of the watercress leaves.

TIME: 30 MINUTES SERVES: 4

| 2 medium onions |
| 30 g unsalted butter |
| 3 cups chicken or vegetable stock |
| 1 kg firm zucchini |
| A large bunch of watercress |
| 1 lemon |
| Salt and black pepper |

1 Peel and finely chop the onions. Heat the unsalted butter in a large saucepan and fry onions over a gentle heat until translucent. Add the stock, cover the saucepan, and bring to the boil.

2 Rinse the zucchini, slice thinly, and add to the boiling stock. Reduce the heat, cover and simmer for 15 minutes.

3 Rinse the watercress, discard the coarse stems and reserve four sprigs for a garnish. Chop the remainder.

4 When the zucchini slices are tender, stir in the watercress. Remove the pan from the heat and leave to stand, covered, for 5 minutes. Meanwhile, squeeze the juice from the lemon and put aside.

5 Blend the soup to a purée, add seasoning and lemon juice to taste. Reheat and garnish with watercress.

NUTRIENTS PER SERVING: kilojoules 498, protein 6 g, carbohydrate 9 g (sugar 7 g), fat 6 g (saturated fat 4 g), good source of vitamins A, B group, C, E and folate, and iron and zinc.

FRENCH VEGETABLE SOUP

This elegant combination of fresh spring vegetables, cooked together then added to a rich tomato-flavoured base, makes a hearty soup that will serve as a light main course for lunch.

TIME: 30 MINUTES SERVES: 4

30 g butter
2 cloves garlic
2 shallots
3 x 425 g canned tomato pieces, with their juice
1¾ cups chicken or vegetable stock
1 teaspoon dried basil
Salt and black pepper
200 g baby new potatoes
12 baby or 4 small carrots
6 large radishes
12 asparagus tips
100 g sugar snap peas or snow peas
2 cups cream
8 large basil leaves
To garnish: Parmesan cheese or mature Cheddar, optional

1 Put a kettle of water on to boil. Heat the butter very slowly in a large saucepan. Peel and chop the garlic and shallots, add to the butter and fry gently for 3 minutes, stirring occasionally.

2 Add the tomatoes and their liquid, the stock, dried basil, and some salt and pepper. Cover and simmer for 15 minutes.

3 Meanwhile, scrub and quarter the potatoes, put into a second saucepan and cover well with boiling water from the kettle. Bring back to the boil, then reduce the heat and boil gently.

4 Trim, scrub and halve the baby carrots or, if you are using larger carrots, peel and cut into 2.5-cm chunks. When the potatoes have been cooking for 5 minutes, add the carrots to the saucepan.

5 Trim and rinse the radishes, then dice and add to the carrots and potatoes. Rinse the asparagus tips and trim and halve the sugar snap peas or snow peas; add both to the saucepan.

6 Cook the vegetables for a total of 10–12 minutes or until they are just tender. Meanwhile, grate the cheese, if using, and put aside.

7 Drain the vegetables and add to the tomato stock. Stir in the cream. Tear and add the basil leaves.

8 Season the soup to taste with salt and pepper. Serve immediately, passing the grated cheese separately to sprinkle over the top, if using.

VARIATION
Add some shredded cooked chicken or turkey to make a delicious poultry and vegetable stew.

NUTRIENTS PER SERVING: kilojoules 938, protein 8 g, carbohydrate 22 g (sugar 14 g), fat 12 g (saturated fat 7 g), good source of vitamins A, B group, C, E and folate.

CRAB AND SESAME SOUP

The creamy richness of the crab meat combines beautifully with the fragrant seasonings in this light and elegant, yet surprisingly satisfying, first-course soup.

TIME: 15 MINUTES SERVES: 4

4 cups chicken stock
Sea salt and black pepper
2 tablespoons cornflour
4 spring onions, white part only
A few sprigs of coriander
125 g cooked crab meat
1 teaspoon sesame seed oil
1 teaspoon chilli paste
1 teaspoon light soy sauce

1 Season stock with sea salt and black pepper and put on to heat.
2 Blend the cornflour with 3 tablespoons cold water to make a smooth paste. When stock is simmering, whisk in the paste until the soup is clear and thickened.
3 Finely chop the spring onions. Add to the soup, along with the spring onions, crab meat, sesame seed oil, chilli paste and soy sauce.

Stir gently over moderate heat for 2–3 minutes, until the crab is just heated through.
4 Divide the soup among four bowls, scatter some coriander leaves on top and serve immediately.

NUTRIENTS PER SERVING: kilojoules 273, protein 7 g, carbohydrate 6 g (sugar 1 g), fat 1 g (saturated fat 0.25 g), good source of vitamin B group, and copper and iodine.

SMOKED HADDOCK, BEAN AND LEEK SOUP

*Modest ingredients add up to a richly flavoured family soup. Creamy butter beans, with a little onion
and leek to sharpen them, have their flavour lifted by the smoky taste of the fish.*

TIME: 30 MINUTES SERVES: 4–6

2 ½ cups fish,
chicken or vegetable stock

1 medium onion

800 g leeks

2 tablespoons extra virgin
olive oil

2 x 445 g canned butter beans,
with their liquid

500 g smoked haddock
or smoked cod

A small handful of parsley

Black pepper

To garnish: 4–6 tablespoons
thick cream, optional

1 Put the stock on to heat in a
medium saucepan. Peel and finely
chop the onion. Trim the leeks, cut
into thin slices and rinse well.
2 Heat the oil in another saucepan
and cook the onion and leeks gently
for 5 minutes, stirring occasionally.
Add the stock, bring to the boil,
reduce the heat, cover and simmer
for 5 minutes.
3 Add the butter beans and their
liquid to the pan and mash roughly.
Return to the boil, reduce the heat,
cover and let simmer.
4 Skin the haddock (see page 11)
and dice the flesh, discarding any

bones. Add the fish to the soup
and simmer until the haddock is
heated through and opaque.
5 Chop the parsley. Season the
soup to taste with the black pepper
(the smoked fish should be salty
enough without adding extra) and
sprinkle over the chopped parsley.
Serve, if you like, with a spoonful of
cream swirled into each bowl.

NUTRIENTS PER SERVING, WHEN SERVING 4:
*kilojoules 1594, protein 38 g, carbohydrate
34 g (sugar 7 g), fat 10 g (saturated fat 1 g),
good source of vitamins B group, C, E,
and folate.*

CHUNKY FISH SOUP

*Chunks of firm fish stay attractively whole in this beautifully simple soup. Herbs, tomatoes and wine
add extra flavour and a warm inviting colour, while a modest addition of cream gives it richness.*

TIME: 30 MINUTES SERVES: 4–6

2 ½ cups fish stock

1 medium onion

1 medium bulb fennel

2 tablespoons sunflower oil

150 ml dry white wine
or vermouth

400 g canned tomato pieces,
with their juice

1 bay leaf

1 teaspoon sugar

Salt and black pepper

500 g firm-fleshed fish fillets
or cutlets

A few sprigs of parsley

1 tablespoon cornflour

2 tablespoons milk

2 tablespoons thick cream

1 Put the stock on to heat. Peel
and finely chop the onion and trim
and finely chop the fennel, reserving
the fronds for a garnish.
2 Heat the oil in a large, heavy
saucepan, then cook the onion and
fennel over moderate heat for
5 minutes, or until softened.

3 Pour off any surplus oil from the
saucepan, then add the stock, the
wine or vermouth, tomatoes, bay
leaf and sugar and season to taste
with salt and pepper. Bring the
mixture to the boil, cover and
simmer for 10 minutes.
4 Meanwhile, skin the fish (see
page 11), discard any bones, cut the
flesh into 2.5-cm cubes and add to
the pan. Reserve a few leaves of
parsley for a garnish, then chop the
rest and add to the soup. Cover and
simmer gently for 5 minutes.
5 Blend the cornflour and milk in
a bowl. When the fish is cooked,
remove the bay leaf, stir the
cornflour into the soup and simmer
until thickened slightly.
6 Stir in the cream and heat gently
for 1–2 minutes. Serve the soup
garnished with the reserved fennel
fronds and parsley.

NUTRIENTS PER SERVING, WHEN SERVING 4:
*kilojoules 1389, protein 22 g, carbohydrate
12 g (sugar 8 g), fat 19 g (saturated fat 8 g),
good source of vitamins A, B group, C and E.*

COOK'S SUGGESTION

*You can use any firm-fleshed
fish, such as snapper, orange roughy,
salmon or shark to make this dish.
Alternatively, you can use equal
quantities of shelled and deveined
prawns and shucked scallops.*

TWO HEARTY FISH SOUPS: *(top)*
SMOKED HADDOCK, BEAN AND LEEK SOUP;
(bottom) CHUNKY FISH SOUP.

SPICY PRAWN AND CHILLI SOUP

Plump green prawns are freshly cooked in this aromatic stock, boosted by the flavoursome addition of lemon grass, ginger and chillies. Lime juice and lime leaves provide the final touch.

TIME: 25 MINUTES SERVES: 4

| 5 cups chicken stock |
| 500 g medium-sized green prawns |
| 2 stalks lemon grass |
| 40 g fresh root ginger |
| 4 small red chillies |
| 4 limes |
| 3 tablespoons fish sauce |
| 6 kaffir lime leaves |
| A small bunch of coriander |

1 Put the stock on to heat in a large saucepan. Shell and devein the prawns and put aside.
2 Finely chop the lemon grass. Peel and cut the ginger into julienne strips. Seed and finely slice the chillies. Squeeze the limes and reserve the juice.
3 Add the lemon grass, ginger, chillies, lime juice and fish sauce to the simmering stock. Continue to simmer, over moderately low heat, for 1–2 minutes.
4 Meanwhile, finely shred 2 lime leaves and chop enough coriander to give 2 tablespoons.
5 Add the shredded lime leaves and prawns to the stock and simmer for a further 10 minutes.
6 Pour the soup into a warmed serving bowl, add the remaining lime leaves and serve immediately.

VARIATION
Yabbies can be used instead of prawns. You could also substitute strips of skinless chicken breast.

NUTRIENTS PER SERVING: kilojoules 536, protein 18 g, carbohydrate 1 g (sugar 0.5 g), fat 1 g (saturated fat 0.2 g), good source of vitamin C and iodine.

COOK'S SUGGESTION

Known as nam pla in Thailand, and nuoc nam in Vietnam, fish sauce is available from Asian food stores and larger supermarkets. It keeps indefinitely without refrigeration.

ORIENTAL CHICKEN BROTH

Shiitake mushrooms, lettuce, cayenne pepper and fresh coriander flavour this classic soup, which is based on chicken stock and made more substantial with vermicelli and threads of beaten egg.

TIME: 15 MINUTES SERVES: 4

5 cups chicken stock
¼ teaspoon cayenne pepper
100 g shiitake mushrooms
70 g Little Gem lettuce
1 large egg
2 sprigs coriander
40 g vermicelli

1 Bring the stock and cayenne pepper to the boil in a large saucepan.
2 Meanwhile, clean, trim and thinly slice the mushrooms. If necessary, remove and discard the outer leaves from the lettuce, then rinse and finely shred the inner leaves. Beat the egg lightly and put aside. Strip the coriander leaves from the stems.
3 When the stock reaches boiling point, add the mushrooms, lower the heat and simmer for 2 minutes. Crush the vermicelli lightly, add to the stock and simmer for 3 minutes, until just barely cooked. Add the lettuce, then raise the heat and bring the soup to a rolling boil.

4 Take the saucepan off the heat and slowly add the egg, stirring gently. It will cook very quickly to form threads. Stir in the coriander leaves and serve immediately.
VARIATION
Oyster mushrooms can be used instead of shiitake, and watercress can be substituted for the lettuce.

NUTRIENTS PER SERVING: kilojoules 335, protein 6 g, carbohydrate 8 g (sugar 0.5 g), fat 2 g (saturated fat 1 g), good source of vitamins B group and E.

STARTERS

Mussels and yabbies, rocket and mangoes, goat's cheese and Camembert – just some of the tempting ingredients that make up these enticing light dishes to launch a great meal.

CHICKEN LIVERS WITH JUNIPER BERRIES

Aromatic juniper berries, juicy grapes, fresh thyme and a dash of dry sherry give earthy, pan-fried chicken livers a new rich flavour and create a dramatic starter.

TIME: 20 MINUTES SERVES: 4

500 g fresh chicken livers
1 shallot
1 clove garlic
10 juniper berries
A large bunch of thyme
A small bunch of flat-leaf parsley
1 tablespoon olive oil
Salt and black pepper
2 tablespoons dry sherry
200 g small, seedless, green and red grapes
8 thick slices white baguette bread

1 Rinse the chicken livers under cold running water, trim off any sinews with scissors, then cut the flesh into bite-sized pieces. Pat dry with paper towels.

2 Peel and finely chop the shallot, peel and crush the garlic and lightly crush the juniper berries. Put aside. Strip enough leaves from the thyme to give 2 tablespoons. Chop the parsley and put aside for a garnish.
3 Heat the oil in a large, heavy frying pan. When it is very hot, add the chicken livers and toss quickly to seal the surfaces. Cook over high heat, stirring, for 2 minutes.
4 Add the shallot, garlic, juniper berries, thyme and plenty of black pepper to the pan, then lower the heat and continue cooking for a further 3–4 minutes, stirring.
5 Add the sherry and grapes to the pan and add salt to taste. Cook for another minute, then turn off the heat, cover and keep warm.
6 Toast the bread and put two slices on each individual serving

plate. Spoon the chicken livers over the toast and sprinkle with the chopped parsley. Serve immediately.
VARIATION
You can add 1 cup pure or sour cream, or natural yoghurt, to the chicken livers and serve them as a sauce for pasta.

NUTRIENTS PER SERVING: kilojoules 1055, protein 25 g, carbohydrate 20 g (sugar 8 g), fat 7 g (saturated fat 1 g), good source of vitamins A, B group, C and folate, and iron and zinc.

COOK'S SUGGESTION
The chicken livers can be washed and trimmed 1–2 hours in advance and kept covered in the refrigerator until you're ready to cook them.

TROPICAL SALAD WITH LIME DRESSING

Two favourite tropical fruits – rich, creamy-smooth avocado and sweet-flavoured pawpaw – are combined with peppery watercress and a fresh lime dressing to make a light and stylish entrée.

TIME: 20 MINUTES   SERVES: 4

| A bunch of watercress |
| 2 ripe but firm avocados |
| 2 ripe but firm pawpaws |

For the dressing:
| 1 lime |
| Salt and black pepper |
| ¼ teaspoon sugar |
| 3 tablespoons extra virgin olive oil |
| 3 tablespoons sunflower oil |

1   First make the dressing. Remove the rind from the lime with a zester, or grate it finely. Squeeze out 2 tablespoons lime juice and put it with the rind in a mixing bowl. Add salt, black pepper and sugar, then whisk in the oils. Taste and add more lime juice, if necessary, then put the dressing aside.

2   Rinse and dry the watercress and trim off the coarse stalks.

3   Halve and stone the avocados (see page 53), then peel and slice widthways. Halve the pawpaws, then remove the seeds and peel and slice the flesh lengthways.

4   Arrange the watercress, avocado and pawpaw on individual serving plates. Pour the dressing over and serve immediately.

VARIATION
Mangoes can be substituted for the pawpaws and the watercress replaced with baby spinach leaves.

NUTRIENTS PER SERVING: kilojoules 1976, protein 4 g, carbohydrate 20 g (sugar 19 g), fat 42 g (saturated fat 7 g), good source of vitamins A, B group and C.

COOK'S SUGGESTION

When choosing an avocado, pick one that feels heavy for its size. An avocado is ripe when it yields to light pressure; it can then be kept for 3–4 days in the refrigerator. Unripe avocados will ripen in 1–2 days if kept in a warm room.

PROSCIUTTO WITH PEAR AND PARMESAN

Served on a bed of mixed salad leaves, this unusual combination makes a lovely appetiser or a very light lunch. Use a fruity extra virgin olive oil as its special flavour really makes the dish sing.

TIME: 12 MINUTES SERVES: 4

1 lime or lemon

4 small dessert pears

Salt and black pepper

100 g mixed salad leaves

12 thin slices prosciutto
or Parma ham, about 200 g in total

100-g piece Parmesan cheese

2–3 tablespoons extra virgin
olive oil

1 Squeeze the lime or lemon and pour the juice into a mixing bowl. Quarter and core the pears. Cut each quarter lengthways into three or four slices, add to the juice, season lightly with black pepper and toss gently.

2 Trim the salad leaves and rinse and dry them if necessary. Tear any large leaves into pieces, then pile the leaves loosely on four plates. Arrange the slices of marinated pear on top of the salad leaves, then weave the slices of prosciutto or Parma ham around the pears. Add salt to taste.

3 Using a potato peeler, shave a few wafer-thin slices of Parmesan cheese directly over the salad (see box, right). Drizzle the olive oil over the salad and serve at once.

NUTRIENTS PER SERVING: kilojoules 1695, protein 20 g, carbohydrate 11 g (sugar 11 g), fat 31 g (saturated fat 11 g), good source of vitamins B group and E, and calcium.

EASY DOES IT!

When you are shaving thin strips of Parmesan, you will need to buy a larger piece of cheese than you actually use to give you a good grip.

GOAT'S CHEESE SOUFFLÉS

Light and dainty, these soufflés are made with strong-flavoured cheese and coated with toasted nuts. They look and taste impressive but are simple to make, rise well and can be served hot or cold.

TIME: 30 MINUTES SERVES: 4

⅓ cup ground hazelnuts,
almonds or walnuts

30 g butter
at room temperature

1½ tablespoons plain flour

4 tablespoons milk

Salt and black pepper

100 g firm goat's cheese

1 large egg yolk

3 large egg whites

1 Preheat the oven to 190°C. Put a kettle of water on to boil. Spread out the ground nuts in a dry frying pan and toast gently, stirring, until golden brown.
2 Use half the butter to grease the insides of four 200-ml ramekins. Divide the nuts equally among the bowls and shake until the sides and bottoms are evenly coated.
3 Melt the remaining butter in a saucepan, stir in the flour and cook,

stirring, for about 30 seconds. Take the pan off the heat and gradually stir in the milk. Bring the sauce to the boil, stirring, until it thickens. Add salt and pepper to taste.
4 Cut the goat's cheese into small dice, add just over half to the sauce and stir well. When the cheese has just melted, take the pan off the heat and stir in the egg yolk.
5 Whisk the egg whites until stiff. Using a large metal spoon, fold a third of the egg white into the cheese sauce to lighten it, then carefully fold in the remainder.
6 Divide the remaining cheese among the four ramekins and spoon the soufflé mixture on top. Stand the ramekins in a large baking dish and pour in boiling water to come halfway up their sides. Bake in the top half of the oven for 10 minutes, or until the soufflés have risen and are lightly set and golden brown. Serve hot, straight from the oven.

VARIATION
The soufflés can be made ahead and served cold on a bed of salad leaves. Let them cool in the ramekins, then chill them. Just before serving, run a knife round the sides of each soufflé and turn out onto a bed of mixed salad leaves.

NUTRIENTS PER SERVING: kilojoules 1193, protein 13 g, carbohydrate 5 g (sugar 2 g), fat 24 g (saturated fat 10 g), good source of vitamins B group and E.

COOK'S SUGGESTION

Use thin, ovenproof china ramekins for the soufflés if you can rather than thicker ceramic ones, as china allows the heat to penetrate faster.

CHEESE WITH VARIATIONS: (*top*) PROSCIUTTO WITH PEAR AND PARMESAN; (*bottom*) GOAT'S CHEESE SOUFFLÉS.

YABBY PÂTÉ

This modern variation on a traditional recipe makes a tasty change from the usual salmon or smoked trout spread.

TIME: 15 MINUTES SERVES: 4

| 12 cooked yabbies |
| 1 white onion |
| 1 clove garlic |
| A small bunch of flat-leaf parsley |
| 1 lime |
| 75 g unsalted butter |
| 1 tablespoon brandy |
| Sea salt and black pepper |
| 1 tablespoon prepared horseradish |
| ½ cup light sour cream |

To serve: **lime wedges, celery stalks, radicchio or lollo rosa leaves and toasted French bread**

1 Shell the yabbies; put the flesh aside. Peel and finely chop the onion and the garlic. Chop the parsley to give 2 tablespoons. Remove the zest from the lime and squeeze the juice; put aside.
2 Heat the butter in a large, heavy-based frying pan and add the chopped onion and garlic. Cook, stirring, until the onion has softened but not coloured.
3 Place the onion and garlic mixture, together with the pan juices, into the bowl of a food processor. Add the yabbies, chopped parsley, the lime zest and juice, and the brandy. Process for 10−15 seconds until the yabbies are coarsely chopped.
4 Season with sea salt and black pepper and add the horseradish. Process for a further 5−6 seconds. Transfer the mixture to a bowl and fold in the sour cream.
5 To serve, arrange lettuce leaves on individual plates, spoon on some pâté, garnish with lime wedges and celery, and accompany with toast.

NUTRIENTS PER SERVING: kilojoules 1212, protein 15 g, carbohydrates 4 g (sugar 2 g), fat 22 g (saturated fat 14 g), good source of vitamins B group and E, and iodine.

COOK'S SUGGESTION

This pâté can be prepared up to 24 hours in advance. Keep it in the refrigerator, tightly covered with plastic wrap, until required.

AVOCADO, PRAWN AND TOMATO SALAD

*Avocado and prawns are famously good together. Here they are joined by tomatoes and a creamy
dressing of lime, yoghurt and coriander gives the combination an elegant new style and exciting taste.*

TIME: 15 MINUTES SERVES: 4

| 1 large avocado |
| ½ lemon |
| 2 medium tomatoes |
| 200 g peeled cooked prawns |

For the dressing:

| ½ lime |
| A small bunch of coriander |
| ½ cup natural yoghurt |
| 1 teaspoon caster sugar |
| Salt and black pepper |

1 To make the dressing, grate the
rind of the lime into a small bowl,
putting a little aside for a garnish,
then squeeze the juice into the
bowl. Reserving a few sprigs of
coriander for a garnish, finely chop

enough to give 1 tablespoon. Add
to the lime juice, then stir in the
yoghurt, caster sugar, salt and black
pepper. Beat well and put aside.
2 Halve and stone the avocado
(see box, right), then peel and slice
the flesh and arrange on separate
serving plates. Squeeze some lemon
juice onto the avocado slices to
prevent browning.
3 Slice the tomatoes and arrange
with the prawns around the
avocado. Spoon over the dressing
and garnish with the reserved lime
rind and sprigs of coriander.

*NUTRIENTS PER SERVING: kilojoules 933,
protein 13 g, carbohydrate 7 g (sugar 6 g),
fat 16 g (saturated fat 4 g), good source of
vitamins B group, C and E.*

EASY DOES IT!

*To halve the avocado, cut lengthways
round then twist to separate the halves.
Carefully stick the blade of a heavy
kitchen knife into the stone. Twist to
loosen the stone, then lift out.*

SARDINES IN A PEPPERCORN CRUST

Fresh sardines are always bursting with flavour, and here they are given a crunchy coating of lemon juice, olive oil, dill, garlic and mixed peppercorns, then grilled with aromatic rosemary.

TIME: 25 MINUTES SERVES: 4

8 large fresh sardines, about 500 g in total
1 teaspoon mixed peppercorns
A small bunch of dill
1 clove garlic
2 lemons
Salt
2 tablespoons olive oil
8 small sprigs rosemary
4 crisp lettuce leaves
8 sprigs watercress

1 Preheat the griller to the highest setting. Cut along the belly of each sardine with kitchen scissors, then pull out the insides. Rinse the fish inside and out, gently rubbing off the scales with your fingers. Dry the sardines on paper towels.

2 Crush the peppercorns and put into a small bowl.

3 Chop the dill, peel and crush the garlic and add both to the bowl. Finely grate the rind of one lemon into the bowl. Add some salt and the olive oil and mix.

4 Put a sprig of rosemary inside each fish, then brush each side with some of the dill mixture, reserving any leftover mixture. Leave the fish to marinate for 5–10 minutes.

5 Meanwhile, finely shred the lettuce leaves, rinse and dry the watercress and arrange on plates. Cut four wedges from the other lemon, remove any pips and put one wedge on each plate.

6 Thread each sardine lengthways onto a metal skewer, then grill for 2–3 minutes on each side.

7 Slide the sardines off the skewers and arrange two on each plate on top of the salad. Spoon over the reserved dill mixture and serve.

VARIATION
As an alternative to grilling, try the skewered sardines cooked on a very hot barbecue.

NUTRIENTS PER SERVING: kilojoules 1109, protein 24 g, carbohydrate 1 g (sugar 0.3 g), fat 19 g (saturated fat 4 g), good source of vitamins B group and E.

COOK'S SUGGESTION

If you have the time, you can spread the peppercorn paste over the sardines an hour or two in advance and leave them to marinate in the refrigerator.

SCALLOP BROCHETTES WITH PROSCIUTTO

The subtle saltiness of Italian dried ham combines perfectly with these marinated scallops and their brilliant orange corals to make handsome starters that can be served on the skewers.

TIME: 30 MINUTES SERVES: 4

24 shucked scallops with their corals, about 350 g in total
16 thin slices prosciutto or Parma ham, about 150 g in total
Black pepper

For the marinade:

2 large cloves garlic
A few sprigs of basil
A few sprigs of coriander
A few sprigs of parsley
½ lemon
2 tablespoons virgin olive oil

1 Rinse and dry the scallops, separate the corals from the white meat and put both into a bowl.

GREAT SEAFOOD GRILLS: *(top)* SARDINES IN A PEPPERCORN CRUST; *(bottom)* SCALLOP BROCHETTES WITH PROSCIUTTO.

2 To make the marinade, peel the garlic cloves and crush into the bowl. Reserve a few sprigs of basil for a garnish, then chop the rest of the basil, coriander and parsley and add to the scallops. Squeeze the lemon juice into the bowl, add the olive oil, stir and leave to marinate at room temperature for 15 minutes. While the scallops are marinating, cut each ham slice in half. Preheat the griller to high.

3 When the scallops are ready, gather a piece of ham into a ruffle, thread it onto a metal skewer, then thread on a scallop and a piece of coral. Repeat twice more and finish with ham. Prepare seven more skewers the same way.

4 Place the skewers across the griller tray, baste with some of the marinade and grill for 5 minutes, turning and basting again halfway through, until the ham is crisp and the scallops are just cooked.

5 Serve on skewers, or remove and pile the scallops and ham onto serving plates. Spoon on the pan juices, then top with black pepper and reserved sprigs of basil.

VARIATION
Shelled green tiger prawns or cubes of firm white fish can be used instead of the scallops.

NUTRIENTS PER SERVING: kilojoules 1318, protein 30 g, carbohydrate 4 g (sugar 0.1 g), fat 20 g (saturated fat 6 g), good source of vitamin E.

COOK'S SUGGESTION

Always use fresh scallops. Frozen scallops are too watery and this will dilute the marinade too much.

SMOKED TROUT WITH PEAR AND ROCKET

Strips of smoked trout and crisp white slivers of pear are set against the brilliant leaves of radicchio and rocket in this very decorative salad, which is served dressed with a creamy horseradish sauce.

TIME: 15 MINUTES SERVES: 4

| 4 fillets smoked trout |
| 2 dessert pears |
| 1 small head radicchio |
| 50 g rocket leaves |
| Salt and black pepper |
| *To serve:* walnut or brown bread |

For the dressing:

| ½ lemon |
| 2 tablespoons extra virgin olive oil |

For the sauce:

| 2 tablespoons crème fraîche |
| 2 teaspoons horseradish cream |

1 Skin the trout fillets (see page 11) and slice across into strips. Halve and core the pears, then cut into narrow slices.

2 Rinse and dry the radicchio and rocket. Tear the radicchio into a bowl, add the rocket and season with salt and pepper.

3 To make the dressing, squeeze 2 teaspoons juice from the lemon into a bowl, add the oil and whisk together. Pour over the salad leaves, add the trout and the pears and toss gently. Divide among four plates.

4 To make the sauce, mix the crème fraîche with the horseradish cream and stir to give a pouring consistency. Spoon over the trout and salad and serve with thinly sliced bread.

NUTRIENTS PER SERVING: kilojoules 2293, protein 39 g, carbohydrate 31 g (sugar 11 g), fat 30 g (saturated fat 9 g), good source of vitamin E.

COOK'S SUGGESTION

Comice and Williams pears are the sweetest and juiciest and will keep their colour if they are served as soon as they are sliced. If you need to keep them for any length of time before serving, brush the slices with lemon juice.

QUAIL ON A MUSHROOM NEST

Tiny quails, nestling on mushroom caps and topped with a garnish of parsley, lemon and garlic,
make a sophisticated starter yet leave you plenty of free time to prepare the main course.

TIME: 30 MINUTES SERVES: 4

2 tablespoons olive oil
30 g butter
4 oven-ready quails
8 sprigs thyme
4 bay leaves
4 large flat mushrooms
Salt and black pepper

For the gremolata:

A small bunch of parsley
1 lemon
1 clove garlic

1 Preheat the oven to 230°C. Put the olive oil and butter in a shallow ovenproof dish and leave to heat in the top half of the oven while you prepare the quails.

2 Pluck any feathers from the quails, rinse and pat dry. Put 2 sprigs thyme and 1 bay leaf into each cavity.

3 Clean the mushrooms and remove the stalks. Place skin side down in the ovenproof dish, and position a quail on the centre of each. Baste the quails and around the edges of the mushrooms with the oil and butter and season well with salt and pepper.

4 Roast the quails in the oven for 15–20 minutes, or until their juices run clear when the flesh is pierced with a skewer. Baste again halfway through cooking.

5 Meanwhile, make the gremolata. Chop enough parsley to give 2 tablespoons. Grate half the rind

from the lemon. Peel and crush the garlic. Mix together in a small bowl.

6 A few minutes before the quails have finished cooking, sprinkle some gremolata over each and return to the oven.

NUTRIENTS PER SERVING: kilojoules 1485, protein 31 g, carbohydrate 1 g (sugar 0.2 g), fat 25 g (saturated fat 4 g), good source of vitamins B group and E.

COOK'S SUGGESTION

Gremolata is an Italian garnish traditionally served with Ossobucco. It can be used to boost the flavour of many simple dishes, including pasta and vegetables.

SWIFT FRUITY STARTERS

A fruit component in a starter adds a tingle to the flavour – think of that uplifting splash of orange juice in a tomato soup or a grated carrot salad. And there's another bonus: ripe, vibrant fruit needs no cooking, so you can add almost instant glamour to the entrée menu.

FRUIT WITH PROSCIUTTO

The classic combination of prosciutto and melon, plus a seasonal variation.

Serve one or two slices of rockmelon on individual plates with thinly sliced, delicately folded prosciutto. Top each serve with some freshly grated black pepper. When figs are in season, serve instead two ripe figs per person, halved to display their flesh and arranged in a cluster beside the folds of prosciutto. Pass the pepper grinder round separately.

STRAWBERRY, CUCUMBER AND AVOCADO SALAD

This colourful summer presentation can be served alone as a starter, or offered as the centrepiece of a sumptuous buffet to complement tender smoked chicken or succulent poached salmon.

Place alternating bands or concentric circles of sliced avocado, strawberries and cucumber on a serving dish (remember to turn the avocado slices in lemon juice if the dish is not to be eaten immediately). Then top the salad with a vinaigrette dressing made of two parts hazelnut oil to three parts olive oil and one part raspberry or wine vinegar.

WATERMELON AND FETA CHEESE

This is the kind of cool fruity starter that is a joy to eat outdoors in the warmth of summer, surrounded by the tempting aroma of hot food sizzling on a barbecue.

Mix bite-sized chunks of peeled watermelon, sprinkled with black pepper, with smaller pieces of crumbled Greek feta cheese. Garnish with rocket or watercress leaves. It is the striking contrasts of flavour and texture that make this salad exciting.

FIRST COURSE FRUIT
FOR THESE SIMPLE PRESENTATIONS CHOOSE RIPE FRUITS IN FLAWLESS CONDITION THAT WILL TASTE AS GOOD AS THEY LOOK.

CITRUS SALAD

A refreshing orange and grapefruit salad is garnished with black olives and red onion rings to make a perfect beginning to a rich meal.

For four people, cut off the rinds and white pith from three oranges and one grapefruit. Separate the fruit into segments over a bowl, cutting between the membranes, or slice thinly across on a plate to catch the juices. Peel a Spanish onion and slice thinly across into rings. Pull the rings apart to separate them.

Measure the orange juice and stir in an equal amount of fruity olive oil and a pinch of salt, then sharpen to taste with lemon juice to make the dressing. Arrange the fruit slices on four plates, garnish with black olives and the onion rings, and pour over the dressing.

LOCKET'S SAVOURY

This dish takes its name from a fashionable London restaurant of the 1970s, where the delicious open sandwich was served as a savoury alternative to dessert. For today's tastes, it works well as an entrée.

Toast one thick slice of wholemeal bread per person and cover with a generous pile of roughly chopped watercress. Then layer overlapping peeled slices of juicy dessert pears on top of the chopped watercress and grind black pepper over the lot. Cover the open sandwich with a thick layer of sliced Stilton cheese and place under the griller until the cheese just reaches melting point. Garnish with lamb's lettuce and tomato halves.

SMOKED MACKEREL WITH GRAPEFRUIT SALSA

The sweet-sharp freshness of lush pink or white grapefruit offsets the smooth saltiness of the fish in this combination of strong smoky flavours.

Take one fillet of smoked mackerel per person, skin it (see page 11) and cut the flesh diagonally into strips. For four people, peel and segment a large grapefruit over a bowl, making sure you catch the juices. Cut the flesh of a ripe avocado into medium dice and add to the bowl. Snip a few fresh chives over the salsa, season generously with black pepper and stir together. Mix in the smoked mackerel strips and garnish the dish with whole chives.

THREE REFRESHING FIRST COURSES:
(*top*) FRUIT WITH PROSCIUTTO;
(*centre*) CITRUS SALAD;
(*bottom right*) SMOKED MACKEREL WITH
GRAPEFRUIT SALSA.

GRILLED OYSTERS

Pacific oysters are topped with a simple mixture of butter, garlic, breadcrumbs and parsley before being lightly grilled on a bed of coarse salt until browned and slightly crunchy on top.

TIME: 30 MINUTES SERVES: 4

| 60 g softened butter |
| 2 cloves garlic |
| 3 tablespoons toasted brown breadcrumbs (see page 14) |
| A small bunch of parsley |
| Salt and black pepper |
| 12 Pacific oysters on the half shell |

To support the oysters: bag of coarse salt

1 Preheat the griller to high. Mash the butter in a small bowl, peel the garlic cloves and crush into the bowl, then mix in the breadcrumbs.

2 Finely chop enough parsley to give about 2–3 tablespoons and add to the butter with a little salt and plenty of pepper.

3 Remove the rack from the griller tray and half fill the tray with coarse salt. Place the oysters firmly in the salt so they do not wobble, and top with some of the seasoned breadcrumb mixture.

4 Grill for 1–2 minutes, or until the topping bubbles and is lightly browned. Serve immediately.

NUTRIENTS PER SERVING: *kilojoules 590, protein 4 g, carbohydrate 7 g (sugar 0.3 g), fat 11g (saturated fat 7 g), good source of vitamins B group and E, and zinc.*

COOK'S SUGGESTION

Pacific oysters taste much better cooked than raw, and they are quite filling. While they are ideal for this recipe, you might prefer to use smaller oysters; if so, you should plan to serve about six per person, so make double the breadcrumb mixture.

PRAWNS WITH CHILLI AND MANGOES

Luscious ripe mango and crunchy spring onions, spiced with hot chilli and fresh ginger, give a sweet and sour flavour to the large stir-fried prawns featured in this exuberant dish.

TIME: 30 MINUTES SERVES: 4

20 peeled green king prawns, about 250 g in total
50 g spring onions
2.5-cm piece fresh root ginger
1 clove garlic
1 small red chilli
2 mangoes, about 400 g each
3 teaspoons tomato paste
1 tablespoon soy sauce
2 tablespoons medium sherry
½ teaspoon sesame seed oil
4–6 red oakleaf or frisée lettuce leaves
2 tablespoons peanut oil
Black pepper

1 Make a deep cut along the back of each prawn. Discard the dark intestinal vein, then put the prawns aside.

2 Trim the spring onions and slice diagonally; peel and grate the ginger; peel and crush the garlic; halve, seed and slice the chilli. Put all into a bowl and put aside.

3 Peel the mangoes, then remove the flesh from the stones and cut into 5-mm-thick slices.

4 Mix the tomato paste, soy sauce, sherry and sesame seed oil in a small bowl.

5 Rinse and dry the lettuce leaves and arrange on individual serving plates. Put aside.

6 Heat the peanut oil in a wok or large frying pan. Add the spring onion mixture and stir-fry for 1 minute. Add the prawns and continue stir-frying until just beginning to turn pink. Add the mango slices and stir-fry until the prawns turn completely pink and the mango is heated through.

7 Add the soy sauce mixture and bring to the boil. Season to taste with black pepper, then spoon over the salad and serve.

NUTRIENTS PER SERVING: kilojoules 912, protein 13 g, carbohydrate 21 g (sugar 20 g), fat 9 g (saturated fat 1 g), good source of vitamins A, B group, C and E.

61

GOAT'S CHEESE AND ROCKET SALAD

This warm salad of roasted goat's cheese served on a bed of smoked bacon and peppery leaves has a dressing flavoured with garlic and wholegrain mustard and is guaranteed to sharpen the appetite.

TIME: 20 MINUTES SERVES: 4

250 g thick bacon rashers
1 tablespoon vegetable oil
2 small, round, soft goat's cheeses, about 100 g each
100 g rocket or watercress

For the dressing:

1 clove garlic
1 teaspoon wholegrain mustard
3 teaspoons white wine vinegar
2 tablespoons extra virgin olive oil
Salt and black pepper

1 Preheat the oven to 240°C. Dice the bacon rashers, discarding the rind. Heat the oil and fry the bacon pieces until crisp then drain on paper towels.

2 To make the dressing, peel the garlic, crush it into a small bowl, then whisk in the mustard, vinegar and olive oil. Season to taste with salt and pepper.

3 Line a baking tray with baking paper. Cut the goat's cheeses in half horizontally and place the rounds on the paper. Bake for 5 minutes or until the cheese begins to melt and turns a toasty brown on top.

4 Meanwhile, trim, rinse and dry the rocket or watercress and put into a mixing bowl with the bacon. Pour over the dressing and toss lightly, then arrange in circles on individual plates.

5 Remove the cheese from the oven, place one round in the centre of each salad and serve immediately.

VARIATION
For a vegetarian version, use lightly toasted pine nuts or almonds instead of the bacon.

NUTRIENTS PER SERVING: kilojoules 1520, protein 17 g, carbohydrate 2 g (sugar 1 g), fat 32 g (saturated fat 11 g), good source of vitamins A, B group, C and E.

MELTED CAMEMBERT WITH CRANBERRIES

Slices of crusty Italian bread topped with creamy cheese and smothered with fresh herbs are lightly grilled and served with a cool green salad and a refreshingly sharp cranberry sauce.

TIME: 25 MINUTES   SERVES: 4

200 g frozen cranberries
3 tablespoons soft brown sugar
1 small orange
2–3 large sprigs parsley
A small bunch of chives
A small sprig of thyme
1 small clove garlic
2 tablespoons olive oil
Black pepper
1 loaf ciabatta or crusty bread
1 round ripe but firm Camembert
Watercress and frisée lettuce leaves

1 Preheat the griller to the highest setting. Remove any stalks from the cranberries, if necessary, then put the berries into a small saucepan along with the sugar and 1 tablespoon water.

2 Grate the rind of the orange into the saucepan, then cover and cook the berries over a moderate heat for 4–5 minutes, or until the berries are soft and the juice has thickened slightly. Remove from the heat and keep warm.

3 Meanwhile, chop the parsley and chives. Strip the leaves from the thyme, then put all the herbs onto a large plate. Peel the garlic and crush it over the herbs, then mix in the oil and black pepper to taste.

4 Cut four thick slices from the loaf. Lightly coat both sides with some of the herb mixture and place on the griller rack.

5 Cut the Camembert vertically into 10 thin slices then discard the slice of rind from each end. Coat the eight remaining slices with the rest of the herb mixture.

6 Lightly toast the bread on one side, then turn and top each with two slices of Camembert. Grill until the cheese begins to run down the sides of the bread.

7 Meanwhile, rinse and dry the salad leaves and arrange on individual serving plates.

8 Place one slice of cheese toast alongside the salad on each plate, then spoon over the warm cranberry sauce and serve.

VARIATION
You can substitute commercially bottled cranberry sauce for the fresh version, or the cranberries can be cooked in advance and warmed through before serving.

NUTRIENTS PER SERVING: kilojoules 1025, protein 11 g, carbohydrate 18 g (sugar 13 g), fat 17 g (saturated fat 7 g), good source of vitamins B group and E.

COOK'S SUGGESTION
To stop the cheese sticking to the knife, wet the blade before you begin to slice.

ONION AND SHALLOT PASTRIES WITH SALAD

Red onions and shallots are particularly well suited to rapid baking as they will not lose any of their flavour or crispness.

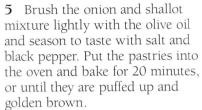

TIME: 30 MINUTES SERVES: 4

2 small red onions
4 large shallots
250 g ready-made puff pastry
1 medium egg
12 sprigs thyme
4 tablespoons olive oil
Salt and black pepper

For the salad:

100 g baby spinach leaves
100 g watercress
¼ cup walnut pieces
40 g Stilton cheese
2 tablespoons thickened cream
3 teaspoons walnut oil
1 teaspoon sherry vinegar

1 Preheat the oven to 220°C. Peel and thinly slice the red onions, then peel the shallots and cut into quarters. Put both aside.

2 Lightly flour a work surface, then cut the pastry in half and roll out each piece to a rectangle of about 30 cm x 15 cm. Cut two large rounds from each, using a 13–15-cm saucer as a guide, and place the pastry rounds on a large baking tray.

3 Beat the egg lightly and brush over the pastry, taking care not to let it trickle over the edges.

4 Pile a quarter of the onions and shallots in the centre of each round, leaving a border of about 2 cm all round. Place 3 sprigs thyme on top of each pile.

5 Brush the onion and shallot mixture lightly with the olive oil and season to taste with salt and black pepper. Put the pastries into the oven and bake for 20 minutes, or until they are puffed up and golden brown.

6 Meanwhile, prepare the salad. Rinse, dry and trim the spinach leaves and watercress and put both into a serving bowl. Roughly chop the walnut pieces and add to the salad leaves.

7 Remove the rind from the Stilton and put the cheese into a small bowl. Pour in the cream and mash the two together thoroughly. Then beat in the walnut oil and sherry vinegar until smooth. Season to taste with a good grinding of black pepper (the Stilton should be salty enough, so no further salt is necessary). Pour the dressing over the salad and toss gently.

8 When the pastries are cooked, serve them on individual plates, accompanied by the bowl of dressed salad on the side.

VARIATION

If you prefer a milder, sweeter blue cheese flavour, you might like to replace the Stilton with either a blue Brie, some Dolcelatte or creamy Blue Castello.

NUTRIENTS PER SERVING: kilojoules 2390, protein 11 g, carbohydrate 28 g (sugar 4 g), fat 47 g (saturated fat 10 g), good source of vitamins A, B group, C, E and folate, and calcium.

COOK'S SUGGESTION

Using a stout wooden spoon and a sturdy bowl makes it an easy job to mash the Stilton cheese and cream together when you are preparing the salad dressing.

LOBSTER TAILS WITH LEMON SAUCE

Luxurious lobster tails deserve the best of sauces, and the lemon and butter used here create superbly succulent juices, which are ideal for soaking up with lots of crusty fresh bread.

TIME: 25 MINUTES SERVES: 4

2 green lobster tails
1 clove garlic
A few sprigs of flat-leaf parsley
3 lemons
250 g unsalted butter
Black pepper
To garnish: lemon halves wrapped in muslin

1 Pre-heat the oven to 200°C. Cut the lobster tails in half lengthways and clean, if necessary; place the halves flesh-side-up in a small baking dish.

2 Peel and crush the garlic. Finely chop enough parsley to give about 2 tablespoons. Remove the zest from the lemons and squeeze the juice; put aside.

3 Combine the garlic with the butter, parsley, lemon zest and juice, and a generous grinding of pepper in a medium-sized saucepan. Heat gently until the butter has melted.

4 Brush the lobsters with the butter mixture. Place in the oven and bake for 10–15 minutes, until the lobster is cooked.

5 Garnish with lemon or lime wedges and serve immediately.

SERVING SUGGESTION
Apart from crusty bread, offer simply dressed salad leaves.

NUTRIENTS PER SERVING: kilojoules 2384, protein 22 g, carbohydrate 3 g (sugar 3 g), fat 53 g (saturated fat 36 g), good source of vitamins B group and C, and iron.

COOK'S SUGGESTION

Choose salad leaves such as mizuna or rocket to accompany this dish. Toss with 1 tablespoon virgin olive oil just before serving.

POTATO PANCAKES WITH SMOKED SALMON

The humble potato is transformed into a sophisticated starter when it is sharpened with onion, made into crisp pancakes and topped with sour cream and strips of smoked salmon.

TIME: 30 MINUTES   SERVES: 4–6

500 g floury potatoes, such as Pontiacs or King Edwards
1 medium onion
1 large egg
2 tablespoons wholemeal flour
Salt and black pepper
Sunflower oil for frying
200 g smoked salmon
150 ml thick sour cream
To garnish: sprigs of dill, onion slices and capers

1 Preheat the oven to low. Peel and grate the potatoes and finely chop the onion; put both in a sieve. Press with a spoon or the base of a saucer to squeeze out as much starchy liquid as possible.

2 Transfer the potato mixture to a bowl, add the egg, flour, salt and pepper and mix well.

3 Pour the oil into a frying pan to a depth of about 10 mm and heat until it shows a haze.

4 Put a tablespoon of the mixture into the oil, flattening to a small pancake about 5 cm in diameter. Keep adding more tablespoons of the mixture to the pan, cooking four to six at a time, until you have made 12 pancakes. Fry for about 1 minute or until golden on the bottom, then turn and cook the other side until crisp and golden but still soft in the centre.

5 Remove the pancakes from the pan, drain on paper towels and keep warm in the oven.

6 Cut the smoked salmon into small strips. Serve each pancake topped with a spoonful of sour cream and a few strips of salmon, and garnish with the sprigs of dill, onion slices or capers.

NUTRIENTS PER SERVING, WHEN SERVING 4:
kilojoules 1431, protein 20 g, carbohydrate 28 g (sugar 4 g), fat 18 g (saturated fat 6 g), good source of vitamins B group, C, E and folate, and selenium.

COOK'S SUGGESTION

Smoked salmon trimmings save time as they do not need to be chopped. They taste as good as the slices and are considerably cheaper.

SCALLOPS WITH VERMOUTH AND TARRAGON

Scallops cooked and served in their shells give a luxury look to a special dinner party meal.
The sauce is based on dry vermouth, a classic culinary companion for most seafood.

TIME: 15 MINUTES SERVES: 4

24 scallops on the shell plus
24 shucked scallops

1 clove garlic

1 small red chilli

1 lemon

A few sprigs of tarragon or
1 tablespoon dried tarragon leaves

60 g unsalted butter

1½ cups dry vermouth

Black pepper

To garnish: lemon or lime wedges,
tarragon sprigs

1 Pre-heat the oven to 200°C. Arrange the scallop shells on baking trays and place an extra scallop on each.

2 Peel and crush the garlic. Seed and finely chop the chilli. Remove the zest from the lemon and squeeze the juice. Chop enough fresh tarragon to give about 2 tablespoons; put aside.
3 Combine the garlic, chilli and butter in a medium-sized saucepan over moderate heat. Add the lemon zest and juice, chopped tarragon, vermouth and a generous grinding of pepper. Cook, stirring, for 3–4 minutes, until the sauce has reduced and thickened slightly.
4 Spoon the sauce over the scallops and place in the oven. Bake for 6–8 minutes, until the scallops have turned opaque and are cooked through.

5 Remove from the oven, arrange on four warmed plates, and garnish with lemon wedges and tarragon sprigs. Serve immediately.

NUTRIENTS PER SERVING: kilojoules 1320, protein 20 g, carbohydrate 17 g (sugar 16 g), fat 14 g (saturated fat 9 g), good source of vitamin B group, and iron and iodine.

COOK'S SUGGESTION

If scallops on the shell are not readily available you can use shucked scallops; buy four dozen, preferably not frozen, and cook them in the oven in small shallow ramekins or gratin dishes.

WARM SALAD OF SCALLOPS WITH GARLIC AND LEMON GRASS

When time is at a premium, quick-cooking scallops provide a stylish start to any meal.
Here they are simply stir-fried and served over salad greens with a tangy Thai-style sauce.

TIME: 20 MINUTES SERVES: 4

1 bunch rocket

1 bunch mizuna

10 shallots

1 red capsicum

2 stalks lemon grass

2 cloves garlic

3 kaffir lime leaves

2 tablespoons olive oil

1 kg shucked scallops

To garnish: lime wedges,
coriander sprigs

For the dressing:

1 clove garlic

1 stalk lemon grass

1 lime

1 teaspoon Thai-style
sweet chilli sauce

4 tablespoons olive oil

1 Make the dressing. Peel and crush the garlic. Peel and finely chop the lemon grass. Remove the zest from the lime and squeeze the juice. Place the garlic and lemon grass in a screwtop jar with the lime zest and juice, chilli sauce and the oil. Shake well and put aside.
2 Remove the leaves from the rocket and mizuna stems and rinse. Peel the shallots and cut in quarters lengthways. Seed and finely slice the capsicum. Arrange the salad vegetables on four individual serving plates.
3 Peel and finely chop the lemon grass and the garlic. Shred the lime leaves.
4 Heat the oil in a large, heavy-based frying pan or wok and add the lemon grass, garlic and lime

leaves. Stir-fry over moderate heat for 30 seconds. Add the scallops and stir-fry for a further 3–4 minutes until the scallops are opaque and cooked through.
5 Remove the scallops from the pan with a slotted spoon and arrange on top of the salad. Spoon over the dressing and garnish with the lime wedges and coriander sprigs. Serve immediately.

NUTRIENTS PER SERVING: kilojoules 2234, protein 56 g, carbohydrate 5 g (sugar 3 g), fat 31 g (saturated fat 6 g), good source of vitamins A and C, and iron and iodine.

A DUO OF SEAFOOD: *(top)* SCALLOPS WITH VERMOUTH AND TARRAGON; *(bottom)* WARM SALAD OF SCALLOPS WITH GARLIC AND LEMON GRASS

EGGPLANT PÂTÉ

*Packed with herbs and spices, this warm spread makes
a fine smoky-flavoured dish to start a meal or serve as a snack.*

TIME: 30 MINUTES   SERVES: 4

2 tablespoons olive oil
1 medium onion
1 large firm eggplant
10 sun-dried tomatoes
6 small gherkins
3 cloves garlic
A few sprigs of thyme
A few sprigs of parsley
1 teaspoon wholegrain mustard
1 teaspoon balsamic vinegar
2 teaspoons capers
1 loaf French bread or crusty Italian bread
Salt and black pepper

1 Heat the oil gently in a frying pan. Peel the onion, chop finely and fry for 5 minutes, or until soft.
2 Cut the eggplant into 1-cm cubes. Add to the onion and stir over moderate heat for 8–10 minutes, or until soft.
3 Drain and chop the sun-dried tomatoes and the gherkins and add to the eggplant. Peel the garlic cloves and crush them in.
4 Strip off the thyme leaves and chop finely. Reserve some parsley for a garnish and chop the rest. Add the chopped herbs to the pan, along with the mustard, vinegar and capers. Simmer, stirring frequently, for 5 minutes.
5 Meanwhile, slice and toast the French bread, or dry fry it on a ridged hotplate.
6 Season the eggplant mixture, then blend in a food processor or mash to a paste by hand.
7 Spoon the pâté onto individual plates, sprinkle with the reserved parsley and serve with the toasted French bread.

NUTRIENTS PER SERVING: kilojoules 1577, protein 10 g, carbohydrate 55 g (sugar 8 g), fat 14 g (saturated fat 1 g), good source of vitamins B group, C and E, and selenium.

COOK'S SUGGESTION

As this pâté tastes equally good either hot or cold, it can be made in advance and served chilled, or reheated just before serving.

YABBIES WITH LIME

Fresh yabbies simply cooked in a white wine stock are enhanced with a tangy lime juice, olive oil and coriander dressing, and served at room temperature.

TIME: 25 MINUTES SERVES: 4

4 cups water
200 ml white wine
½ cup sugar
2 tablespoons salt
16 green yabbies

To garnish: mesclun leaves, lime wedges, julienne of lime rind

For the dressing:

1 small green chilli
2 cloves garlic
A small bunch of coriander
1 lime
4 tablespoons virgin olive oil
1 tablespoon sugar
Salt and black pepper

1 Place water, wine, sugar and salt in a large saucepan. Bring to the boil and add the yabbies. Simmer for 5–6 minutes until the shells have turned red and the yabbies are cooked. Remove from the pan with a slotted spoon and put aside to cool.

2 Meanwhile, seed and finely chop the chilli. Peel and finely chop the garlic. Finely chop enough coriander to give ½ cup. Remove the zest from the lime and squeeze the juice; put aside.

3 Place 1 tablespoon oil, along with the chilli and garlic in a small frying pan. Add the sugar, salt and pepper, and cook, stirring, for 1–2 minutes.

4 Spoon the chilli and garlic mixture into a bowl. Allow to cool then add the remaining oil, the chopped coriander and the reserved lime zest and juice. Mix well to combine; put aside.

5 Arrange mesclun on a serving platter. Remove the shells from the yabbies and arrange the flesh on the leaves. Pour over the dressing, garnish with lime wedges and lime rind, and serve.

NUTRIENTS PER SERVING: kilojoules 1586, protein 18 g, carbohydrate 32 g (sugar 5 g), fat 19 g (saturated fat 3 g), good source of vitamins B group and E, and copper.

COOK'S SUGGESTION

This recipe is nicest made with green yabbies. However, if they are not available, buy freshly cooked ones and eliminate Step 1 of the instructions.

THAI CHILLI CHICKEN BROCHETTES

*Sweet chilli sauce adds a delightful zing to the marinade that accompanies these simple skewers
of chicken. They make a tangy starter or light meal, and can also be cooked on a barbecue.*

TIME: 20 MINUTES SERVES: 4–6

| 6 chicken half breast fillets |
| A small bunch of coriander |
| 1 clove garlic |
| ½ cup light olive oil |
| 1 tablespoon Thai-style sweet chilli sauce |
| 1 tablespoon sesame seed oil |
| 4 tablespoons medium dry sherry |
| 1 tablespoon sugar |
| *To garnish:* fresh red chillies, lime wedges, coriander sprigs |

1 Pre-heat the griller. Cut the chicken into 2–3-cm cubes and place in a medium-sized mixing bowl; put aside.

2 Finely chop enough coriander to give about ¼ cup. Peel and crush the garlic.

3 Combine the coriander, garlic, olive oil, chilli sauce, sesame oil, sherry and sugar with the chicken and toss well. Leave to marinate for 5–10 minutes.

4 Thread the chicken on to 4–6 metal skewers and place under the griller. Grill for 5–6 minutes, or until chicken is cooked through. Meanwhile, place the marinade in a small saucepan over moderate heat and cook until it has reduced and thickened.

5 Arrange the skewers on heated serving plates and spoon the sauce over. Garnish with the chillies, lime wedges and coriander, and serve.

SERVING SUGGESTION
To make a light yet satisfying lunch, serve the brochettes over steamed rice with a simple green salad on the side.

*NUTRIENTS PER SERVING, WHEN SERVING 4:
kilojoules 2275, protein 38 g, carbohydrate 6 g
(sugar 6 g), fat 39 g (saturated fat 5 g), good
source of vitamin B group, and iron and zinc.*

PESTO AND GOAT'S CHEESE CROÛTES

Grilled croûtes spread with spicy red pesto and topped with melted goat's cheese are teamed with an unusual tomato salad that marries fresh tomatoes with the intense flavour of the sun-dried version.

TIME: 15 MINUTES SERVES: 4

6–8 small tomatoes

12 sun-dried tomatoes in oil

2 tablespoons extra virgin olive oil

3 teaspoons balsamic vinegar

Salt and black pepper

1 loaf French bread

4–5 tablespoons red pesto or
2 tablespoons wholegrain mustard

200 g fresh goat's cheese

1 Preheat the griller to high. Cut the fresh tomatoes into thin slices and arrange on four plates. Drain and slice the sun-dried tomatoes and scatter over the fresh ones.

2 Drizzle the oil and vinegar over the tomatoes and season to taste with salt and pepper.

3 To make the croûtes, cut 12 diagonal slices, each about 2.5 cm thick, from the French bread. Spread each slice with some red pesto or mustard, put a spoonful of goat's cheese on top and season with black pepper.

4 Put the croûtes under the hot griller for 1–2 minutes, or until the cheese has melted slightly.

5 Place three grilled croûtes on each plate alongside the tomato salad and serve.

NUTRIENTS PER SERVING: *kilojoules 2373, protein 17 g, carbohydrate 27 g (sugar 6 g), fat 44 g (saturated fat 11 g), good source of vitamins A, B group, C and E.*

COOK'S SUGGESTION

The cheese croûtes can be assembled ahead of time, kept in the refrigerator and grilled just before serving.

GREAT BARBECUE STARTERS

AVOCADO AND WATERCRESS CREAM

A blend of creamy avocado and hot watercress, this pretty purée can be eaten with a spoon or served as a dip.

TIME: 18 MINUTES   SERVES: 4

1 bunch watercress
A few sprigs of parsley
A few sprigs of basil
4 spring onions
1 clove garlic
1 lemon
2 large avocados
Salt and black pepper
1 tablespoon green peppercorns in brine
To serve: frisée lettuce, Melba toast

1   Discard the stalks from the watercress, then rinse and dry the leaves and put aside. Strip the parsley and basil leaves from the stems and put aside.
2   Chop the green tops of the spring onions, leaving the whites for another dish, and put them into a blender or food processor with the watercress, parsley and basil.
3   Peel the garlic and crush it into the herbs. Grate the rind from the lemon, squeeze out the juice and add both rind and juice to the blender or processor.
4   Halve and stone the avocados (see page 53). Spoon the flesh into the blender or processor, season with salt and black pepper, and add the olive oil. Process until smooth.
5   Garnish serving plates with frisée lettuce. Spoon the purée into a bowl, sprinkle with the peppercorns and serve immediately, accompanied by the Melba toast.
VARIATION
The cream can also be spooned back into the shells before serving.

NUTRIENTS PER SERVING: kilojoules 845, protein 3 g, carbohydrate 2 g (sugar 1 g), fat 20 g (saturated fat 4 g), good source of vitamins B group, C and E.

WARM CHEESE AND TOMATO DIP

A hot dip to get any barbecue off to a glowing start, especially when served with some chilled tequila.

TIME: 25 MINUTES   SERVES: 4

1 large onion
2 teaspoons olive oil
5 medium tomatoes
2 jalapeno chillies or 1 tablespoon chopped jalapeno chillies in brine
200 g Gloucester or Cheddar cheese
100 ml thick cream
Salt and black pepper
Tabasco sauce
To garnish: 1 red chilli, 2 lime wedges
To serve: corn chips, soft tortillas or pita breads

1   Preheat the oven to moderate. Put a kettle of water on to boil.
2   Peel and chop the onion and fry in the oil in a small saucepan over low heat for 10–15 minutes.
3   Peel the tomatoes and cut into quarters. Remove and discard the seeds, slice the flesh finely, and put aside.
4   Halve, seed and finely chop the jalapeno chillies, if necessary, and put aside. Grate the cheese into a small bowl and put aside.
5   Put the corn chips, tortillas or pita breads into the oven to heat.
6   Add the cream to the softened onion in the pan and raise the heat. Just before the cream reaches simmering point, add the cheese and stir until it melts.
7   Add the tomatoes and chillies and stir gently. Season to taste with salt, pepper and Tabasco sauce.
8   Pour the dip into a heated serving bowl, garnish with the chilli and lime wedges and serve.

NUTRIENTS PER SERVING: kilojoules 2814, protein 17 g, carbohydrate 31 g (sugar 7 g), fat 53 g (saturated fat 22 g), good source of vitamins A, B group, C and E, and calcium.

SALMON PÂTÉ

Cream cheese is given a kick with hot chilli sauce for an almost instant salmon pâté. Great as a starter, it could also fill a glamorous sandwich.

TIME: 30 MINUTES   SERVES: 4

A small bunch of chives
A small bunch of dill
A small bunch of parsley
415 g canned salmon
150 g cream cheese
1 lemon
1 teaspoon Tabasco sauce
Salt and black pepper
To serve: brown bread, toast fingers or triangles, Melba toast or water biscuits

1   Chop and mix the chives, dill and parsley.
2   Drain the salmon and discard any bones and skin. Put it into a bowl and thoroughly mix in the cream cheese.
3   Squeeze the lemon and add the juice to the salmon mixture a little at a time, until it is sharp enough to suit your taste. Stir in the Tabasco sauce and the chopped herbs and blend to a smooth purée using a hand blender. If you prefer a slightly coarser texture, you can use a potato masher or a wooden spoon to do the blending.
4   Season to taste with salt, black pepper, and more lemon juice, then spoon into a serving bowl or individual ramekin dishes and chill for 15 minutes.
5   Serve the pâté with bread, toast or water biscuits as desired.

NUTRIENTS PER SERVING: kilojoules 1515, protein 22 g, carbohydrate 16 g (sugar 2 g), fat 24 g (saturated fat 12 g), good source of vitamins A, B group and E, and selenium.

THREE CREAMY SAVOURIES:
(*top left*) AVOCADO AND WATERCRESS CREAM; (*centre*) WARM CHEESE AND TOMATO DIP; (*bottom*) SALMON PÂTÉ.

HOT CORN CAKES WITH SALAD

Crispy sweetcorn pancakes spiced with Tabasco sauce and served hot are accompanied by a salad of cool lettuce, sweet capsicum and rich avocado, with a sour cream dressing on the side.

TIME: 30 MINUTES   SERVES: 4

200 g canned or frozen sweetcorn	
⅓ cup milk	
Salt and black pepper	
A few drops of Tabasco sauce, or more as desired	
1 medium iceberg lettuce	
2 avocados	
1 yellow capsicum	
3 tablespoons olive oil	
3 teaspoons wine vinegar	
¾ cup self-raising flour	
2 large eggs	
2 tablespoons vegetable oil	

For the dressing:

3 spring onions
4–5 sprigs dill
150 ml sour cream
Salt and black pepper

1 Drain canned sweetcorn, put aside and mix the milk, salt, pepper and Tabasco in a bowl. Or put frozen sweetcorn into a pan with the milk, salt, pepper and Tabasco and shake over a low heat for 1 minute. Turn off the heat and leave to thaw.

2 To make the dressing, trim and finely slice the spring onions, chop the dill, reserving 1 sprig for a garnish, then mix into the sour cream and season to taste.

3 Rinse and dry the lettuce leaves and put them into a salad bowl. Peel and slice the avocados, seed and slice the capsicum and add both to the bowl. Mix the olive oil and vinegar together, season and toss gently into the salad.

4 Put the flour into a bowl, make a well in the centre and break in the eggs. Add the seasoned milk, or strain in the milk from the defrosted corn, beat until smooth, then stir in the corn.

5 Take two frying pans and heat 1 tablespoon vegetable oil in each. Drop six scant tablespoons of batter into each pan. Fry gently for 4–5 minutes until golden underneath and set at the edges. Turn and fry another 1–2 minutes.

6 Divide the salad among four plates. Drain the corn cakes and arrange three alongside each salad. Garnish with fronds of dill and serve the dressing separately.

NUTRIENTS PER SERVING: kilojoules 2792, protein 13 g, carbohydrate 40 g (sugar 12 g), fat 52 g (saturated fat 13 g), good source of vitamins A, B group, C, E and folate, and calcium.

THAI CHICKEN SALAD

Tender chicken fillets are lightly grilled then sliced and marinated in a tangy sauce.
Creamy avocado slices and crisp salad leaves provide fresh colour and taste.

TIME: 25 MINUTES SERVES: 4

2 chicken half breast fillets
2 limes
1 tablespoon Thai-style sweet chilli sauce
1 tablespoon fish sauce
6 spring onions, white part only
3 stems lemon grass
A bunch of mint
1 large avocado
½ lemon
Salad greens

1 Grill the chicken fillets under moderate heat for 5–6 minutes.

Meanwhile, squeeze enough juice from the limes to give ⅓ cup and put aside.

2 When the chicken is cooked, cut into fine strips. Place in a bowl and pour over the lime juice, chilli sauce and fish sauce. Toss with a spoon to combine well. Put aside.

3 Finely chop the spring onions. Peel and finely chop the lemon grass. Finely chop enough mint to give 4 tablespoons. Add to the chicken mixture and toss to combine well.

4 Peel and slice the avocado and arrange on four serving plates.

Sprinkle with some juice from the half lemon to prevent discoloration.

5 Rinse the salad greens, if necessary, and arrange with the avocado slices on individual plates. Spoon the chicken mixture onto the salad just before serving.

VARIATION
Instead of chicken breast fillets, you can use tender lamb fillets; if you do, omit the fish sauce.

NUTRIENTS PER SERVING: kilojoules 1006, protein 14 g, carbohydrate 4 g (sugar 4 g), fat 17 g (saturated fat 4 g), good source of vitamins A, B group, C and E, and iron.

KING PRAWNS WITH SUN-DRIED TOMATOES

Freshly cooked prawns in an intensely flavoured sauce of sun-dried tomatoes with a touch of sweet chilli top an aromatic mix of rocket leaves and avocado slices.

TIME: 20 MINUTES   SERVES: 4

500 g medium-sized green king prawns
100 g sun-dried tomatoes, drained
1 lime
3 tablespoons olive oil
2 tablespoons Thai-style sweet chilli sauce
Black pepper
1 bunch rocket leaves
1 avocado

For the dressing:

1 lime
1 tablespoon virgin olive oil
1 tablespoon light soy sauce
A pinch of sugar

1 Peel and devein the prawns. Finely chop the sun-dried tomatoes. Remove the zest from the lime with a zester, or grate finely, and squeeze the juice; put aside.

2 Heat the oil in a large, heavy-based frying pan. Add the prawns and cook over moderately high heat for 1–2 minutes.

3 Add the sun-dried tomatoes and chilli sauce and cook, stirring, for a further 3–4 minutes or until the prawns are opaque.

4 Add the reserved lime zest and juice to the pan and season with pepper. Remove the pan from the heat and put aside.

5 To make the dressing, squeeze 2 teaspoons juice from the extra lime and combine with the oil, soy sauce and sugar.

6 Rinse the rocket leaves. Peel and slice the avocado. Arrange the rocket and avocado on four serving plates and spoon over the dressing.

7 Pile the prawns, with their pan juices, on top of the salad and serve immediately.

NUTRIENTS PER SERVING: *kilojoules 1734, protein 18 g, carbohydrate 7 g (sugar 7 g), fat 34 g (saturated fat 6 g), good source of vitamins B group, C and E, and iodine.*

MUSSELS WITH TOMATO AND GARLIC

Sweet black mussels are teamed with a traditional tomato and garlic sauce in this hearty starter which can also double as a light yet thoroughly satisfying main course.

TIME: 30 MINUTES   SERVES: 4

2 kg mussels
3 cloves garlic
500 g very ripe tomatoes
1 bunch spring onions, white part only
A small bunch of basil or continental parsley
2 tablespoons olive oil
1 cup white wine
1 cup fresh tomato sauce
A pinch of sugar
Black pepper

1   Prepare the mussels by rinsing them under cold running water. Thoroughly scrub with a scourer to remove any mud or seaweed and remove the beards by pulling firmly.
2   Peel and finely chop the garlic. Coarsely chop the tomatoes. Finely chop the spring onions. Chop enough basil or parsley to give about ½ cup; put aside.
3   Heat the oil in a large, heavy-based pan with a tight-fitting lid. Add the garlic, tomatoes and spring onions and cook, stirring, for 2–3 minutes.
4   Add the wine, tomato sauce and sugar and simmer for a further 2–3 minutes.
5   Add the mussels to the pan, along with the chopped basil and a generous grinding of pepper. Cover with the lid and cook for 5 minutes over high heat, shaking the pan from time to time.
6   Discard any mussels that have not opened and divide the rest between four serving bowls. Spoon over the sauce and serve immediately, accompanied by lots of crusty bread to soak up the flavoursome sauce.

VARIATION
You can use a mixture of seafood, such as prawns and fish pieces, instead of the mussels.

NUTRIENTS PER SERVING: kilojoules 1327, protein 35 g, carbohydrate 12 g (sugar 11 g), fat 15 g (saturated fat 3 g), good source of vitamin C, and calcium, iron and zinc.

COOK'S SUGGESTION

Fresh tomato sauce – a mixture of chopped tomatoes with onion, garlic, oil, salt and pepper – can be made in minutes on top of the stove. If time is limited, however, you can substitute a good-quality commercial Italian pasta sauce.

SALADS

The refreshing taste of summer leaves and herbs, the aroma of oils and spices, a wealth of appealing ingredients – here are salads from the simple to the substantial for every meal.

SALMON AND ASPARAGUS SALAD

A velvety mango, yoghurt and mustard dressing with a subtle hint of aniseed gives the freshly cooked salmon in this salad a tropical taste that is just right for a summer dinner party.

TIME: 25 MINUTES SERVES: 4

4 salmon fillets, about 750 g in total
1 tablespoon olive or sunflower oil
200 g asparagus spears
1 large stalk celery
250 g mixed salad leaves

For the dressing:
2 large mangoes
4 chives
100 g natural yoghurt
1 teaspoon wholegrain mustard
1 tablespoon Pernod or ouzo
Black pepper

1 Put a kettle of water on to boil. Skin the salmon, discard any bones, and cut into large cubes. Heat the oil in a frying pan and stir-fry the salmon for 2–3 minutes until just cooked through and lightly browned. Drain on paper towels.

2 Rinse and trim the asparagus spears, cut into 4-cm pieces, cover with the boiling water and blanch for 2 minutes. Rinse under cold water and drain.

3 To make the dressing, peel the mangoes and cut into cubes: you need about 500 g. Place in a food processor or blender. Snip the chives into the mango. Add the yoghurt, mustard and Pernod or ouzo. Purée until dressing is smooth. Add black pepper to taste.

4 Trim and finely slice the celery. Put into a bowl with the salmon and asparagus. Pour the dressing over the top, holding a little back in case there is more than you need. Toss gently, taking care not to break up the salmon.

5 Trim, rinse and dry the salad leaves, then arrange on four individual plates and top with the salmon salad.

VARIATION
You can use dry vermouth as a substitute for the aniseed flavour of the Pernod or ouzo.

NUTRIENTS PER SERVING: kilojoules 2452, protein 48 g, carbohydrate 33 g (sugar 32 g), fat 29 g (saturated fat 5 g), good source of vitamins A, B group, C, E and folate, and selenium and zinc.

COOK'S SUGGESTION

The dressing can be made and the fish cooked in advance and both stored in the refrigerator, leaving the salad to be assembled at the last minute.

WILD RICE AND FENNEL SALAD

Grapes, orange juice and a handful of raisins add sweetness to a salad redolent with the earthy flavours of wild rice, chopped hazelnuts and a nut oil, herb and white wine vinegar dressing.

TIME: 30 MINUTES SERVES: 4–6

185 g easy-cook wild rice and long grain mixture	
Salt	
250 g cucumber	
250 g fennel	
6 spring onions	
125 g seedless red grapes	
½ cup skinned hazelnuts	
¼ cup raisins	
1 orange	
To garnish: 4–6 sprigs tarragon	

For the dressing:

3 sprigs chervil
2 sprigs tarragon
2 sprigs parsley
4 tablespoons hazelnut or walnut oil
3 teaspoons white wine vinegar
Salt and black pepper

1 Bring 1¾ cups water to the boil, add the rice mixture and a little salt, cover and simmer for about 18–20 minutes, or until the rice is cooked and all the water absorbed (alternatively, follow the directions on the packet).

2 Meanwhile, finely dice the cucumber; trim and thinly slice the fennel and spring onions; halve the grapes. Put all into a salad bowl.

3 Chop the hazelnuts and add to the bowl with the raisins. Then grate in the rind of the orange.

4 To make the herb dressing, squeeze 2 tablespoons juice from the orange and pour into a small bowl. Finely chop the tarragon and parsley and add to the juice with the oil and vinegar. Whisk together then season to taste.

5 Drain the cooked rice and rinse briefly under cold running water. Drain well again, mix carefully into the salad vegetables and pour over the dressing.

6 Just before serving, garnish the salad with sprigs of tarragon.

NUTRIENTS PER SERVING, WHEN SERVING 4: kilojoules 1921, protein 7 g, carbohydrate 50 g (sugar 12 g), fat 26 g (saturated fat 2 g), good source of vitamins B group, C and E.

COOK'S SUGGESTION

This salad can be made in advance and left to stand for 30 minutes before serving. The mix of fruit and nuts makes it an excellent accompaniment to game or chicken.

ORANGE AND WATERCRESS SALAD WITH TOASTED WALNUTS

This refreshing combination of sweet citrus and peppery watercress is offset by the satisfying crunch of freshly toasted walnuts. The walnut theme is continued in the fragrant dressing.

TIME: 10 MINUTES   SERVES: 4–6

1 cup walnut halves
6 navel oranges
1 bunch spring onions
½ bunch watercress leaves

For the dressing:
⅓ cup walnut oil
2 tablespoons red wine vinegar
1 tablespoon orange flower water
1 teaspoon Dijon mustard
or wholegrain mustard
Black pepper

1 Put the walnuts in a large frying pan and toast over low heat for 4–5 minutes, tossing occasionally.
2 While the walnuts are toasting, peel the oranges, removing all white pith. Slice finely, discarding seeds. Cut spring onions into fine strips.
3 Arrange the walnuts, orange segments, spring onions and watercress leaves on serving plates.
4 Combine the walnut oil, vinegar, orange flower water, mustard, salt and pepper in a screwtop jar and shake well to combine.

5 Spoon the dressing over the salad and serve immediately.

NUTRIENTS PER SERVING, WHEN SERVING 4:
kilojoules 1789, protein 6 g, carbohydrate 18 g (sugar 18 g), fat 37 g (saturated fat 4 g), good source of vitamins B group, C and E.

COOK'S SUGGESTION

The walnuts can also be toasted in the oven. Spread out flat on a baking tray and cook at 180°C for 5–10 minutes.

THAI NOODLE SALAD

This easy salad of crisp fresh vegetables and prawns, stirred into simple rice noodles, is accompanied by the sharp taste of chillies and lemon grass to make a cold dish full of hot flavours.

TIME: 30 MINUTES   SERVES: 4

200 g snow peas
1 yellow capsicum
200 g rice noodles
8 spring onions
250 g peeled cooked prawns

For the dressing:

2 stems lemon grass
2 red chillies
7.5-cm piece fresh root ginger
A large handful of coriander leaves
2 limes
3 tablespoons sunflower oil
1 tablespoon sesame seed oil
2 tablespoons soy sauce
To serve: prawn crackers

1 Put a kettle of water on to boil. Top and tail the snow peas. Put into a saucepan, cover with boiling water, bring back to the boil, then reduce the heat and simmer for 3 minutes. Seed the capsicum and slice thinly.

2 Take the snow peas off the heat. Add the capsicum and noodles; leave to stand for 2 minutes, transfer to a colander, rinse and drain.

3 To make the dressing, peel away the outer layers of the lemon grass and slice the stems into chunks. Seed and slice the chillies. Peel and slice the ginger. Chop the coriander. Put them all into a food processor or blender.

4 Squeeze the limes and add their juice with the sunflower and sesame oils and the soy sauce. Blend just long enough to make a thick, chunky dressing. Alternatively, chop or grind the dressing ingredients with a pestle and mortar.

5 Trim the spring onions. Cut diagonally into 1-cm pieces and put into a serving bowl. Add the prawns and the noodle mixture, pour in the dressing and toss well.

6 Serve the salad accompanied by a bowl of prawn crackers.

NUTRIENTS PER SERVING: kilojoules 2737, protein 21 g, carbohydrate 71 g (sugar 7 g), fat 31 g (saturated fat 4 g), good source of vitamins B group, C and E.

COOK'S SUGGESTION

The thread-like noodles used for this dish are sold in Asian food stores and larger supermarkets, and are sometimes called rice sticks. The salad can be made in advance and stored for an hour or two in the refrigerator.

THAI BEEF SALAD

Rare lean beef and a variety of crunchy fresh vegetables are combined with the fragrant Asian flavourings of lemon grass, lime and pungent herbs in this main-course salad.

TIME: 30 MINUTES SERVES: 4

350 g crisp lettuce leaves	
185 g cucumber	
2 medium carrots	
125 g fresh bean sprouts	
1 clove garlic	
1 stalk lemon grass	
500 g lean beef steak	
A small bunch of coriander	
A small bunch of basil	

2 teaspoons vegetable oil	
2 limes	
2 tablespoons olive oil	
1 tablespoon sweet chilli sauce	

1 Rinse, dry and shred the lettuce. Dice the cucumber. Peel and coarsely grate the carrots. Rinse and drain the bean sprouts. Arrange all on a large serving dish or on individual entrée plates.

2 Peel and crush the garlic. Remove and discard the outer leaves from the lemon grass and chop enough of the inner stalk to give 1 teaspoon. Thinly slice the beef and put aside. Finely chop the herbs and put aside.

3 Heat the vegetable oil in a large frying pan and gently cook the garlic and lemon grass for about 30 seconds, until just golden brown.

4 Add the beef to the pan and fry over high heat for 1–2 minutes, stirring continuously to keep the slices separate. Then remove the meat from the pan and place on top of the salad vegetables.

5 Squeeze 2 tablespoons juice from the limes and add to the pan with the herbs, olive oil and chilli sauce. Cook, stirring, for 1 minute, then pour the dressing over the beef and salad and serve.

NUTRIENTS PER SERVING: kilojoules 1152, protein 29 g, carbohydrate 7 g (sugar 6 g), fat 16 g (saturated fat 4 g), good source of vitamins A, B group, C, E, and folate.

GREEK SALAD

This pretty variation on the classic Mediterranean salad mixes sweet cherry tomatoes with salty feta cheese and olives.

TIME: 15 MINUTES SERVES: 4–6

| 20 cherry tomatoes |
| 1 cucumber |
| 375 g feta cheese |
| 3 tablespoons extra virgin olive oil |
| ½ lemon |
| 12 good black olives |
| Black pepper |

1 Rinse and dry the cherry tomatoes, then cut in half and place in a serving bowl. Halve the cucumber, then cut each half into 1-cm slices and add to the bowl with the tomatoes.

2 Cut the cheese into cubes and add to the bowl. Sprinkle in the oil and 1 tablespoon juice from the half lemon. Add the black olives and pepper to taste (the cheese is salty already). Toss well and serve.

NUTRIENTS PER SERVING, WHEN SERVING 4: kilojoules 1528, protein 16 g, carbohydrate 5 g (sugar 5 g), fat 31 g (saturated fat 15 g), good source of vitamins A, B group, C and E, and calcium.

VEGETABLES WITH COCONUT DRESSING

Creamy coconut milk, smooth peanut butter and fiery chilli sauce are combined with lime to dress this Asian-style salad of fresh crunchy vegetables and Chinese leaves.

TIME: 25 MINUTES SERVES: 4

200 g Chinese cabbage
3 medium stalks celery
2 medium carrots
4 spring onions
200 g baby corn

For the dressing:

2 limes
4 tablespoons coconut milk
2 tablespoons smooth peanut butter
½ teaspoon chilli sauce
1 teaspoon Thai fish sauce or light soy sauce, optional
Salt and black pepper

1 Rinse and dry the Chinese leaves, tear into pieces and put into a salad bowl.

2 Trim the celery and peel the carrots. Cut into thin matchsticks and add to the bowl.

3 Trim the spring onions and slice them and the baby corn diagonally; add both to the salad.

4 To make the coconut dressing, squeeze 2 tablespoons juice from the limes and pour it into a screwtop jar. Add the coconut milk, peanut butter, chilli sauce, fish or soy sauce, if using, and season. Shake well to combine. Taste and adjust the seasoning.

5 Pour the dressing over the salad vegetables and toss well together to combine. Serve immediately.

NUTRIENTS PER SERVING: kilojoules 691, protein 6 g, carbohydrate 15 g (sugar 6 g), fat 9 g (saturated fat 2 g), good source of vitamins A, B group, C, E and folate.

COOK'S SUGGESTION

Chinese cabbage looks like pale, elongated cos lettuce, which can be substituted if necessary. The whole vegetable can be eaten, apart from any tattered outer leaves.

MOZZARELLA WITH TOMATO DRESSING

A simple salad of mild mozzarella cheese and mixed lettuce leaves is given a rich tomato and fresh herb dressing, which can also be used as a sauce for pasta or as a pizza topping.

TIME: 15 MINUTES SERVES: 4

125 g mixed salad leaves

500 g fresh
mozzarella cheese

For the dressing:

150 g sun-dried
tomatoes in oil

A small bunch of basil

A small bunch of parsley

A small bunch of marjoram
or oregano

1 tablespoon balsamic vinegar

1 tablespoon capers

1 clove garlic, optional

Black pepper

1 To make the dressing, take the sun-dried tomatoes from the jar and put into a food processor or blender. Pour 150 ml oil from the jar into a measuring jug. If there is not enough, top it up with some olive or vegetable oil. Rinse and dry the fresh herbs, if necessary.

2 Add the herbs, vinegar and capers to the processor. Peel the garlic, if using, and add it, with the oil, then process to a thick purée. Or process the ingredients in a bowl with a hand-held mixer.

3 Season the dressing to taste with pepper. It should not need any salt because the capers are salty.

4 Trim, rinse and dry the mixed salad leaves and arrange on four serving plates.

5 Drain and slice the mozzarella and arrange on top of the salad leaves. Spoon the dressing over the top and serve.

VARIATION

Bocconcini cheese – tiny balls of mozzarella – when served whole make an attractive alternative to the sliced cheese.

NUTRIENTS PER SERVING: *kilojoules 2176, protein 33 g, carbohydrate 7 g (sugar 1 g), fat 40 g (saturated fat 17 g), good source of vitamins A, B group and E, and calcium.*

SALMON TABBOULEH

Tabbouleh are salads made with nutty wheat grains. This stylish dish of burghul and poached salmon has the clean light taste that comes from fresh herbs and lemon.

TIME: 30 MINUTES SERVES: 4

100 g burghul
600 g skinned salmon fillet
175–200 g flat-leaf parsley
60 g mint
8 spring onions
1 large lemon
Leaves of cos or Little Gem lettuce
4 tablespoons olive oil
Salt and black pepper
To serve: lemon wedges and pitta bread

1 Put a kettle of water on to boil. Put the burghul in a saucepan with 300 ml cold water. Bring to the boil, then reduce the heat and simmer for 8–10 minutes, until the burghul has absorbed all the water.

2 Meanwhile, cut the salmon into four equal pieces, put into a shallow pan and cover with boiling water. Bring back to the boil, reduce the heat and simmer for 3 minutes. Transfer to a plate to cool.

3 Chop the parsley and finely shred the mint leaves. Trim and finely chop the spring onions. Put all three into a salad bowl.

4 Squeeze the lemon and put the juice aside, then rinse and dry the lettuce and warm the pitta bread.

5 Rinse the burghul in cold water, then squeeze dry in handfuls and add to the salad bowl with the lemon juice and oil. Season to taste and mix thoroughly.

6 Flake the salmon, removing any bones, add to the salad and toss.

7 Line a platter with the lettuce leaves and pile the tabbouleh on top. Garnish the salad with lemon wedges and the warm pitta bread.

NUTRIENTS PER SERVING: kilojoules 3160, protein 33 g, carbohydrate 66 g (sugar 4 g), fat 41 g (saturated fat 15 g), good source of vitamins A, B group, C, E and folate, and calcium and iron.

COOK'S SUGGESTION

The herbs and spring onions can be chopped together in a food processor, but use a pulsing action and check regularly to avoid chopping them too finely as they will turn into a damp mess.

SUMMER TABBOULEH

Burghul is perfect with crisp, just-cooked summer vegetables mixed with handfuls of fresh herbs and tossed with a lively honey and mustard dressing to give it an extra bite.

TIME: 30 MINUTES SERVES: 4

250 g burghul
200 g small green beans
200 g frozen peas
Salt
5 large spring onions
300 g tomatoes
1 lemon
A large handful of parsley
A large handful of mint
A large handful of chives or dill
To serve: 2 Little Gem lettuces

For the dressing:

2 tablespoons extra virgin olive oil
3 teaspoons red wine vinegar
1 teaspoon honey
3 teaspoons Dijon mustard
Salt and black pepper

1 Put a kettle of water on to boil. Put the burghul in a large saucepan with 700 ml cold water. Bring to the boil, reduce the heat and simmer for 8–10 minutes, just until the burghul has absorbed all the water.

2 Meanwhile, top and tail the green beans and chop into 2.5-cm pieces. Put into a saucepan with the frozen peas. Cover with the boiling water, add a little salt, and return to the boil. Cook for 1–2 minutes, then drain.

3 Trim and thinly slice the spring onions. Dice the tomatoes. Grate the rind of the lemon and squeeze the juice. Add them all to the burghul and fluff up the mixture with a fork.

4 Add the cooled beans and peas to the tabbouleh. Chop the parsley, mint, chives or dill and add to the salad. Rinse and dry the lettuce leaves and put aside.

5 To make the honey and mustard dressing, whisk all the ingredients together in a bowl, then pour over the tabbouleh and mix well. Serve with the lettuce leaves.

NUTRIENTS PER SERVING: kilojoules 1599, protein 12 g, carbohydrate 60 g (sugar 8 g), fat 11 g (saturated fat 1.5 g), good source of vitamins A, B group, C, E and folate, and iron.

COOK'S SUGGESTION

In the Middle East this salad is eaten by rolling a spoonful of the tabbouleh inside a lettuce leaf and picking it up with the fingers.

TWO WHEAT GRAIN SALADS:
(top) SALMON TABBOULEH;
(bottom) SUMMER TABBOULEH.

WARM DUCK BREAST SALAD WITH RED WINE AND APPLE

Crunchy apple and lettuce make a delicious base for fried duck breast, sliced and served warm with a red wine dressing.

TIME: 30 MINUTES SERVES: 4

4 boneless duck breasts, about 185 g each
Salt and black pepper
2 oakleaf lettuces
50 g radicchio
75 g watercress
1 small red onion
1 red dessert apple
1 tablespoon olive oil
2 – 3 tablespoons red wine

For the dressing:

A handful of mint or parsley
1 clove garlic
Salt and black pepper
1 teaspoon caster sugar
2 teaspoons Dijon or wholegrain mustard
1½ tablespoons red wine
2 tablespoons olive oil

1 Remove the skin and sinew from each duck breast. If the breasts are uneven in size, cut the larger ones in half horizontally. Season the meat generously with salt and black pepper and put aside.

2 For the dressing, chop the mint or parsley and put into a salad bowl. Peel the garlic and crush it into the bowl. Season with salt and black pepper, add the sugar, mustard, red wine and oil and whisk to a creamy emulsion.

3 Trim, rinse and dry the lettuces and radicchio. Tear into small pieces and add to the salad dressing. Trim, rinse and dry the watercress. Halve, peel and thinly slice the red onion. Quarter, core and slice the apple. Add all three to the salad bowl and toss gently.

4 Heat 1 tablespoon oil in a frying pan, add the duck breasts and fry over moderate heat for 4–5 minutes on each side until golden brown but still slightly pink in the centre. If you prefer duck well done, you might like to fry the breasts for a few minutes longer.

5 Transfer the duck breasts to a board and leave to stand for about 2–3 minutes. Meanwhile, pour off the excess fat from the frying pan, raise the heat, add the red wine and bring to the boil, stirring and scraping the residue from the bottom of the pan.

6 Slice the duck breasts thinly on the diagonal and add to the salad. Pour the pan juices over the salad, then toss well and serve.

VARIATION

Chicken breasts may be substituted for the duck, using white wine with the juices instead of red. Chicken needs to be cooked thoroughly, so allow a little longer.

NUTRIENTS PER SERVING: kilojoules 1704, protein 36 g, carbohydrate 8 g (sugar 7.5 g), fat 24 g (saturated fat 5 g), good source of vitamins B group, C, E and folate, and iron and zinc.

CREAMY MIXED BEAN SALAD

This hearty salad mixes a variety of fresh and canned vegetables into a nutritious dish packed with strong flavours. Fresh basil infuses a creamy yoghurt and mustard dressing.

TIME: 25 MINUTES SERVES: 4

| 250 g stringless green beans |
| 465 g canned kidney beans |
| 375 g canned cannellini beans |
| 430 g canned lentils |
| 300 g artichoke hearts in oil |
| 150 g button mushrooms |
| 75 g spring onions |
| 1 soft lettuce, such as butterhead |

For the dressing:

| 1 cup natural yoghurt |
| ½ lemon |
| 1–2 teaspoons Dijon mustard |
| A large handful of basil |
| Salt and black pepper |

1 Bring a saucepan of water to the boil. Top, tail and halve the green beans. Cook for 5–6 minutes or until just tender. Rinse under cold water then drain.

2 Rinse the kidney beans and cannellini beans and lentils; drain and spread on a tea towel to dry.

3 Drain the artichoke hearts on paper towels and cut into quarters. Clean and slice the mushrooms; trim and slice the spring onions.

4 To make the dressing, put the yoghurt into a large bowl, squeeze in the juice from the lemon, add mustard to taste, and stir well.

5 Reserve a few sprigs of basil for a garnish, then tear the rest and add to the dressing. Season to taste with salt and pepper.

6 Rinse and dry the lettuce leaves and arrange on a serving dish. Mix the vegetables into the yoghurt and mustard dressing. Spoon on top of the lettuce leaves and garnish with the reserved basil.

VARIATION
Diced cheese, strips of cooked ham, chicken or turkey or some small peeled prawns can be added to this creamy salad.

NUTRIENTS PER SERVING: kilojoules 2503, protein 32 g, carbohydrate 64 g (sugar 9 g), fat 24 g (saturated fat 5 g), good source of vitamins B group, C and folate.

MELON, AVOCADO AND PRAWN SALAD

Ripe and richly scented melon and avocado combined with pale pink prawns and garnished with aromatic coriander leaves make a pretty summer salad that is filling but not too rich.

TIME: 20 MINUTES SERVES: 6

A few sprigs of coriander
1 rockmelon
2 avocados
50 g mixed salad leaves
350 g peeled cooked prawns

For the dressing:
1 small shallot
½ cup crème fraîche
2 tablespoons extra virgin olive oil
1 tablespoon cider vinegar
A pinch of sugar
Salt and black pepper

1 To make the dressing, halve, peel and finely chop the shallot. Put into a bowl and add the crème fraîche, olive oil, cider vinegar and sugar. Stir well, season to taste with salt and a good grinding of pepper and put aside.
2 Strip off the coriander leaves and put aside for a garnish.
3 Cut the rockmelon into quarters and discard the seeds. Remove the skin and cut the flesh lengthways into narrow slices.
4 Halve and stone the avocados (see page 53), then peel and cut the flesh lengthways into slices the same thickness as the melon.
5 Trim, rinse and dry the salad leaves and divide among six plates. Arrange the slices of melon and avocado among them. Scatter the prawns on top and, using a spoon, drizzle over the dressing.
6 Garnish the salad with the reserved coriander leaves and serve.

NUTRIENTS PER SERVING: kilojoules 1439, protein 16 g, carbohydrate 7 g (sugar 6 g), fat 28 g (saturated fat 9 g), good source of vitamins B group, C and E.

CHICORY, PEAR AND ROQUEFORT SALAD

*This simple but elegant salad, a mixture of fruit, blue cheese, fresh nuts and bitter leaves,
is at its best in autumn when the new season's crop of walnuts is available.*

TIME: 15 MINUTES SERVES: 4–6

6 whole fresh walnuts
or 12 shelled walnut halves

3 heads chicory

2 Comice or Williams pears

100 g Roquefort cheese

To garnish: a small bunch of chervil
or 4 sprigs tarragon, optional

For the dressing:

3 teaspoons wine vinegar

Salt

1½ tablespoons virgin olive oil

2 tablespoons walnut oil

1 If using fresh walnuts, crack
the shells and remove the kernels
(see box, right). Roughly chop the
kernels or halves and put aside.

2 Rinse, dry and separate the
chicory leaves and arrange on
individual plates. Quarter and core
the pears. Cut each quarter into
three slices and arrange decoratively
over the chicory.
3 Crumble the cheese and scatter
it, along with the walnuts, over the
pears. Strip off the chervil or
tarragon leaves, if using; put aside.
4 To make the dressing, put the
vinegar into a bowl, add salt and
both oils and whisk, then pour a
little over each salad. Scatter with
the chervil or tarragon, if using.

NUTRIENTS PER SERVING, WHEN SERVING 4:
*kilojoules 1281, protein 6 g, carbohydrate 9 g
(sugar 7 g), fat 28 g (saturated fat 7 g), good
source of vitamin B group.*

EASY DOES IT!

*Fresh walnuts, available
April–May, have an incomparable
flavour and should feel heavy in the
hand. To prepare them, crack the
shells, remove the kernels, and rub
off the thin, dark inner skin.*

SALAD NIÇOISE

*A popular summer lunch dish, this classic Provençal salad of eggs and fish has many variations,
so it can be made up from ingredients on hand and enjoyed at any time of the year.*

TIME: 25 MINUTES SERVES: 4

| 4 medium eggs |
| 375 g canned tuna |
| 1 medium red onion |
| 50 g canned anchovy fillets |
| 50 g capers |
| 125 g pitted black olives |
| 3 Little Gem lettuces |
| 200 g cherry tomatoes |

For the croutons:

| 2 thick slices wholemeal bread |
| 1 clove garlic |
| 2 tablespoons olive oil |

For the dressing:

| ½ teaspoon caster sugar |
| 3 teaspoons white wine vinegar |
| Salt |
| 1 clove garlic |
| 1–2 teaspoons Dijon mustard |
| 2 tablespoons extra virgin olive oil |

1 Put the eggs into a small saucepan and cover with water. Bring to the boil, then reduce the heat and simmer for 4 minutes. Take the pan off the heat, cover and leave the eggs to stand.

2 To make the croutons, cut the bread into 1-cm cubes. Peel the garlic, crush it into a frying pan, add the oil and fry over moderate heat. Add the croutons and fry until crisp and golden, stirring frequently, then drain on paper towels and put aside to cool.

3 To make the dressing, put the sugar and vinegar into a large salad bowl with salt to taste. Peel the garlic and crush it into the bowl, then add the mustard and oil and mix to a thick emulsion.

4 Drain the tuna and flake it into the dressing. Peel the onion, slice thinly and add to the salad bowl, with the anchovies and their oil, the capers and olives. Toss gently.

5 Separate, rinse and dry the lettuce leaves, slicing the heart into small pieces, and add to the tuna

mixture. Halve the cherry tomatoes and scatter them in the bowl.

6 Shell the eggs and slice into quarters, lengthways. Toss the salad, making sure every leaf is coated with dressing, then add the egg quarters. Serve the croutons in a separate dish.

VARIATION
You can also add artichoke hearts, sliced red capsicum or cooled steamed green beans to the salad when you add the tomatoes.

NUTRIENTS PER SERVING: kilojoules 2239, protein 33 g, carbohydrate 17 g (sugar 6 g), fat 38 g (saturated fat 6 g), good source of vitamins A, B group, C, E and folate, and selenium and zinc.

COOK'S SUGGESTION
Anchovies are very salty, so add only a little salt to this salad. If you are using sea salt, remember that it is not as strong as table salt.

BROAD BEAN, PRAWN AND FETA SALAD

A pretty salad of broad beans and cubes of salty feta cheese, flavoured with fresh mint and scattered with juicy prawns, gets added punch from a refreshing lemon and garlic dressing.

TIME: 20 MINUTES SERVES: 4

| 500 g frozen broad beans |
| 200 g feta cheese |
| 500 g peeled cooked prawns |

For the dressing:

| 1 large lemon |
| 5 tablespoons extra virgin olive oil |
| 1 clove garlic |
| A small bunch of mint |
| Salt and black pepper |

1 Put a kettle of water on to boil. Put the beans into a saucepan, cover with boiling water and simmer for 6 minutes. Drain and rinse the beans, then drain again.
2 Dice the cheese into a shallow salad bowl; add the beans.
3 To make the dressing, halve the lemon and squeeze one half to give 2 tablespoons juice. Mix with the olive oil, then peel the garlic and crush it into the dressing. Chop enough mint to give 2 tablespoons,

and put a few sprigs aside for a garnish. Whisk the chopped mint into the dressing, then add salt and black pepper to taste.
4 Arrange the prawns in the bowl and pour over the dressing. Serve with mint sprigs and wedges cut from the remaining half lemon.

NUTRIENTS PER SERVING: kilojoules 1875, protein 29 g, carbohydrate 16 g (sugar 2 g), fat 30 g (saturated fat 9 g), good source of vitamins B group, C and E, and calcium

BEAN SPROUT, FETA AND HAZELNUT SALAD

A nutritious mix of crunchy salad vegetables, salty white cheese, fresh citrus fruit and roasted hazelnuts with a tangy orange dressing makes a great salad for the winter months.

TIME: 20 MINUTES SERVES: 4

5-cm piece cucumber
2 stalks celery
350 g fresh bean sprouts, or a mixture of mung and alfalfa sprouts
100 g hazelnut kernels, ready-skinned
1 orange
150 g feta cheese
To garnish: 1 punnet salad cress

For the dressing:

1 orange
2 tablespoons hazelnut or walnut oil
Salt and black pepper
1 teaspoon wholegrain mustard

1 Preheat the oven to 200°C and bring a large saucepan of water to the boil.

2 Trim the cucumber and celery, chop into small pieces and place in a salad bowl.

3 Place the bean or mung sprouts in the boiling water for 1 minute to blanch, then drain and rinse. Alfalfa sprouts do not need blanching.

4 Press the hazelnuts in half with a rolling pin. Toast on a tray in the oven for 3–4 minutes until golden.

5 Cut the peel and pith from the orange then, holding it over the celery to catch any juice, cut the segments from the connecting tissue and let them fall into the bowl.

6 To make the dressing, squeeze the juice from the orange into a small bowl or jug and whisk in the oil, salt and pepper and mustard.

7 Drain the cheese and crumble into the salad bowl, then add the bean sprouts and hazelnuts. Rinse and dry the cress. Pour the dressing onto the salad, toss gently and garnish with cress.

NUTRIENTS PER SERVING: *kilojoules 1473, protein 13 g, carbohydrate 9 g (sugar 7 g), fat 30 g (saturated fat 7 g), good source of vitamins B group, C , E and folate, and calcium.*

SPECIAL SALADS FOR SIDE DISHES

SNOW PEA AND PICKLED GINGER SALAD

The sharp taste of pickled ginger blended into natural yoghurt turns a simple salad into a great accompaniment for plain roasts or grills of beef, chicken or fish.

TIME: 15 MINUTES SERVES: 4

| 350 g snow peas |
| Salt |
| A small bunch of chives |

For the dressing:
| 50 g pickled ginger |
| 1 tablespoon light olive oil |
| 1 teaspoon sesame seed oil |
| Black pepper |

1 Put a pan of water on to boil. Top and tail the snow peas. Add to the pan with a little salt, bring back to the boil and cook for 1–2 minutes, until tender but still crisp. Drain and put aside.
2 To make the dressing, shred the pickled ginger into a salad bowl. Add the black pepper to taste and mix well.
3 Add the snow peas to the bowl and toss to coat with the dressing. Snip the chives over the salad.
VARIATION
You can substitute 1 tablespoon pickled green peppercorns, rinsed but left whole, for the ginger.

NUTRIENTS PER SERVING: kilojoules 251, protein 5 g, carbohydrate 7 g (sugar 6 g), fat 1 g (saturated fat 0.6 g), good source of vitamins B group, C and E.

COOK'S SUGGESTION

Finely sliced pickled ginger, sometimes called sushi ginger, is served with Japanese dishes and may be found in Asian food markets, larger supermarkets and in specialty food and health-food shops. It also teams well with slices of cold ham.

CARROT AND GINGER SALAD

A simple salad with a surprising citrus dressing, sharpened with ginger and sweetened with honey, this makes an excellent accompaniment to grilled fish.

TIME: 30 MINUTES SERVES: 4

| 1 cup sultanas |
| 400 g young carrots |
| Salt |
| ½ teaspoon honey or sugar |
| ½ cup chopped peanuts, pecans or walnuts |

For the dressing:
| 5-cm piece fresh root ginger |
| 1 lemon |
| 1 orange |
| 1 cup sour cream or natural yoghurt |

1 Put a little water into a kettle and put on to boil. Tip the sultanas into a small bowl, then cover with the boiling water and put aside.
2 To make the citrus dressing, peel and finely grate the ginger into a small mixing bowl. Finely grate half the rind from the lemon and the orange into the bowl. Squeeze the juice from half of each of them and add to the ginger in the mixing bowl.
3 Stir in the sour cream or yoghurt until well blended and put the dressing aside.
4 Peel the carrots and grate into a serving bowl, then drain the sultanas and add to the carrots.
5 Stir the dressing into the carrot and sultana mixture, then season with salt and add the honey or sugar. Finally, stir in the chopped peanuts, pecans or walnuts and serve immediately.

NUTRIENTS PER SERVING: kilojoules 1318, protein 7 g, carbohydrate 35 g (sugar 33 g), fat 18 g (saturated fat 8 g), good source of vitamins A, B group and E.

FRISÉE, CUCUMBER AND RED ONION SALAD

Curly frisée, chicory and radicchio make a bitter-sweet salad which is particularly good served after a hearty stew or to accompany a rich main course such as roast goose.

TIME: 10 MINUTES SERVES: 4

| 1 head frisée or curly endive |
| 1 head chicory |
| 1 head radicchio |
| 250 g cucumber |
| 1 small red onion |
| ½ cup walnut halves |

For the dressing:
| 1 clove garlic |
| 2 tablespoons walnut oil |
| 3 teaspoons white wine vinegar |
| Salt and black pepper |

1 Separate, rinse and dry the leaves of the frisée or endive, chicory and radicchio – you will save time if you use a salad spinner. Put all the leaves into a large salad bowl and mix together.
2 Peel and finely slice the cucumber and peel and finely slice the onion. Put them into the salad bowl, then add the walnuts.
3 To make the dressing, peel the garlic and crush it into a small bowl, then pour the walnut oil into the bowl along with the wine vinegar. Add salt and black pepper to taste, then whisk well together.
4 Just before serving, trickle the walnut dressing over the salad and toss gently.

NUTRIENTS PER SERVING: kilojoules 783, protein 4 g, carbohydrate 5 g (sugar 4 g), fat 17 g (saturated fat 2 g), good source of vitamin B group.

VERSATILE SIDE SALADS:
(top) FRISÉE, CUCUMBER AND RED ONION; *(centre)* SNOW PEA AND PICKLED GINGER; *(bottom)* CARROT AND GINGER.

CAESAR SALAD

Anchovies add extra zing to this strongly flavoured combination of hearty lettuce, Parmesan cheese and crunchy croutons, bathed in a velvety dressing of olive oil, egg and lemon juice.

TIME: 25 MINUTES SERVES: 4

2 heads cos lettuce
5 thick slices white bread
2 tablespoons peanut oil
6 tablespoons olive oil
2 cloves garlic
1 large egg
8 anchovy fillets
1 lemon
Salt and black pepper
100 g Parmesan cheese

1 Discard the outer leaves from the lettuces, rinse and dry the rest and put into a salad bowl.

2 Put a small saucepan of water on to boil for the egg.

3 To make the croutons, remove and discard the crusts from the bread and cut the slices into 1-cm cubes. Heat the peanut oil with 2 tablespoons olive oil in a frying pan. Peel the garlic, crush it into the pan, add the bread and fry, stirring, until the croutons are crisp. Drain on paper towels.

4 When the water boils, add the egg and cook for 1 minute, then remove from the water and put aside. Roughly chop the anchovy fillets and put aside.

5 To make the dressing, squeeze 1 tablespoon juice from the lemon, mix in the remaining olive oil and some salt and black pepper, then whisk in the egg.

6 Pour the dressing over the lettuce, toss, then add the anchovies and croutons and toss again.

7 Cut thin strips of cheese, scatter on top of the salad and serve.

NUTRIENTS PER SERVING: kilojoules 2272, protein 18 g, carbohydrate 27 g (sugar 3 g), fat 41 g (saturated fat 9 g), good source of vitamins B group, E and folate, and calcium and selenium.

CUCUMBER, RADISH AND MELON SALAD

This wonderful combination of fruit, vegetables and crunchy almonds mixed with a honey and walnut oil dressing makes an ideal accompaniment to cold or smoked meats and poultry.

TIME: 20 MINUTES SERVES: 4

500 g piece watermelon or honeydew melon
100 g cucumber
Salt
Olive oil for frying
¼ cup flaked almonds
100 g fresh bean sprouts
150 g radishes
4 spring onions
A small bunch of watercress

For the dressing:

1½ teaspoons clear honey
2 tablespoons walnut oil
3 teaspoons cider vinegar
Black pepper

1 Peel, seed and dice the melon, then dice the cucumber. Put both into a colander, add a little salt and toss together. Place a saucer on top and leave to drain.

2 Heat a little oil in a frying pan and fry the almonds until golden, then drain on paper towels.

3 Rinse the bean sprouts and drain well, then trim the radishes and spring onions. Quarter the radishes, slice the onions and mix all three together in a salad bowl.

4 Whisk the honey, walnut oil and vinegar together; season with pepper and pour over the salad.

5 Trim the watercress, rinse and dry it and arrange in a shallow serving dish. Add the melon and cucumber to the salad bowl, toss gently, then spoon onto the watercress. Scatter the almonds over the top just before serving.

NUTRIENTS PER SERVING: kilojoules 967, protein 4 g, carbohydrate 15 g (sugar 14 g), fat 18 g (saturated fat 2 g), good source of vitamins B group, C and E.

103

CAJUN POTATO SALAD

Capsicum, celery and onion are called the 'holy trinity' of Cajun cooking and form the basis of many dishes, including this substantial salad which is ideal for picnics and barbecues.

TIME: 30 MINUTES SERVES: 4

| 500 g waxy salad potatoes |
| Salt and black pepper |
| 1 small green capsicum |
| 2 stalks celery |
| 1 small red onion |

For the dressing:
| 150 ml mayonnaise |
| 2 teaspoons Dijon mustard |
| A few dashes of Tabasco sauce |

1 Put a kettle of water on to boil. Scrape the potatoes and put into a pan with the boiling water and some salt. Return to the boil and simmer for 15–20 minutes or until the potatoes are tender.

2 Halve and seed the capsicum, slice into strips and put into a salad bowl. Trim the celery; reserve the leaves for a garnish and finely slice the rest. Add to the capsicum. Peel the onion, halve lengthways and slice lengthways again into crescents. Add to the bowl.

3 To make the dressing, mix the mayonnaise and mustard in a small bowl and add Tabasco to taste.

4 Drain the potatoes, cool under cold running water, drain again and add to the salad. Spoon in the dressing, grind pepper over the top and mix well. Garnish the salad with celery leaves.

VARIATION

Add chopped hard-boiled eggs to the salad to turn it into a meal.

NUTRIENTS PER SERVING: kilojoules 1448, protein 3 g, carbohydrate 19 g (sugar 4 g), fat 29 g (saturated fat 4 g), good source of vitamins B group, C and E.

COOK'S SUGGESTION

Small waxy potato varieties such as Patrones and Kipflers are the best type to use when you are making potato salads.

SPINACH AND BABY CORN SALAD

Succulent morsels of rich avocado in oil and vinegar are strewn throughout this pretty combination of tender spinach and rocket leaves tossed with tiny cobs of crunchy corn.

TIME: 15 MINUTES SERVES: 4

100 g baby corn
Salt
100 g rocket leaves
250 g baby spinach leaves

For the dressing:

1 avocado, about 125 g
1 clove garlic
2 tablespoons extra virgin olive oil
3 teaspoons white wine vinegar
1 teaspoon sugar
1 teaspoon Tabasco sauce

1 Bring a small saucepan of water to the boil. Cut the baby corn across in half and add to the boiling water with some salt. Simmer for 1 minute then drain.

2 Rinse the rocket and spinach leaves and leave to drain.

3 Meanwhile, make the dressing. Cut the avocado in half, remove the stone (see page 53) and scoop the flesh into a large salad bowl.

4 Peel the garlic and crush it into the bowl, then add the oil, vinegar, sugar and Tabasco sauce. Season to taste with salt, then stir the dressing

together: some of the avocado will merge into the oil, but some small chunks should remain,

5 Add the well-drained corn, rocket and spinach leaves to the dressing and toss well. Serve as soon as possible.

VARIATION

If rocket is unavailable, peppery watercress makes a good substitute.

NUTRIENTS PER SERVING: kilojoules 728, protein 3 g, carbohydrate 8 g (sugar 3 g), fat 15 g (saturated fat 3 g), good source of vitamins A, B group, C, E and folate.

FISH &
SHELLFISH

*From grilled whole fish to stir-fried salmon,
from char-grilled octopus to scallops with Thai flavourings,
here are tempting recipes for all manner of seafood.*

FRESH TROUT WITH WALNUT DRESSING

Plain grilled trout is dramatically transformed by the addition of herbs and nuts, spiced vinegar and a pinch of paprika.

TIME: 25 MINUTES SERVES: 4

2 teaspoons vegetable oil
4 trout fillets, about 185 g each
¼ teaspoon paprika
10 walnut halves
125 g rocket, watercress or mixed salad leaves

For the dressing:

1 shallot or 2 spring onions
A few sprigs of dill or celery leaves
1½ tablespoons spiced rice vinegar or sherry vinegar
4 tablespoons walnut oil
Salt and black pepper

1 Preheat the griller to the highest setting. To make the dressing, peel and finely chop the shallot, or trim and finely chop the spring onions, and place in a small bowl. Chop the dill or celery leaves and add to the bowl along with the vinegar, walnut oil, salt and pepper. Mix well and put aside.

2 Grease the griller tray with half the vegetable oil and place the trout fillets on top, skin side down. Season with salt and paprika. Grill the fish for 5–8 minutes, on one side only, until the flesh is opaque in the centre and delicately brown at the edges.

3 While the fillets are cooking, heat the remaining vegetable oil in a small frying pan and gently fry the walnuts, shaking and stirring constantly so that they colour but do not burn. Drain on paper towels, then chop roughly.

4 Rinse and dry the salad greens and arrange on four plates. Place a fillet of trout on each. Stir the dressing, spoon it over the fish, and scatter the walnuts on top.

SERVING SUGGESTION
Tiny new potatoes go well with the clear flavours of this dish. Put them on to boil before you start grilling the trout.

NUTRIENTS PER SERVING: kilojoules 1888, protein 37 g, carbohydrate 1 g (sugar 0.5 g), fat 33 g (saturated fat 4 g), good source of vitamins B group and C.

SEAFOOD CAKES

These rich crab and prawn cakes are spiced with mustard, Worcestershire sauce and a little cayenne pepper then coated with breadcrumbs and fried until the outside is a crunchy golden brown.

TIME: 30 MINUTES SERVES: 4

2 slices dry bread, about 125 g in total
100 ml milk
200 g fresh crab meat
200 g peeled cooked prawns
2 large eggs
2 teaspoons Dijon mustard
1 tablespoon Worcestershire sauce
½ cup ground almonds
A large pinch of cayenne pepper
1 tablespoon mayonnaise
A handful of parsley

For the coating:

⅓ cup plain flour
1½ cups dried breadcrumbs
Sunflower oil for frying

1 Soak both slices of bread in the milk for 5 minutes. Flake the crab, put into a bowl, then chop the prawns and add to the crab.

2 Separate the eggs and put the whites aside. Add the yolks, mustard, Worcestershire sauce, almonds, cayenne and mayonnaise to the crab. Rinse, dry and chop enough parsley to give 1 tablespoon and add to the bowl.

3 Squeeze the bread dry, add to the crab and stir until soft but not sloppy: add some breadcrumbs if the mixture is too moist.

4 To make the coating: put the flour onto one plate and the breadcrumbs onto another. Whisk 1 tablespoon water into the egg whites. Divide the crab mixture into eight portions and shape into patties. Dip each one into the flour, shake off the excess, then dip into the egg whites; finally, coat with the breadcrumbs.

5 Heat 1 cm oil in a large frying pan over fairly high heat. Fry the fish cakes for 2–3 minutes on each side until crisp and golden, then drain on paper towels. Serve two cakes per person.

SERVING SUGGESTION
Serve with lemon wedges, tartare or seafood sauce, lettuce and tomatoes, or a spicy salsa. To make a heartier meal, use the seafood cakes and salad to fill burger buns.

NUTRIENTS PER SERVING: kilojoules 2490, protein 38 g, carbohydrate 56 g (sugar 6 g), fat 26 g (saturated fat 4 g), good source of vitamins B group and E, and calcium, selenium and zinc.

SALMON PIZZAS WITH YOGHURT AND DILL

Salmon makes an unusual topping for pizza, and thick yoghurt flavoured with dill adds a creamy texture that complements the richness of the fish better than the cheese normally used for pizzas.

TIME: 30 MINUTES SERVES: 4

| 2 small skinless salmon fillets, about 350 g in total |
| 2 large tomatoes |
| 1 small white or red onion |
| 2 thin 25-cm pizza bases |
| Salt and black pepper |
| 8 sprigs dill |
| ½ cup natural yoghurt |
| *To serve:* 4 tablespoons mango chutney, optional |

1 Preheat the oven to 220°C. Discard any bones from the salmon, then dice the flesh.

2 Finely chop the tomatoes and peel and finely chop the onion. Place the pizza bases on baking trays; cover with the tomatoes and onion. Arrange the salmon on top and add salt and pepper to taste.

3 Bake for 15–20 minutes, or until lightly browned, swapping the trays round half way through.

4 Put aside a few sprigs of dill for a garnish, then finely chop the remainder and mix into the yoghurt, along with some pepper.

5 Remove the pizzas from the oven, spoon some yoghurt over each and garnish with the reserved dill.

6 Cut each pizza into quarters and serve, accompanied by the mango chutney, if using.

NUTRIENTS PER SERVING: *kilojoules 2130, protein 25 g, carbohydrate 37 g (sugar 6 g), fat 29 g (saturated fat 15 g), good source of vitamins B group and E.*

COOK'S SUGGESTION

Salmon is quite a fatty fish so the pizzas do not need to be brushed with oil before baking, making this a healthy alternative to conventional pizzas.

CRAB AND AVOCADO SALAD

Both aromatic and tangy, the Asian-style marinade for the crab doubles as a dressing for the creamy avocado. Together they create a superbly flavoursome entrée or light lunch dish.

TIME: 30 MINUTES SERVES: 4

4 cooked sand or spanner crabs
1 small red chilli
A small bunch coriander
1 clove garlic
15 g fresh root ginger
2 spring onions
3 stalks lemon grass
4 limes
¼ cup Thai fish sauce
¼ cup sherry vinegar
1 tablespoon sugar
3 tablespoons light soy sauce
2 ripe firm avocados
To garnish: coriander sprigs, lime wedges

1 Cut the sand or spanner crabs in half and clean; place in a large bowl and put aside.

2 Seed and finely chop the chilli. Put aside a few sprigs of coriander for a garnish, and finely chop the remainder. Peel and crush the garlic and peel and finely chop the ginger. Trim the spring onions and the lemon grass and chop finely. Squeeze the juice from the limes. Combine in the bowl of a food processor with the fish sauce, vinegar, sugar and soy sauce and process for 10–15 seconds.

3 Pour the dressing over the crabs; allow to marinate for 10 minutes.

Meanwhile, halve, peel and slice the avocados lengthways.

4 Arrange the crab and the avocado on four serving plates and spoon over the remaining marinade. Serve immediately, garnished with coriander sprigs.

VARIATION

Freshly cooked king prawns, or strips of char-grilled chicken breast, can be used instead of the crab.

NUTRIENTS PER SERVING: kilojoules 1579, protein 13 g, carbohydrate 7 g (sugar 6 g), fat 31 g (saturated fat 7 g), good source of vitamins B group, C and E, and iodine, calcium, potassium and zinc.

SNAPPER PARCELS WITH CREAMY BROCCOLI

Fish parcels cook easily in the oven while you make a delicious accompaniment of broccoli florets with cream and tarragon.

TIME: 30 MINUTES SERVES: 4

4 thick fresh snapper cutlets, about 185 g each
2 tablespoons extra virgin olive oil
Salt and black pepper
1 shallot
350 g broccoli
10 sprigs tarragon
1 cup thick cream

1 Preheat the oven to 180°C. Dry the snapper cutlets then brush with 1 tablespoon oil and season well.

2 Cut four pieces of foil, each large enough to enclose a cutlet. Put one cutlet on each piece of foil, fold the edges together to make a roomy parcel and crimp to seal. Place the four parcels on a baking tray and cook for 15 minutes.

3 Meanwhile, peel and grate the shallot. Trim the broccoli into small florets.

4 Heat the remaining oil in a medium frying pan and fry the shallot until translucent.

5 Add the broccoli to the pan, stems down, with 150 ml water. Bring to the boil, then cover and simmer for 4–5 minutes until the broccoli is barely tender. Remove the lid, raise the heat, and cook until only 1–2 tablespoons water remain in the pan. Do not let the broccoli burn.

6 Reserve four sprigs of tarragon for a garnish, then strip the leaves off the rest and add to the broccoli. Stir in the thick cream to heat through, season to taste with salt and pepper and keep warm.

7 Remove the foil parcels from the oven, unwrap them and transfer the fish to four warmed plates. Serve the broccoli alongside the fish and garnish with the tarragon.

SERVING SUGGESTION
Serve the snapper cutlets sitting on top of individual portions of Sweet Potato Rösti (see page 272), as photographed.

NUTRIENTS PER SERVING: kilojoules 2063, protein 37 g, carbohydrate 3 g (sugar 3 g), fat 37 g (saturated fat 18 g), good source of vitamins A, B group, C, E and folate, and selenium.

BAKED FISH PLAKI

Plaki is a baked dish with a thick sauce made in many forms all over Greece. This is a simpler version of the original, but still has the robust flavours of capsicums, tomatoes, lemon and garlic.

TIME: 30 MINUTES SERVES: 4–6

2 tablespoons olive oil
1 medium onion
1 green capsicum
6 egg tomatoes
1 clove garlic
750 g skinless firm white fish fillet
1½ lemons
A handful of parsley
3 tablespoons dry white wine
3 tablespoons tomato paste
Salt and black pepper

1 Slowly heat the olive oil in a large flameproof casserole. Peel the onion and slice thinly. Seed the capsicum and slice into thin strips. Slice the tomatoes.
2 Put the vegetables into the casserole, peel the garlic and crush it in. Cover and cook over high heat for 6–8 minutes, shaking the casserole occasionally so that the vegetables do not stick.
3 Meanwhile, cut the fish fillet into 5-cm cubes and sprinkle with the juice from the half lemon. Finely chop the parsley and put aside.
4 Stir the wine and tomato paste into the vegetables. Cut the whole lemon into very fine slices and arrange in a single layer on top.
5 Put the fish on top of the lemon slices. Season with salt and pepper and sprinkle with the parsley. Reduce the heat to moderate, cover and simmer for 15 minutes; uncover for the last 5 minutes if the sauce seems too liquid. The fish is cooked when the flesh turns opaque and flakes easily.

SERVING SUGGESTION
Serve the fish with plenty of crusty bread or a big bowl of steamed rice with which to soak up the juices, and a green salad tossed with feta or soft goat's cheese and black olives, on the side.

NUTRIENTS PER SERVING, WHEN SERVING 4:
kilojoules 1154, protein 35 g, carbohydrate 11 g (sugar 10 g), fat 10 g (saturated fat 1 g), good source of vitamins A, B group, C and E, and selenium.

COOK'S SUGGESTION

Any type of firm white fish can be used in this recipe, as long as the fillets are not too thin. And if fresh egg tomatoes are not available, you can use canned whole plum tomatoes or tomato pieces, drained.

GEMFISH BAKED WITH PESTO

Firm fresh fish given a flourish of herby pesto and baked in the oven makes a fine family dish accompanied by crushed garlic potatoes enriched with butter and cream.

TIME: 30 MINUTES SERVES: 4

650 g floury potatoes, such as Desirée
Salt and black pepper
4 thick gemfish fillets, or cutlets, about 185 g each
1 tablespoon green or red pesto
1 tablespoon olive oil
1 clove garlic
2 tablespoons butter
3 tablespoons cream
***To garnish:* 4 sprigs basil**

1 Preheat the oven to 200°C and put a kettle of water on to boil.
2 Scrub the potatoes and cut into 2-cm cubes. Put the cubes into a saucepan, cover with boiling water and add salt. Cover, bring back to the boil and boil the potatoes for 10–15 minutes, until cooked.
3 Meanwhile, line a small baking dish with foil. Wipe the fish with paper towels and place the fillets in the baking dish. Spread the pesto evenly over each and season with the salt and pepper. Drizzle with olive oil and bake on the top shelf of the oven for 15–20 minutes or until the flesh flakes easily.
4 Drain the potatoes and return to the pan. Peel the garlic, crush it into the potatoes and mash. Stir in the butter and cream and reheat gently.
5 Serve the fish resting on a bed of potato and garnish with the basil.
SERVING SUGGESTION
Accompany with a simply cooked vegetable such as steamed beans, char-grilled vegetables, or Italian Baked Chicory (page 264).

NUTRIENTS PER SERVING: kilojoules 1804, protein 37 g, carbohydrate 23 g (sugar 2 g), fat 22 g (saturated fat 10 g), good source of vitamins B group, C and E.

COOK'S SUGGESTION

Pesto is made from fresh basil, pine nuts, garlic, olive oil and Parmesan or Pecorino cheese, pounded together with a pestle and mortar. Red pesto also includes sun-dried tomatoes. When there is a glut of basil in the summer, pesto can be made quickly in a food processor and then stored in batches in the freezer for several months.

LEATHERJACKET WITH PEA PURÉE

A creamy pool of sweet-tasting green pea purée complements the earthy flavour of Indian spices which are roasted to form a golden brown crust around firm-textured white leatherjacket.

TIME: 30 MINUTES SERVES: 2

1 large leatherjacket tail, skinned, or tail end of other firm white fish, about 400–500 g
1 clove garlic
1 red chilli
1 tablespoon olive oil
1 teaspoon ground cumin
1 teaspoon ground coriander
½ teaspoon sugar
½ lemon
To garnish: 2 sprigs mint

For the pea purée:
150 g frozen peas
350 ml vegetable stock
1 clove garlic
1 tablespoon cream
Salt and black pepper

1 Preheat the oven to 200°C. Trim the leatherjacket tail of any fins and tough outer membrane and place on a rack in a baking tray.
2 Peel and crush the garlic. Seed and finely chop the chilli and place both in a small bowl with the olive oil, cumin, coriander and sugar. Add 1 teaspoon juice from the half lemon to the bowl; stir to make a thick paste.
3 Spread the paste evenly over both sides of the fish tail, then roast in the oven for 20 minutes or until just cooked.
4 Meanwhile, make the pea purée. Put the peas into a saucepan with the vegetable stock and bring to the boil. Peel the garlic, crush it into the peas and simmer, uncovered, for

5 minutes, skimming off any scum that comes to the surface.
5 When the peas are tender, drain the stock into a measuring jug. Blend the peas with the cream and 150 ml stock to make a textured purée. Season to taste with salt and pepper and keep warm.
6 When the fish is cooked, cut the fillets from both sides of the central bone. Pour the purée onto two warmed plates and serve the fish fillets on top, garnished with the sprigs of mint.

NUTRIENTS PER SERVING: kilojoules 1203, protein 37 g, carbohydrate 10 g (sugar 4 g), fat 13 g (saturated fat 3 g), good source of vitamins B group, C and E, and chloride and phosphorus.

115

FISH WITH FLAVOURED BUTTERS

SALMON WITH LIME HERB BUTTER

This aromatic butter is infused with the Southeast Asian flavours of ginger, coriander and lime.

TIME: 30 MINUTES SERVES: 4

5-cm piece fresh root ginger

12 sprigs coriander

2 limes

125 g butter

Salt and black pepper

Cayenne pepper

2 tablespoons sunflower oil

4 salmon fillets, about 185 g each

1   Preheat the oven to 220°C. Peel and slice the ginger and put into a food processor. Put some sprigs of coriander aside and add the rest to the ginger. Cut 1 lime into wedges for a garnish. Grate the zest of the other, squeeze the juice, and add to the mixing bowl with the butter, salt, pepper and cayenne, then blend.
2   Shape the butter into a sausage, wrap in foil and chill in the freezer.
3   In the meantime, brush a baking tray with a little oil, place the salmon fillets on it and brush with the remaining oil. Sprinkle with salt and bake for 8 minutes, or until the flesh flakes easily.
4   Take the butter from the freezer and cut into thick rounds. Transfer the fish to four plates, place a round of butter on each and garnish with the lime and coriander.
SERVING SUGGESTION
Serve with couscous, which you can leave to soak while you cook the salmon. Or try Glazed Onions (page 278) and Spinach and Baby Corn Salad (page 105).
VARIATION
You can also use rainbow trout or ocean trout in this recipe.

NUTRIENTS PER SERVING: kilojoules 2695, protein 26 g, carbohydrate 2 g (sugar 0.4 g), fat 59 g (saturated fat 33 g), good source of vitamins A and E.

TUNA WITH WASABI BUTTER

East meets West in this exciting, well-flavoured butter containing hot wasabi, sesame seeds and soy sauce.

TIME: 25 MINUTES SERVES: 4

1 teaspoon sesame seeds

½ lemon

A few sprigs each of basil, chives, coriander and parsley

125 g unsalted butter

1 tablespoon wasabi paste

1 tablespoon soy sauce

3 drops Tabasco sauce

4 tuna steaks, about 185 g each

1 tablespoon olive or vegetable oil

1   Dry roast the sesame seeds in a small frying pan until lightly coloured then put aside.
2   Squeeze 1 teaspoon juice from the lemon and add to the seeds. Finely chop the herbs, reserving a few sprigs for a garnish, then stir the chopped herbs into the sesame seeds along with the butter, wasabi paste, soy sauce and Tabasco. Beat until smooth.
3   Shape the butter into a sausage, wrap in foil and chill in the freezer.
4   Heat a ridged griller plate or frying pan over moderately high heat. Brush both sides of the tuna steaks with the oil and fry for 3–4 minutes on each side.
5   Cut the butter into rounds. Transfer the steaks to four plates, place a round of butter on each and garnish with the herb sprigs.
SERVING SUGGESTION
Radishes, pickled ginger, bean sprouts and watercress all make good garnishes for this dish. Steamed new potatoes are a good foil for the flavoured butter.

NUTRIENTS PER SERVING: kilojoules 2185, protein 42 g, carbohydrate 1 g (sugar 0.8 g), fat 39 g (saturated fat 19 g), good source of vitamins A, B group and E, and selenium.

JEWFISH WITH HORSERADISH BUTTER

The pungent flavour of chive and horseradish butter is a zesty finishing touch for quickly pan-fried fish.

TIME: 25 MINUTES SERVES: 4

A small bunch of chives

1½ tablespoons hot horseradish cream

125 g butter

4 jewfish cutlets, about 185 g each

Salt and black pepper

2 teaspoons vegetable oil

1   Snip about 2 tablespoons fresh chives into a small mixing bowl and combine with the horseradish cream and all but 15 g of the butter.
2   Shape the butter into a sausage, wrap in foil and chill in the freezer.
3   Wipe the jewfish cutlets with paper towels and season on both sides with salt and pepper. Heat the remaining butter and the oil in a pan. Cook the fish over high heat for about 4–6 minutes, until it flakes easily.
4   Cut the butter into rounds, then transfer the cooked fish to four serving plates and place a round of butter on each.
SERVING SUGGESTION
A bowl of simply steamed spinach, or maybe Orange and Sesame Carrots (page 262), would go well with this recipe.
VARIATION
If you prefer, you can substitute snapper cutlets or fillets, or kingfish cutlets, for the jewfish.

NUTRIENTS PER SERVING: kilojoules 1833, protein 38 g, carbohydrate 1 g (sugar 1 g), fat 31 g (saturated fat 18 g), good source of vitamins A, B group and E.

THREE TASTY FISHES: (*top*) JEWFISH WITH HORSERADISH BUTTER; (*centre*) TUNA WITH WASABI BUTTER; (*bottom*) SALMON WITH LIME HERB BUTTER.

CHAR-GRILLED BABY OCTOPUS WITH ROASTED CAPSICUM

The smoky flavours of the grilled octopus and the roasted capsicum are complemented by the tang of the rocket leaves in a dish that is just as delicious cooked on the barbecue.

TIME: 30 MINUTES SERVES: 4

| 2 red capsicums |
| ½ cup sun-dried tomatoes, drained |
| 1 lime |
| 1 lemon |
| A small bunch of thyme |
| 1 kg baby octopus, cleaned and debeaked by the fishmonger |
| ½ cup olive oil |
| 1 bunch rocket |
| 2 tablespoons extra virgin olive oil |
| Sea salt and black pepper |
| *To garnish:* lime or lemon wedges |

1 Pre-heat oven to maximum setting. Pre-heat the char-grill or barbecue to very hot.

2 Slice the capsicum across the stem end to remove the base, then remove the seeds with your fingertips. Arrange the capsicums on a baking tray and place in the oven. Roast for 10–12 minutes until the skin is charred. Remove from the oven and put aside to cool.

3 Meanwhile, finely chop the sun-dried tomatoes. Remove the zest from the lime and the lemon and squeeze the juices. Finely chop enough thyme to give about 2 tablespoons. Combine in a bowl with the octopus and the ½ cup oil. Marinate for 10–15 minutes.

4 When the capsicums are cool, remove skins with fingertips. Slice the flesh into wide strips.

5 Place the octopus on the char-grill or barbecue and cook over high heat for 5–6 minutes, spooning the marinade over regularly.

6 Arrange the capsicum, rocket leaves and octopus on four serving plates. Drizzle each plate with 2 teaspoons extra virgin olive oil, season with salt and pepper, and garnish with lime or lemon wedges.

NUTRIENTS PER SERVING: kilojoules 2620, protein 45 g, carbohydrate 7 g (sugar 7 g), fat 48 g (saturated fat 6 g), good source of vitamins A, B group, C and folate, and iodine.

COOK'S SUGGESTION

The octopus can be marinated for up to 24 hours in the refrigerator. Remove from the refrigerator about 10–15 minutes before cooking.

CALAMARI WITH OLIVES AND CAPERS

Tender calamari comes to the table as a main course in a hearty tomato, anchovy, olive, garlic, white wine and caper sauce inspired by the flavours of the Mediterranean.

TIME: 25 MINUTES SERVES: 4–6

| 1 kg calamari, cleaned by the fishmonger |
| 2 cloves garlic |
| 6 anchovy fillets |
| ¼ cup olive oil |
| 1 cup dry white wine |
| 2 tablespoons capers, drained |
| 2 x 425 g canned tomato pieces |
| A pinch of sugar |
| A bunch of flat-leaf parsley |
| 1 cup black olives |
| Freshly ground black pepper |

1 Cut the calamari into rings. Peel and finely chop the garlic. Finely chop the anchovy fillets.
2 Heat the oil in a large, heavy-based saucepan. Add the calamari and garlic. Cook, stirring, over moderate heat until the garlic is golden.
3 Add the anchovies, wine, capers, tomato pieces with their juice and the sugar. Simmer gently over low heat for 15 minutes. Meanwhile, finely chop enough parsley to give about ½ cup.

4 When the calamari is cooked, add the olives, parsley, and pepper to taste. Serve immediately.
SERVING SUGGESTION
Good crusty bread is essential to soak up the rich juices in this dish. If you like, you can also serve some simply cooked pasta.

NUTRIENTS PER SERVING, WHEN SERVING 4:
kilojoules 1836, protein 44 g, carbohydrate 4 g (sugar 3 g), fat 20 g (saturated fat 2 g), good source of vitamins B group and C, iodine and calcium.

BAKED SKATE

Tender skate wings dotted with nuts of butter and sprinkled with shallots and vinegar are simply baked in the oven. A final flourish of capers and chopped gherkins adds extra flavour.

TIME: 30 MINUTES SERVES: 4

2 shallots
3 small gherkins
90 g butter
2 large skate wings, about 500 g each
2 tablespoons balsamic or sherry vinegar
Salt and black pepper
2 tablespoons capers

1 Preheat the oven to 190°C. Peel and chop the shallots, chop the gherkins and put aside separately.
2 Use a little of the butter to grease a shallow baking dish, which should be large enough to hold the skate wings flat in one layer. Rinse the skate, cut each wing into two pieces, then place in the baking dish and dot with the remaining butter.
3 Sprinkle the skate wings with the chopped shallots and the balsamic or sherrry vinegar and season with salt and pepper. Bake the fish, uncovered, for 20 minutes, or until the thickest part of the wing flakes easily when tested gently with a fork.
4 Sprinkle the pieces of fish with the capers and chopped gherkins and baste with the cooking juices just before serving.

SERVING SUGGESTION
Accompany with some tomato halves, roasted alongside the fish. New potatoes can be boiled or steamed while the fish is baking.

VARIATION
If you have difficulty finding skate, slices of fresh tuna can be used successfully in this recipe.

NUTRIENTS PER SERVING: kilojoules 1344, protein 38 g, carbohydrate 0.5 g (sugar 0.5 g), fat 18 g (saturated fat 12 g), good source of vitamins A, B group and E.

SALMON WITH TROPICAL FRUIT SALSA

Hearty pieces of grilled salmon are given a tropical taste when served with an exciting salsa – a finely chopped mixture of mango and pawpaw, laced with lime, ginger and fresh mint.

TIME: 25 MINUTES SERVES: 4

4 salmon fillets, 185 g each
1 tablespoon olive oil

For the salsa:

1 small mango
1 small pawpaw
2.5-cm piece fresh root ginger
A handful of mint leaves
1 lime
Salt and black pepper

1 Preheat the griller to moderate and cover the rack with foil.
2 To make the salsa, cut the mango in half, remove the flesh, dice finely and put into a bowl. Cut the pawpaw in half, scoop out and discard the seeds, finely dice the flesh and add to the mango.
3 Peel the ginger and grate it into the bowl. Chop the mint and add to the bowl.
4 Remove a few shreds of zest from the lime for a garnish, then grate the rest and add to the salsa. Squeeze the juice and add half to the bowl, reserving the rest.
5 Season the salsa with salt and plenty of pepper and mix well.
6 Put the salmon, skin side down, onto the foil on the rack. Brush with the oil, season with salt and pepper and sprinkle with the remaining lime juice. Grill for 6–8 minutes without turning. The fish is done when the flesh flakes easily.

7 Serve the grilled salmon garnished with the lime zest and accompanied by the salsa.
SERVING SUGGESTION
Serve with a plain green salad and perhaps some new potatoes.

NUTRIENTS PER SERVING: kilojoules 1816, protein 26 g, carbohydrate 15 g (sugar 14 g), fat 30 g (saturated fat 15 g), good source of vitamins A, C and E.

COOK'S SUGGESTION

If you grill the salmon skin side down on a piece of ungreased foil it does not need turning, and is easy to lift away from the skin to serve.

QUICK FROM THE CAN

A well-stocked cupboard is the best defence against sudden pangs of hunger and cooks have always reached for the can opener in emergencies. Canned fish, in particular, provides a good basis for a wide range of dishes from starters and quick light lunches to filling main courses.

SARDINE BRUSCHETTA

Sardines on toast never tasted so good. Here they are given a new twist by the addition of strong Mediterranean flavours.

SERVES: 2

1 crusty Italian bread loaf
1 clove garlic
2–3 firm ripe tomatoes
Salt and black pepper
Olive oil
105 g canned sardines
Basil, rocket or watercress
Lemon juice or balsamic vinegar

Toast or grill four thick slices from the bread, then rub one surface of each with the cut clove of garlic. Cut the tomatoes into chunks, pile onto the bruschetta, season with salt and pepper, and drizzle generously with olive oil. Drain the sardines and arrange on top. Scatter leaves of basil, rocket or watercress over the bruschetta. Sprinkle a little lemon juice or balsamic vinegar on the salad.

SMOKED OYSTER PAN-FRY

Canned smoked oysters need no cooking and they add an unusual flavour to this one-dish meal.

SERVES: 2

1 clove garlic
2 tablespoons olive oil
400 g waxy potatoes
A bunch of spring onions or chives
105 g canned smoked oysters
4 sun-dried tomatoes
Salt and black pepper

Peel and thickly slice the garlic and fry very gently for 3–4 minutes in the olive oil in a large, non-stick frying pan. Peel or scrub the potatoes and cut into 1-cm cubes. Remove the garlic from the pan and discard it. Add the diced potatoes and fry over fairly high heat until golden. Chop the spring onions or chives. Drain the oysters and cut in half, then drain and chop the tomatoes. When the potatoes are nearly done, add the onions and cook for 1 minute. Stir in the oysters and tomatoes and heat through for 2 minutes. Season with salt and pepper and serve.

SALMON FILO PARCELS

Chilled filo pastry means you don't have to wait for the pastry to defrost to make these delicious fish parcels.

SERVES: 2 AS A MAIN COURSE,
4 AS A STARTER

3 tablespoons butter
¼ cup plain flour
1 cup milk
210 g canned red salmon
340 g canned asparagus tips
A sprig of dill
Salt and black pepper
2 sheets filo pastry

Preheat the oven to 190°C. Make a sauce by whisking together half the butter with the flour and milk in a saucepan over moderate heat, until it comes to the boil and thickens. Simmer for 1 minute, then pour into a bowl. Drain the salmon and flake the flesh into the sauce. Spoon out half the asparagus tips (keep the rest for another dish), drain and add to the sauce. Snip in the dill; season generously with salt and pepper.

Melt the remaining butter. Place the sheets of pastry on top of each other, cut out four 18-cm squares and brush with melted butter. Spoon a quarter of the salmon mixture into the centre of each square and draw up the corners to make a bundle. Brush the outside with butter and place on a greased baking tray. Bake for 12–15 minutes, until golden.

CRAB AND PEA TART

A prebaked pastry case is quickly filled with crab in a creamy sauce to make a mouth-watering flan.

SERVES: 4

2 medium eggs
Salt and black pepper
½ teaspoon ground mace
170 g canned crab meat
100 g frozen peas
2 spring onions
100 ml thick cream
2 tablespoons Amontillado sherry
2 tablespoons grated Parmesan cheese
23-cm prebaked pastry case

Preheat the oven to 200°C. Beat the eggs with salt, pepper and mace in a medium bowl. Stir in the crab. Defrost the peas in boiling water and drain. Chop the spring onions and add both to the bowl. Stir in the cream, sherry and half the cheese.

Use the mixture to fill the flan case and place, in its foil container, on a heavy baking tray. Sprinkle the rest of the cheese on top and bake high in the oven for 20 minutes.

TUNA AND POTATO SALAD

A very substantial salad that tastes especially good made in the morning to eat outdoors for lunch.

SERVES: 4

4 eggs
250 g frozen peas
440 g canned new potatoes
425 g canned tuna in oil
2 medium carrots
1 lemon
Salt and black pepper
300 ml mayonnaise
A bunch of chives or flat-leaf parsley

Hardboil the eggs and put the peas into a saucepan of boiling water to cook for 3 minutes. Drain the potatoes, then slice into a serving bowl. Drain the oil from the tuna into a measuring jug then flake the tuna onto the potatoes. Peel the carrots and grate into the bowl.

Drain the peas and rinse under cold running water. Cool and shell the eggs, cut into quarters and add along with the peas to the bowl.

Squeeze the juice from the lemon into the tuna oil. Add salt, black pepper and enough mayonnaise to make it up to 350 ml. Whisk the dressing and stir through the salad Sprinkle with chopped chives or parsley, cover and chill.

NOODLES WITH ANCHOVY SAUCE

A truly simple sauce from Sicily and Venice gets its impact from the intense flavour of anchovies.

SERVES: 4

250 g wholemeal or plain noodles
2 tablespoons currants
1 large clove garlic
1 sprig rosemary
2 tablespoons olive oil
1 lemon
2 x 50 g canned anchovies
2 tablespoons pine nuts
Black pepper
A sprig of mint

Bring a saucepan of water to the boil, add the noodles and cook according to packet directions. Soak the currants in a little boiling water from the pasta pan. Fry the garlic and rosemary in the oil over moderate heat until they begin to colour, then remove from the oil and discard. Grate the lemon rind.

Place the frying pan on top of the pan of boiling pasta (the next step needs only gentle heat). Stir in the anchovies, pine nuts, drained currants and lemon rind.

Cook until the anchovies form a sauce. If the mixture seems dry, add a little hot water. Season with pepper, pour over the drained noodles and garnish with chopped mint.

CANNED FISH TRANSFORMATION:
SARDINE BRUSCHETTA.

SMOKED SALMON WITH STIR-FRIED VEGETABLES

This unusual dish features delicate baby vegetables and smoked salmon with a light touch of Asian flavourings.

TIME: 25 MINUTES SERVES: 4

250 g mixed salad leaves
1 green chilli
100 g small green beans
100 g baby carrots
100 g shallots
100 g thin asparagus
1 tablespoon olive oil
1 tablespoon sesame seed oil
1 clove garlic
100 ml dry sherry
125 g smoked salmon trimmings, or slices
1 tablespoon light soy sauce
½ teaspoon caster sugar
To garnish: a few coriander leaves

1 Rinse and dry the salad leaves and arrange on a serving plate.
2 Seed and slice the chilli. Top and tail the beans and carrots, halving the carrots lengthways if they are thick.
3 Peel the shallots and cut into halves or quarters if large. Trim the asparagus and cut the stalks into 2.5-cm lengths.
4 Heat the olive oil and sesame oil in a large frying pan. Peel the garlic and crush it into the pan, then add the sliced chilli and stir-fry over moderate heat for 1 minute. Add the beans and carrots and continue to fry for 1–2 minutes more.
5 Add the shallots and asparagus and stir-fry for 1 minute. Then add the sherry, cover the pan and cook for 1 minute more.
6 Cut the smoked salmon into strips, if necessary, add to the pan, cover and cook for 1 minute. Then add the soy sauce and caster sugar and stir well. Leave the sauce to heat through.
7 To serve, spoon the smoked salmon mixture over the prepared salad leaves and sprinkle with the coriander leaves.

SERVING SUGGESTION
A bowl of steamed new potatoes is an excellent accompaniment to this crunchy stir-fry.

NUTRIENTS PER SERVING: kilojoules 732, protein 10 g, carbohydrate 5 g (sugar 4 g), fat 10 g (saturated fat 1 g), good source of vitamins A, B group, C, E and folate.

PAN-FRIED OCEAN TROUT WITH LEEKS AND CREAM

Succulently fresh fillets of ocean trout are gently cooked on a bed of lightly fried leeks, then enhanced with a white wine and cream sauce subtly flavoured with chives.

TIME: 20 MINUTES SERVES: 4

| 4 leeks, white part only |
| 1 bunch chives |
| 2 tablespoons unsalted butter |
| 4 ocean trout fillets, about 150 g each |
| ½ cup white wine |
| ½ cup thickened cream |
| Black pepper |
| *To serve:* steamed spinach |

1 Clean and finely chop the leeks; finely chop the chives.

2 Heat the butter gently in a large, heavy-based frying pan, add the leeks, and sauté for 4–5 minutes, until just tender.

3 Add the trout to the pan and cook for 2–3 minutes on each side, until just cooked. Remove fish from the pan and keep warm.

4 Add the wine, cream and most of the chopped chives to the pan and season with pepper. Increase the heat and cook, stirring, for 3–4 minutes, until the sauce has reduced and thickened.

5 Place some steamed spinach on individual plates and pour over a little sauce. Top with a trout fillet, drizzle over some more sauce, and scatter over the remaining chives.

SERVING SUGGESTION
Offset the creaminess of the sauce with some crispy sautéed potatoes.

NUTRIENTS PER SERVING: kilojoules 2049, protein 30 g, carbohydrate 4 g (sugar 4 g), fat 37 g (saturated fat 13 g), good source of vitamins B group, C and D, and potassium, iron, selenium and iodine.

GRILLED SOLE WITH BUTTERY ZUCCHINI

A delicate dish of grilled white fish and buttery shredded zucchini is a perfect choice for an elegant summer meal.

TIME: 30 MINUTES   SERVES: 4

600 g zucchini
Salt and black pepper
4 whole sole or flounder, about 500 g each, dark skin and heads removed by the fishmonger
A few sprigs of dill
A small bunch of chives
A few sprigs of parsley
4 tablespoons butter
Oil for greasing
1½ lemons

1 Preheat the griller to high. Trim the zucchini then shred coarsely in a food processor or grate by hand. Put into a colander with a little salt, toss gently together and put aside to drain thoroughly.

2 Rinse and dry the fish and make three diagonal cuts through the white skin on each one.

3 Put 4 sprigs dill aside for a garnish, then chop enough dill, chives and parsley to give 1 tablespoon of each. Put into a small bowl with half the butter, season well with pepper, and mash with a fork until well mixed. Divide the mixture into four and put aside.

4 Melt the remaining butter in a frying pan. Fry the zucchini over moderate heat for 10 minutes, until cooked but still slightly firm. Shake the pan gently from time to time.

5 Meanwhile, lightly oil a large griller tray and place the sole in it, white skin side up. Grill the fish for 5 minutes, then turn and sprinkle with the juice from the half lemon. Cook for 2–3 minutes, until the flesh flakes easily.

6 Cut the whole lemon into eight wedges and put aside. Place a portion of herb butter on each sole and warm under the griller for a few seconds until butter starts to melt.

7 Serve the fish on individual plates, accompanied by the zucchini and the lemon wedges.

SERVING SUGGESTION

Grill some halved tomatoes with the sole and serve with Roast New Potatoes with Rosemary (page 273).

VARIATION

Salmon, jewfish, snapper or bream fillets can be used instead of sole or flounder. Brush them with melted butter before cooking.

NUTRIENTS PER SERVING: kilojoules 2319, protein 84 g, carbohydrate 2 g (sugar 2 g), fat 23 g (saturated fat 10 g), good source of vitamins A, B group, C, E and folate, and iron, selenium and zinc.

COOK'S SUGGESTION

If your griller tray is not big enough for four sole, you can cook them on a large baking tray in the oven instead. Preheat the oven to 220°C, then bake the fish, white skin side up, for 15–20 minutes.

SMOKED HADDOCK WITH NOODLES

Lightly smoked haddock is served on a bed of choice baby vegetables which are stir-fried with rice noodles and enriched with a sweet and sour sauce to make an easy and unusual dish.

TIME: 30 MINUTES   SERVES: 4

4 smoked haddock fillets, 185 g each
250 g rice vermicelli noodles (rice sticks)
1 green chilli
100 g baby carrots
100 g small green beans
250 g thin asparagus
1 tablespoon peanut oil
1 clove garlic
1–2 tablespoons Thai fish sauce (nam pla or nuoc mam) or soy sauce
2 tablespoons white wine
3 teaspoons clear honey
1 teaspoon sesame seed oil

1 Put a kettle of water on to boil. Skin the fish (see page 11). Put the noodles into a bowl, cover with boiling water, leave to stand for 5 minutes, then drain.

2 Meanwhile, seed and chop the chilli. Peel the carrots; trim the green beans and asparagus. Slice the asparagus into lengths to match the beans.

3 Heat the oil in a wok or large frying pan with a lid. Peel the garlic and crush it into the oil, then add the chilli and sweat over low heat for 2 minutes to flavour the oil.

4 Add the vegetables, increase the heat, then add the fish or soy sauce, wine and honey.

5 Place the smoked haddock fillets on top of the vegetables, cover and cook for 5 minutes. Remove the fish with a slotted spoon; keep warm.

6 Add the drained noodles to the pan, toss with the vegetables in the pan juices and then stir in the sesame oil. Toss the mixture for a minute or two longer to warm the noodles through.

7 Divide the stir-fried vegetables among four serving plates and arrange the haddock fillets on top.

NUTRIENTS PER SERVING: kilojoules 1929, protein 38 g, carbohydrate 59 g (sugar 7 g), fat 7 g (saturated fat 1 g), good source of vitamins A, B group, E and folate.

STEAMED WHOLE FISH CHINESE STYLE

A whole fish flavoured with ginger, soy sauce and sesame oil looks quite spectacular yet is easy to prepare.

TIME: 30 MINUTES SERVES: 4

1 whole round fish, ready-gutted, such as bream or snapper, about 1 kg
Salt
5-cm piece fresh root ginger
4 spring onions
2 tablespoons soy sauce
1 tablespoon sesame seed oil
1 small red chilli
2 tablespoons peanut or vegetable oil
To garnish: coriander sprigs

1 Clean and rinse the fish and pat dry with paper towels. Make three or four diagonal slashes down to the bone on each side of the fish and gently rub with salt, inside and out. Put aside for 10 minutes.

2 Peel the ginger and cut into julienne strips, then trim the spring onions, cut into 7.5-cm lengths, shred finely and put aside. Stir the soy sauce and sesame oil together in a small bowl and put aside.

3 Fill a steamer or wok with water to a level of 5–7.5 cm and bring to the boil. If using a wok, place a trivet in the bottom.

4 Rinse the salted fish under cold running water then dry with paper towels. Place on a heatproof plate and lower into the steamer basket or wok; do not let the plate touch the water. Cover, reduce the heat and steam gently for 15–20 minutes, or until the fish is cooked.

5 While the fish is steaming, seed the chilli and cut into fine shreds. Heat the oil in a small frying pan and cook the chilli and ginger over high heat until softened.

6 Transfer the fish to a warmed serving dish and sprinkle with the spring onions, ginger and chilli shreds. Pour the soy sauce and sesame oil mixture over the top, garnish with coriander sprigs and serve immediately.

SERVING SUGGESTION
White rice would go well with this dish and can be cooked while the fish is steaming. Asian noodles cook even faster and can be garnished with sesame seeds and some finely chopped red chilli. A side dish of crisp stir-fried vegetables can also be cooked while the fish is steaming.

NUTRIENTS PER SERVING: kilojoules 1599, protein 50 g, carbohydrate 2 g (sugar 0.4 g), fat 19 g (saturated fat 2 g), good source of vitamin B group, and calcium and iron.

COOK'S SUGGESTION

If you do not have a wok or steamer large enough to hold a whole fish, use a baking dish with a wire rack. Place the fish on its plate on the rack and cover the dish with foil, tucking it under the rim to keep the steam in.

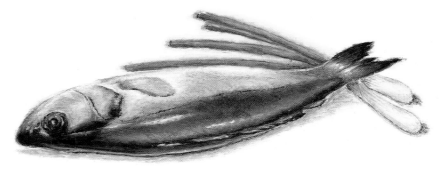

STIR-FRIED YABBIES WITH GINGER AND SHALLOTS

Under a glaze of chilli sauce sweetened with brown sugar, freshly cooked yabbies take pride of place on the dinner table.

TIME: 20 MINUTES SERVES: 4

| 24 large green yabbies |
| 1 bunch shallots |
| 30 g fresh root ginger |
| 2 cloves garlic |
| 1 lime |
| 2 tablespoons vegetable or peanut oil |
| ¼ cup brown sugar |
| ½ cup chicken stock |
| 2 tablespoons Thai-style sweet chilli sauce |
| *To garnish:* lime wedges, whole red chillies |

1 Shell the yabbies, leaving the heads on. Peel and finely chop the shallots, the ginger and the garlic. Remove the zest from the lime and squeeze the juice; put aside.

2 Heat the oil in a large, heavy-based frying pan. Add the yabbies and cook, stirring, over moderate heat until they change colour and are cooked. Remove from the pan with a slotted spoon; put aside.

3 Add the shallots, ginger and garlic to the pan and cook, stirring, over low heat for 3–4 minutes.

4 Increase the heat and add the sugar, stock, chilli sauce and reserved lime zest and juice. Cook, stirring, until the sauce has reduced and thickened slightly.

5 Reduce the heat again, return the yabbies to the pan and heat through. Serve immediately.

SERVING SUGGESTION
Serve the yabbies with a bowl of steaming rice, put on to cook at the same time, or some simply cooked boiled noodles.

NUTRIENTS PER SERVING: kilojoules 1139, protein 27 g, carbohydrate 11 g (sugar 11 g), fat 10 g (saturated fat 2 g), good source of vitamins B group and C, and copper.

COOK'S SUGGESTION

The small round bulbs of golden or purple shallots are used in this dish, rather than the green and white slender vegetables more correctly known as spring onions.

GRILLED YABBIES WITH ALMOND AND GARLIC

Yabbies cooked with garlic butter gain an extra dimension by the addition of finely ground almonds in the topping, making a subtly flavoured variation of the more traditional breadcrumbs.

TIME: 20 MINUTES SERVES: 4

24 large green yabbies
2 cloves garlic
A bunch of flat-leaf parsley
1 lemon
125 g unsalted butter, at room temperature
⅓ cup ground almonds
Black pepper

1 Pre-heat the griller. Shell the yabby tails and flatten slightly with a meat mallet. Place in a baking dish and put aside.

2 Peel and crush the garlic. Put 4 sprigs parsley aside for a garnish, then finely chop enough to give 3 tablespoons. Remove the lemon zest and squeeze the juice.

3 Combine the garlic, butter, almonds and parsley and spread the mixture over the yabbies. Sprinkle with lemon zest and juice and a good grinding of pepper.

4 Place the yabbies under the pre-heated griller and cook for 4–5 minutes, until golden brown. Serve immediately with the pan juices and garnish with parsley.

SERVING SUGGESTION
Crusty bread to soak up the juices, and a green salad on the side, are the only accompaniments this succulent seafood dish needs.

VARIATION
Large green king prawns, shelled and deveined – or scampi, when available – can be used instead of the yabbies.

NUTRIENTS PER SERVING: kilojoules 1902, protein 29 g, carbohydrate 2 g (sugar 2 g), fat 8 g (saturated fat 0.5 g), good source of vitamins B group, C and E, and copper.

SCALLOPS WITH A HERB DRESSING

A piquant dressing made with a heady bunch of fresh herbs, capers and olives accompanies
sweet-flavoured scallops, seared over high heat and served with long strands of pasta.

TIME: 30 MINUTES   SERVES: 4

500 g fresh scallops, with or without corals	
350 g dried tagliatelle	
2 tablespoons olive oil	

For the dressing:

A bunch of parsley
A bunch of mint
A bunch of chives
1 lemon
2 tablespoons white wine vinegar or sherry vinegar
4 tablespoons extra virgin olive oil
1 tablespoon capers
6 large pitted black olives
Salt and black pepper

1 Put a large pan of water on to boil for the pasta. To start making the dressing, finely chop the parsley and mint and snip the chives. Put a mixture of all three herbs in a measuring jug; you will need about ¾ cup.

2 Grate the rind of the lemon and add to the jug with the wine vinegar or sherry vinegar and the extra virgin olive oil. Roughly chop the capers and black olives and add them to the jug, then season to taste with salt and black pepper. Mix well and put aside.

3 Check each scallop has had the small tough muscle removed, then rinse and dry on paper towels. Season with salt and pepper.

4 Add the tagliatelle to the saucepan of boiling water and cook for 5–7 minutes, or according to packet instructions.

5 Meanwhile, heat the olive oil in a large frying pan over high heat and gently fry the scallops for 2–3 minutes until lightly browned and only just cooked. Remove from the heat, pour on the dressing, and toss well.

6 Drain the pasta and serve on individual plates topped with the dressed scallops.

NUTRIENTS PER SERVING: kilojoules 2917, protein 39 g, carbohydrate 77 g (sugar 9 g), fat 25 g (saturated fat 4 g), good source of vitamin E, and iodine and iron.

SCALLOPS WITH THAI FLAVOURINGS

The fragrant flavours of Thailand – lemon grass and kaffir lime leaves – are combined with the tropical taste of coconut milk to give stir-fried fresh scallops an intriguing flavour.

TIME: 20 MINUTES SERVES: 4

½ cup chicken stock
2 shallots
1 stalk lemon grass
3 fresh or dried kaffir lime leaves
350 g fresh scallops
185 g snow peas
2 tablespoons peanut oil
2 teaspoons Thai green curry paste
150 ml coconut milk
A few sprigs of coriander

1 Heat the stock in a small saucepan over moderate heat.
2 Meanwhile, peel the shallots and chop finely. Remove and discard the outer section of the lemon grass, then chop the stalk finely. Chop or crumble the kaffir lime leaves.

3 Rinse the scallops and pat dry, leaving any corals intact. Top and tail the snow peas and cut in half crossways.
4 Heat the oil in a large, heavy-based frying pan until it shows a faint haze. Add the shallots, lemon grass, kaffir lime leaves, scallops and snow peas and stir-fry for 3 minutes.
5 Stir the curry paste into the stock, then add to the frying pan along with the coconut milk. Bring to the boil, reduce the heat and simmer for 3 minutes. In the meantime, finely chop the coriander leaves for the garnish.
6 Transfer the cooked scallops to a serving dish and sprinkle the coriander on top.

SERVING SUGGESTION
For a Thai feast, match this dish with Thai Salad with Coconut Dressing (page 88), Thai Beef Salad (page 86) and rice.

NUTRIENTS PER SERVING: *kilojoules 862, carbohydrate 7 g (sugar 4 g), protein 23 g, fat 10 g (saturated fat 1 g), good source of vitamins B group, C and E.*

COOK'S SUGGESTION

Kaffir lime is a Southeast Asian citrus fruit whose leaves and rind both have a strong, flowery, lime-and-lemon scent. You will find fresh and/or dried leaves in larger supermarkets or Asian grocery shops.

SEARED TUNA WITH CAPSICUM SAUCE

A richly flavoured, peppery-hot purée of char-grilled capsicums, chilli, onion and garlic makes the perfect partner for a meaty fish steak that is cooked quickly over high heat.

TIME: 20 MINUTES SERVES: 4

4 tuna, or swordfish, steaks, about 185 g each

For the sauce:

2 medium red capsicums
1 medium onion
2 cloves garlic
1 small red chilli
1 large slice wholemeal bread
1 lime
3 teaspoons tomato paste
3 tablespoons olive oil
Salt and black pepper

1 Preheat the griller to high. To make the sauce, seed and halve the capsicums lengthways. Halve the onion across. Put both under the griller, skin sides up, with the unpeeled cloves of garlic. Grill for 10 minutes or until the skins are slightly charred.

2 While the vegetables are grilling, seed and chop the chilli. Dice the bread. Grate the rind of the lime and squeeze the juice.

3 When the grilled capsicums, onion and garlic are cool enough to handle, peel them and put the flesh into a food processor with the chilli, bread, tomato paste and 2 tablespoons olive oil. Add half the lime rind and juice, reserving the rest. Process the mixture to a purée, then season to taste with salt and black pepper. Transfer the sauce to a serving bowl and put aside.

4 Brush a ridged griller plate or a large, heavy-based frying pan with the remaining oil and place over very high heat. Lightly season the fish steaks and fry for 4–6 minutes, until golden brown on the outside and cooked through, turning once.

5 Sprinkle the steaks with the remaining lime rind and juice and serve with the capsicum sauce, either spooned round the fish or offered separately in a bowl.

SERVING SUGGESTION

The cool flavours of Spinach and Baby Corn Salad (page 105) would complement the hot sauce.

VARIATION

The sauce is best served slightly warm, but it can be made in advance and served cold.

NUTRIENTS PER SERVING: kilojoules 1712, protein 44 g, carbohydrate 14 g (sugar 7 g), fat 20 g (saturated fat 4 g), good source of vitamins A, B group, C and E, and selenium.

COOK'S SUGGESTION

This dish is suitable for barbecuing. Start by grilling the capsicums, onion and garlic then finish off the sauce while the tuna is cooking on the barbecue.

BLACKENED WHITE FISH

Thick fillets of fish are given a crunchy polenta crust, seasoned with a fiery mixture of spices and herbs, before being seared over a fierce heat in the Cajun style and served with lemon.

TIME: 20 MINUTES SERVES: 4

1 teaspoon black peppercorns
1 teaspoon each fennel seeds, dried oregano and thyme
½–1 teaspoon cayenne pepper
Salt
3 cloves garlic
2 tablespoons polenta
4 firm white fish fillets, about 185 g–250 g each
2 tablespoons peanut oil
To garnish: 1 lemon

1 Crush the peppercorns and put into a large bowl. Add the dried herbs, cayenne pepper and some salt. Peel the garlic and crush it into the bowl, then add the polenta and stir thoroughly.

2 Skin the fish fillets if necessary (see page 11), add to the herb and spice mixture and press it on firmly to coat well.

3 Heat the peanut oil in a large, heavy-based frying pan until it begins to smoke. Add the fish and fry for 1½ minutes on each side, or until the fillets are lightly browned and cooked through.

4 Meanwhile, cut the lemon into wedges. Drain the cooked fish on paper towels, then transfer the fillets to a warmed serving dish and garnish with the lemon wedges.

SERVING SUGGESTION

Serve this spicy fish with steamed new potatoes and a green salad or, to continue the Louisiana theme, the Cajun Potato Salad (page 104).

NUTRIENTS PER SERVING, USING BREAM: kilojoules 1080, protein 34 g, carbohydrate 9 g (sugar 0.1 g), fat 10 g (saturated fat 2 g), good source of vitamin E.

COOK'S SUGGESTION

Any round white fish fillets are suitable for this dish. Fish cutlets can be used too, but you will have to allow them a little longer to cook – they will need about 6–8 minutes. Flatfish, such as sole and flounder, are too thin and too delicate to be cooked this way.

TWO HOT FISH DISHES: *(top)* SEARED TUNA WITH CAPSICUM SAUCE; *(bottom)* BLACKENED WHITE FISH.

SEARED SQUID WITH BUTTER AND MINT

Fresh squid, quickly fried, is juicy and tender. Tossed with shredded lettuce that is bathed in a buttery onion and lime sauce, it makes a perfect light lunch or an elegant first course.

TIME: 30 MINUTES SERVES: 4

500 g prepared squid (the pouch without head and tentacles)
3 Little Gem lettuces
2 shallots
2 limes
6 sprigs mint
4 tablespoons butter
2 cloves garlic
2 tablespoons cooking oil
Salt and black pepper
To serve: French or Italian bread

1 Halve the prepared squid lengthways. If the flat triangles are more than 10 cm long, cut in half again. Score the inner surfaces in a diamond pattern with a sharp knife, then put aside.

2 Trim the lettuces, discarding the outer leaves, then slice across into fine strips and put into a large serving bowl.

3 Peel and chop the shallots. Grate the rind of one lime and squeeze out the juice. Slice the other lime and put aside. Finely chop the mint leaves and put aside.

4 Warm the butter in a saucepan. Peel the garlic and crush it into the pan. Add the shallots and cook very gently for about 1 minute. Stir in the lime rind and juice and pour the mixture over the strips of lettuce.

5 Heat the oil in a large frying pan until very hot and fry the squid in batches, for 2–3 minutes each batch, until the pieces have become opaque and tightened into curls.

6 Transfer the squid to the serving bowl with all the juices and residue from the pan. Season to taste with salt and pepper and toss gently into the lettuce.

7 To serve, scatter the finely chopped mint over the salad and garnish each plate with the reserved slices of lime.

SERVING SUGGESTION

The squid can be served with warm bread rolls and paired with the sunny Mediterranean flavour of Greek Salad (page 87).

NUTRIENTS PER SERVING: kilojoules 2326, protein 28 g, carbohydrate 47 g (sugar 3 g), fat 28 g (saturated fat 13 g), good source of vitamins A, B group, E and folate, and selenium.

PRAWNS MASALA

This simple Indian-inspired dish of sweet-tasting prawns has a spicy flavour, balancing the coolness of coconut cream with the heat of cumin, coriander, turmeric and aromatic ginger.

TIME: 20 MINUTES SERVES: 4

1 medium onion
2 cloves garlic
5-cm piece fresh root ginger
2 tablespoons vegetable oil
2 teaspoons ground coriander
2 teaspoons ground cumin
1 teaspoon ground turmeric
400 g peeled green prawns
200 ml coconut cream
Salt and black pepper
A small bunch of coriander

1 Peel and chop the onion. Peel and finely chop the ginger.

2 Heat the oil in a heavy frying pan, add the onion and garlic and fry for a few minutes until softened. Then add the ginger and the ground coriander, cumin and turmeric and cook for another 1–2 minutes until the spices have released their fragrance.

3 Add the prawns and the coconut cream to the frying pan, taste and season with salt and black pepper. Then bring the mixture to the boil, reduce the heat, and simmer for 2–3 minutes. Meanwhile, put aside a few sprigs of coriander to use as a garnish and chop the rest.

4 Pour the prawn mixture into a serving dish. Just before serving, scatter the chopped coriander over the top and garnish with the sprigs.

SERVING SUGGESTION

This light dish could be served with steamed long-grain rice or some naan bread. Or you could add Potato and Green Bean Curry (page 259) and Dhal (page 258) to make a more substantial meal.

VARIATION

The prawns could be replaced by chunks of firm white fish.

NUTRIENTS PER SERVING: kilojoules 1510, protein 26 g, carbohydrate 7 g (sugar 5 g), fat 26 g (saturated fat 16 g), good source of vitamins B group and E, and selenium and zinc.

MEATS

Please the family or delight guests with nourishing, richly flavoured main-course dishes that range from classic steaks to spiced lamb kebabs and gingered pork.

BEEF STROGANOFF

Pickled cocktail gherkins and hot green peppercorns offset the richness of sour cream and mushrooms in this stroganoff, and bring a new dimension to a traditional favourite.

TIME: 30 MINUTES SERVES: 4

2 tablespoons olive oil
1 large red onion
250 g small mushrooms
600 g beef fillet
2 teaspoons green peppercorns in brine
Salt
2 tablespoons Dijon mustard
300 ml sour cream
100 g drained cornichons (pickled cocktail gherkins)
A small bunch of chives

1 Heat 2 teaspoons oil in a large frying pan. Halve, peel and thinly slice the onion, then fry over moderate heat for 2–3 minutes, until slightly softened.

2 Meanwhile, clean and halve the mushrooms. Add to the pan, increase the heat and cook, stirring, for about 5 minutes, until the mushrooms have softened and most of the liquid has evaporated.

3 While the mushrooms are cooking, slice the beef fillet very thinly, then cut across the grain into thin strips (piling several slices on top of one another will speed up this process).

4 When the mushrooms are cooked, tip them with the onion into a large bowl and put aside.

5 Add half the remaining oil to the pan and increase the heat to high. Add half the beef and stir-fry for 2–3 minutes, or until very lightly browned, then remove. Heat the remaining oil and cook the rest of the beef the same way.

6 Return the onion, mushrooms and the first batch of beef with any juices to the frying pan. Crush the green peppercorns, add to the pan with salt to taste, and heat through for 1–2 minutes.

7 Blend the mustard and sour cream together and stir into the beef along with the cornichons. Heat through gently without boiling. Snip the chives over the top and serve immediately.

SERVING SUGGESTION
Serve with rice, mashed potatoes or noodles, which can be steamed or boiled while the beef is cooking, and a green side salad.

VARIATION
The stroganoff can also be made with pork fillet, lean lamb fillet, or skinless chicken breasts. You can use any type of mushroom and, if you prefer, the cornichons can be coarsely chopped.

NUTRIENTS PER SERVING: kilojoules 2356, protein 35g, carbohydrate 14g (sugar 11g), fat 41g (saturated fat 16g), good source of vitamins A, B group, E and folate, and iron, selenium and zinc.

SPICED STEAK WITH SPEEDY RATATOUILLE

*Zucchini, eggplant and tomato, gently flavoured with wine and herbs, produce a melting ratatouille
that perfectly complements tender steak rubbed with a mixture of hot spices.*

TIME: 30 MINUTES   SERVES: 4

3 tablespoons olive oil
2–3 shallots
2 cloves garlic
500 g zucchini
300 g baby eggplants
½ teaspoon dried thyme
½ teaspoon dried oregano
3 tablespoons red wine
425 g canned tomato pieces
2 tablespoons tomato paste
Salt
1 teaspoon ground coriander
1 teaspoon ground cumin
1 teaspoon ground paprika
½ teaspoon cayenne pepper
4 sirloin or rump steaks, about 175 g–200 g each

1 Heat 2 tablespoons oil in a
large saucepan. Peel and chop the
shallots and garlic, add to the pan
and cook over moderate heat for
3–4 minutes.

2 Meanwhile, trim the zucchini
and eggplants and cut into 1-cm
chunks. Stir into the shallots along
with the thyme and oregano, and
cook gently for 5 minutes.

3 Add the wine, the tomatoes and
their juice, tomato paste and a little
salt, then cover and simmer gently
for about 15 minutes, stirring
occasionally, until the vegetables
have softened.

4 While the ratatouille is cooking,
put the coriander, cumin, paprika
and cayenne pepper into a small
bowl, add a pinch of salt and mix
well. Season each steak on both
sides with the spice mixture.

5 Heat the remaining olive oil in
a heavy-based frying pan until a
faint haze rises, then cook the
steaks for 4–4½ minutes each side
for rare, 5½–6 minutes for
medium, or 6–8½ minutes for well
done, depending on the thickness of
the meat.

6 Serve on individual plates,
accompanied by the ratatouille.

SERVING SUGGESTION
For a hearty meal, add Polenta with
Provolone (page 220).

*NUTRIENTS PER SERVING: kilojoules 1703,
protein 46 g, carbohydrate 9 g (sugar 8 g),
fat 20 g (saturated fat 5 g), good source of
vitamins A, B group, C, E and folate, and iron
and zinc.*

COOK'S SUGGESTION

*Baby eggplants have tender skins
that do not need peeling but, if you can
get only larger ones, you will have to peel
them first. You will also have to salt the
flesh of the larger ones before cooking,
so more time will be needed.*

STYLISH SAUCES FROM THE FRYING PAN

When you pan-fry meat, whether it is steak, chicken breasts, lamb or pork chops, there is a great bonus. After you remove the meat, it leaves behind in the pan the delicious juices exuded during cooking, just waiting to be made into a quick sauce.

Each of the following sauces uses the technique known as deglazing, and will make enough to serve four people. For each recipe, first remove the cooked meat from the frying pan and put in a low oven to keep warm. Then pour off all but 1 tablespoon fat or oil from the pan, being careful to leave all the sticky residue behind. Finally, make the sauce.

SPICED RED WINE AND RED CURRANT SAUCE

This is an excellent dressing for lamb chops or venison steaks.

Stir 2 teaspoons cumin seeds and ½ teaspoon each paprika, ground cinnamon and ground coriander into the pan juices with 300 ml red wine. Swirl and stir, scraping up the sediment, until the wine comes to the boil then add 2 – 3 teaspoons red currant jelly, mashing it to help it melt. Cook, stirring frequently, for 5 minutes, until the liquid is reduced by almost half. Season with salt and pepper and pour over the meat.

MUSTARD AND CREAM SAUCE

A sophisticated finish for butter-fried chicken or veal.

Stir 300 ml thick cream into the pan, then mix in 2 tablespoons Dijon or tarragon mustard (tarragon is particularly good with chicken). As soon as the sauce begins to bubble, season with salt and black pepper to taste and pour over the meat.

To make an even faster sauce, mix the mustard, salt and pepper with the cream while the meat is cooking, then stir the mixture into the pan juices to deglaze.

PAN-FRIED STEAK

One of the most delicious meat dishes of all is a tender pan-fried steak with a dark and crusty exterior surrounding juicy meat.

1 Brush a large, heavy-based pan with oil and heat until very hot.
2 Sprinkle the meat with pepper and fry for 1 minute each side.
3 Turning the meat half-way through, cook for a further 3 minutes for rare steak, for 4½ minutes for medium and for 5–7 minutes for well done. For rare, keep the heat very high all the time. For medium and well done, lower the heat to moderate after the initial browning.

CHUNKY TOMATO SAUCE

A favourite sauce for sausages, this goes well with lamb or pork chops.

Finely chop 1 clove garlic, fry in the pan until soft, then add 215 g canned tomato pieces and their juice. Boil rapidly for a couple of minutes to thicken, scraping up the sediment from the bottom of the pan. Season to taste with salt and pepper, add 1 teaspoon Worcestershire sauce and, if you like, a dash of Tabasco sauce, and serve.

BRANDY CREAM SAUCE

A smooth sauce for any lean red meat, but particularly beef or venison steaks.

Stir 4 tablespoons brandy into the pan and allow to bubble gently for 1–2 minutes, stirring and scraping up the residue. Add 1 tablespoon chopped fresh thyme (or 1 teaspoon dried thyme), 1 tablespoon tomato paste and 1 tablespoon balsamic vinegar, and simmer for 1 minute, stirring until smooth. Finally stir in 100 ml thick cream and bring to the boil. Add salt and black pepper to taste and spoon over the meat.

SAGE AND APPLE SAUCE

This traditional sauce is particularly good with pork chops or ham steaks.

Grate in 1 large, unpeeled cooking apple, discarding the core. Shred 8 fresh sage leaves and add half, along with 1 tablespoon cider vinegar and 2 –3 tablespoons water. Stir over the heat until the apple is soft. Add more water if necessary, but keep the sauce chunky. Finely chop half a small red onion and add to the pan with the remaining sage. Heat through, season with salt and black pepper, and serve.

SHALLOTS IN RED WINE

The classic sauce for sirloin or New York cut steaks.

Peel and slice 4 shallots, then peel and crush 1 clove garlic. Sizzle both in the pan juices for 1–2 minutes, then stir in 1 cup red wine and 1 tablespoon chopped parsley. Bring to the boil over medium heat, stirring and scraping the deposits from the bottom of the pan, until the liquid is reduced to about one third. Season to taste with salt and black pepper, then spoon the sauce over the steaks and sprinkle with more chopped parsley.

FLASH IN THE PAN SAUCE: SHALLOTS IN RED WINE.

BEEF AND BEAN CHILLI

*Nothing is quite as hearty as a bowl of tingling-hot chilli con carne made with prime minced beef,
cooked with kidney beans and served with tortillas in the easy Mexican style.*

TIME: 30 MINUTES SERVES: 4

1 medium onion
1 small red capsicum
1 small red chilli
2 tablespoons sunflower oil
500 g lean minced beef
1 tablespoon paprika
1 tablespoon ground cumin
3 cloves garlic
425 g canned tomato pieces, with their juice
2 teaspoons tomato paste
1 teaspoon dried oregano
½ cup red wine or beef stock
½ teaspoon sugar
Salt
2 spring onions
425 g canned kidney beans
8 soft flour tortillas
4 tablespoons sour cream, or to taste

1 Peel and chop the onion. Seed and chop the capsicum and the chilli; put the chilli aside.

2 Heat the oil in a large flameproof casserole and fry the onion, capsicum, beef, paprika and cumin over moderate heat. Stir constantly until the meat browns.

3 Peel and crush the garlic. Add to the casserole along with the chilli, the tomatoes and their juice, tomato paste, oregano, wine or stock, sugar and salt to taste. Bring to the boil, reduce the heat, cover and simmer for 15 minutes.

4 Chop the spring onions; put aside. Preheat the griller to high.

5 When the beef has been cooking for 15 minutes, drain and rinse the kidney beans, stir into the casserole and cook for a further 5 minutes. Meanwhile, place the tortillas under the griller.

6 Transfer the chilli to four serving dishes, then add 1 tablespoon sour cream to each, sprinkle the spring onions over the top, and serve with the heated tortillas.

SERVING SUGGESTION
A simple green salad, perhaps with some hard cheese, adds a cool contrast to this rugged chilli.

NUTRIENTS PER SERVING: kilojoules 2489, protein 39 g, carbohydrate 53 g (sugar 12 g), fat 24 g (saturated fat 8 g), good source of vitamins A, B group, C and E, and iron and zinc.

COOK'S SUGGESTION

*Tortillas are thin pancakes
made from corn or wheat flour, which
you can roll and stuff with a spicy meat
or bean sauce. Corn tortillas can also be
cut into small triangles which are then
deep-fried and sprinkled with
salt to make corn chips.*

144

MEATBALLS WITH CREOLE SAUCE

Tender meatballs are easy to prepare for a filling family meal and come with a tasty sauce of crunchy fresh vegetables spiced with cayenne pepper and hot paprika.

TIME: 30 MINUTES SERVES: 4

1 large onion
600 g minced beef
1 large egg
2 tablespoons plain flour
¼ teaspoon cayenne pepper
¼ teaspoon hot paprika
Salt and black pepper
2 tablespoons olive oil

For the sauce:

1 tablespoon olive oil
1 medium green capsicum
1 medium red capsicum
2 cloves garlic
2 stalks celery
425 g canned tomato pieces, with their juice
1 bay leaf
1 teaspoon cayenne pepper
1 teaspoon hot paprika
1 teaspoon molasses or treacle

1 To make the meatballs, peel and chop the onion. Put half into a large bowl with the beef, egg, flour, cayenne, paprika, salt and pepper. Combine well, then put aside.

2 To make the sauce, heat the oil in a large saucepan over moderate heat and fry the remaining onion until softened. Seed and chop the capsicums and stir into the onion.

3 Peel the garlic and crush it into the pan. Chop the celery and stir into the pan. Cook the mixture for another 2 minutes.

4 Add the tomatoes and their juice, the bay leaf, cayenne, paprika, molasses or treacle. Measure out 100 ml water, add to the pan and bring to the boil. Reduce the heat and simmer, uncovered, for about 15 minutes, or until the sauce is thick but the vegetables still retain a little crunch.

5 While the sauce is simmering, cook the meatballs. Heat the 2 tablespoons oil slowly in a very large frying pan. With wet hands, shape the meat mixture into 16 balls, each about the size of a golf ball, and put into the hot oil. Fry over high heat for 10 minutes, until browned all over and just cooked on the inside.

6 Season the sauce to taste with salt and black pepper and pour over the meatballs. Serve immediately.

SERVING SUGGESTION
A steaming mound of mixed white and wild rices, or some Cajun Potato Salad (page 104), would be a good accompaniment.

NUTRIENTS PER SERVING: kilojoules 2326, protein 35 g, carbohydrate 19 g (sugar 10 g), fat 38 g (saturated fat 13 g), good source of vitamins A, B group, C, E and folate, and zinc.

145

BEEF BALTI

Balti dishes are stir-fried curries that originated in Kashmir and are traditionally served with a bread accompaniment.

TIME: 25 MINUTES   SERVES: 4

2 tablespoons sunflower oil	1 red capsicum
1 medium onion	3 medium tomatoes
500 g rump or fillet steak	½ lemon
1 clove garlic	3 teaspoons garam masala
4-cm piece fresh root ginger	1 teaspoon ground cumin
1 small red chilli	Salt
1 green capsicum	2 tablespoons desiccated shredded coconut
	To serve: 4 naan breads

1 Preheat the oven to low to keep the beef warm later. Heat 1 tablespoon oil in a large balti pan, wok or frying pan. Peel and thinly slice the onion and fry over fairly high heat for 3–4 minutes, stirring occasionally, until softened and lightly browned.

2 Meanwhile, trim any excess fat from the steak, then slice into very thin strips. Peel and crush the garlic, then peel and grate the ginger and seed and chop the chilli. Add them all to the onion and cook over fairly high heat for 5 minutes, stirring occasionally, until the meat is lightly coloured. Remove from the pan and keep warm in the oven.

3 Seed and thinly slice the capsicums. Add to the same pan, with the remaining oil, if necessary, and continue frying for 3 minutes, stirring occasionally, until softened and lightly browned.

4 Meanwhile, roughly chop the tomatoes, then squeeze the juice from the half lemon and preheat the griller to high.

5 Stir the garam masala and the cumin into the frying pan and cook, stirring continuously, for 1 minute. Add the tomatoes, lemon juice and some salt and simmer, stirring, for about 3–4 minutes. If the mixture becomes dry, add a little water.

6 Sprinkle the naan with water and grill for about 1 minute each side. Return the beef to the pan and heat through.

7 Sprinkle with the shredded coconut and serve with the naan.

NUTRIENTS PER SERVING: kilojoules 3946, protein 43 g, carbohydrate 90 g (sugar 16 g), fat 48 g (saturated fat 12 g), good source of vitamins A, B group, C, E and folate, and calcium, iron, selenium and zinc.

COOK'S SUGGESTION

Naan is a flat, tear-shaped bread from India that is authentically baked on the walls of a tandoor oven. To approximate this at home, sprinkle each naan with water before grilling to help them puff up and become deliciously soft and light.

STEAK AND ONION KEBABS

A powerfully aromatic basting sauce made by combining Dijon mustard, Worcestershire sauce and red wine vinegar tenderises cubes of steak grilled on skewers with crunchy onions.

TIME: 25 MINUTES SERVES: 4

750 g sirloin or rump steak, trimmed of all fat
2 medium red onions
4 fat spring onions
3 teaspoons Dijon mustard
1 teaspoon Worcestershire sauce
½ teaspoon red wine vinegar
Salt and black pepper
3 tablespoons light olive oil

For the sauce, optional:
½ cup red wine

1 Preheat the griller to high. Cut the meat into 20 equal cubes. Peel, top and tail the red onions, cut in half widthways and cut each half into four wedges. Trim the spring onions to 4-cm lengths and cut in half lengthways.

2 Thread five pieces of meat onto each of four metal skewers, about 38 cm long, alternating the meat with a combination of red and spring onions.

3 Place the skewers across the griller tray or a small baking dish, balancing their ends on the rim.

4 Mix the mustard, Worcestershire sauce, vinegar, salt and pepper in a small bowl, then whisk in the oil.

5 Brush half the mixture over the top of the kebabs, then grill, close to the heat source, for 3–5 minutes. Turn the skewers, brush with the remaining mixture and grill for a further 3–5 minutes. If the kebabs start to burn, lower the griller tray a little.

6 The kebabs can be served on their own, but taste even better with a sauce made from the pan juices.

Put the kebabs in the oven to keep warm. Pour the wine into the griller tray and stir over moderate heat, scraping up any sediment. Cook until the sauce is reduced by half, then season to taste and pour over the kebabs.

SERVING SUGGESTION
Serve with mashed potatoes and a green vegetable or Orange and Sesame Carrots (page 262).

VARIATION
These kebabs are ideal for a quick and easy barbecue. The skewers can be cooked over the griller rack then put to one side to keep warm while you make the sauce.

NUTRIENTS PER SERVING: kilojoules 1570, protein 43 g, carbohydrate 8 g (sugar 6 g), fat 20 g (saturated fat 5 g), good source of vitamins B group and E, and zinc.

BEEF FAJITAS WITH FLAT BREAD

Minced meat with pine nuts, flavoured with cumin and allspice, is served with salad in this easy Middle Eastern-style dish.

TIME: 30 MINUTES SERVES: 4

⅔ cup pine nuts
1 tablespoon olive oil
1 large onion
500 g lean minced beef or lamb
3 teaspoons ground cumin
1 teaspoon ground allspice
215 g canned tomato pieces, with their juice
A bunch of coriander
1 cucumber
½ crisp lettuce

To serve: **200 ml sour cream, 8 soft flour tortillas or small pita breads**

EASY DOES IT!

If you use pita bread instead of tortillas, make a pocket for the filling by cutting a slit in the side of the warm bread. Place a spoonful of the meat mixture inside, then stuff with shredded lettuce and chopped cucumber. Top the salad with a spoonful of sour cream.

---

1 Preheat the oven to warm the bread. Meanwhile, dry-fry the pine nuts in a large pan, shaking the pan and stirring the nuts frequently until just lightly browned. Transfer to a small bowl and put aside.

2 Add the olive oil to the pan and heat slowly. Halve, peel and chop the onion, then fry over moderate heat for 3 minutes, or until softened. Add the meat and fry until brown, stirring to break up any lumps. Then stir in the cumin, allspice and tomatoes with their juice; simmer for 10–15 minutes, stirring occasionally.

3 Chop enough coriander to give 4 tablespoons and put aside. Chop the cucumber and rinse and finely shred the lettuce; place in separate serving bowls. Put the bread into the oven to warm.

4 When the meat is cooked, stir in the coriander and pine nuts, heat through for 1–2 minutes, then transfer to a serving dish. Spoon the sour cream into a serving bowl. Put the bread into a napkin-lined serving basket to keep hot.

5 At the table, each diner takes a tortilla, places a spoonful of meat in the centre, tops it with lettuce, cucumber and some sour cream, then rolls it up, holds it in the fingers and eats it. If using pita bread, make a slit in one side of each and spoon the meat and salad into the pocket (see box, above).

NUTRIENTS PER SERVING: kilojoules 2925, protein 38 g, carbohydrate 41 g (sugar 10 g), fat 44 g (saturated fat 13 g), good source of vitamins A, B group, C, E and folate, and iron and zinc.

RACK OF VEAL ROASTED WITH GARLIC

Coated with a succulent mixture of sage, orange marmalade, black pepper and oil, tender veal chops are cooked in one piece with whole garlic cloves for added flavour.

TIME: 30 MINUTES SERVES: 2

1 orange
6 sage leaves
2 teaspoons bitter orange marmalade
1 tablespoon olive oil
Black pepper
1 veal rack with 2 thick chops, about 350 g in total
8 cloves garlic
½ cup medium dry sherry
½ cup chicken stock

1 Preheat the oven to 220°C. Use a zester to remove the rind from the orange, or grate finely. Squeeze the juice into the same bowl.
2 Chop the sage leaves and combine with the orange juice and zest, marmalade, oil and pepper.

3 Place the veal and the garlic, whole and unpeeled, in a lightly oiled baking dish. Baste the veal with the orange mixture, being sure to coat the rack thoroughly, then cook in the oven for 20 minutes.
4 Move the baking dish from the oven to the stove top and transfer the veal to a serving platter; allow to rest in a warm place. Meanwhile, add the sherry and stock to the garlic in the baking dish and cook, stirring, over moderately high heat for 2–3 minutes, until the sauce has reduced and thickened slightly.
5 To serve, carve the veal into individual chops and spoon over the garlic and pan juices.

SERVING SUGGESTION
A simple accompaniment of steamed new potatoes and wilted English spinach complements the flavoursome sauce in this dish.

VARIATION
A rack of tender young lamb cutlets can be substituted for the veal; if you use lamb, add rosemary leaves to the coating mixture.

NUTRIENTS PER SERVING: kilojoules 1555, protein 35 g, carbohydrate 9 g (sugar 8 g), fat 15 g (saturated fat 2 g), good source of vitamins B group and C, and iron and zinc.

COOK'S SUGGESTION

To save preparation time, ask your butcher to trim the veal of any fat and membrane and to scrape the bones. As the cooking time is so short, there is no need to cover the bone ends with foil.

VEAL BUTT FILLET WITH ROSEMARY AND RED CURRANT

The pungency of fresh rosemary and the sweetness of the red currant jelly combine to turn quickly cooked fillets of veal into sumptuous dinner party fare.

TIME: 25 MINUTES SERVES: 4

1 tablespoon butter
2 tablespoons olive oil
1 veal butt fillet, about 800 g in total, cut into 4 pieces
2 sprigs rosemary
Black pepper
1 cup medium dry sherry
1½ tablespoons red currant jelly
1 tablespoon unsalted butter

1 Preheat the oven to 220°C. Heat the butter and olive oil, over moderate heat, in a baking dish on top of the stove.

2 Add the veal and rosemary to the baking dish, season generously with pepper, and cook for about 5 minutes, until the meat is golden and sealed on all sides.
3 Transfer the baking dish to the oven and cook the veal for a further 10 minutes. Remove the dish from oven and keep the veal in a warm place while you make the sauce.
4 Place the baking dish back on the stove top and add the sherry, red currant jelly and butter. Cook, stirring, over moderate heat for about 5 minutes, until the sauce has reduced and thickened slightly.

5 Cut the veal fillets in half, arrange on individual plates and pour over the sauce.
SERVING SUGGESTION
A purée of parsnips and some steamed baby beans will accompany this dish perfectly.
VARIATION
You can use eye fillet of beef instead of the veal. To serve rare, it will take the same cooking time.

NUTRIENTS PER SERVING: kilojoules 2166, protein 59 g, carbohydrate 7 g (sugar 7 g), fat 21 g (saturated fat 8 g), good source of vitamins A, B group and E, and iron and zinc.

CHEESY VEAL SCHNITZEL

Simple schnitzels take on an extra dimension when Parmesan and sage leaves are added to the breadcrumb coating.

TIME: 25 MINUTES   SERVES: 4

2 eggs
100 g Parmesan cheese
8–10 sage leaves
1 cup soft breadcrumbs, made from day-old Italian-style bread
8 small veal escalopes, about 600 g in total, and flattened to a thickness of approximately 3 mm
½ cup plain flour
4 tablespoons olive oil
2 tablespoons butter
To serve: lemon slices

1   Lightly beat the eggs; put aside.
2   Grate enough Parmesan to give ½ cup and finely chop the sage to give 1 tablespoon. Combine the cheese and sage in a bowl with the breadcrumbs and put aside.
3   Coat the veal with flour, then dip in egg and then breadcrumbs.
4   Heat half the oil and butter over moderate heat in a large frying pan. Add four escalopes and cook for 1–2 minutes, until golden on each side. Remove and keep warm while you cook the other escalopes in the remaining oil and butter.

SERVING SUGGESTION
Serve with sliced tomatoes and basil and a crisp green salad on the side.

NUTRIENTS PER SERVING: kilojoules 2707, protein 47g, carbohydrate 21 g (sugar 1 g), fat 39 g (saturated fat 12 g), good source of vitamins A, B group and E, and calcium.

CHAR-GRILLED VEAL CUTLETS

Prime young veal cutlets assume a starring role when served grilled or barbecued and topped with herbed butter.

TIME: 25 MINUTES   SERVES: 4

A small bunch of tarragon
1 lemon
125 g unsalted butter, softened
Sea salt and black pepper
4 well-trimmed veal cutlets, about 600 g in total
2 tablespoons olive oil

1   Preheat the char-grill or griller.
2   Chop enough tarragon to give 2 tablespoons; put some sprigs aside for a garnish. Squeeze the lemon to give 2 tablespoons juice.
3   Beat the butter and chopped tarragon together, then beat in the lemon juice and season well with sea salt and black pepper. Form into a cylinder, wrap in plastic wrap and place in the freezer.
4   Brush the veal cutlets with oil and a good grinding of pepper on both sides. Place on the char-grill or under the griller and cook for 5–7 minutes each side, until golden brown outside and pink inside.
5   Serve the cutlets with a slice of tarragon butter on each. Garnish with the reserved tarragon sprigs.

SERVING SUGGESTION
A good accompaniment is sliced capsicum and whole salad onions char-grilled at the same time.

VARIATION
If you prefer, the veal cutlets can be cooked on a hot barbecue.

NUTRIENTS PER SERVING: kilojoules 2112, protein 34g, carbohydrate 3 g (sugar 3 g), fat 40 g (saturated fat 19 g), good source of vitamins A, B group and E, and iron and zinc.

SIMPLE YET SPECIAL:
(top) CHEESY VEAL SCHNITZEL;
(bottom) CHAR-GRILLED VEAL CUTLETS.

VEAL PICCATA WITH SAGE AND LEMON

A single fresh sage leaf pressed onto each tender slice of veal before cooking adds extra flavour and a delicate fragrance to these escalopes, which are served in a refreshing lemon and butter sauce.

TIME: 15 MINUTES SERVES: 2

1 tablespoon plain flour
Salt and black pepper
2 veal escalopes, about 125 g each
6 sage leaves
1 tablespoon oil
2 tablespoons butter
½ lemon
4 tablespoons chicken stock or water

1 Preheat the oven to low to keep the veal warm later. Sprinkle the flour onto a board or large plate and season well with salt and pepper. Cut each veal escalope into three equal pieces, press a sage leaf firmly onto each, then turn in the flour until well coated.

2 Heat the oil and half the butter in a large, heavy-based frying pan until the butter has melted. Add the veal to the pan and cook for 2 minutes on each side, then remove and keep warm.

3 Squeeze the juice from the half lemon into the pan, then add the stock or water and swirl over medium heat until the liquid has reduced by half. Add the remaining butter and continue to swirl the mixture until all the butter has been absorbed into the sauce.

4 Return the veal escalopes to the pan and cook for a few seconds on each side to heat through. Transfer to individual plates.

SERVING SUGGESTION

Serve the veal with boiled new potatoes and a simply prepared green vegetable, such as frozen beans or peas, or fresh broccoli, or a side dish of Italian Baked Chicory (page 264) or Zucchini, Apples and Persillade (page 266).

NUTRIENTS PER SERVING: kilojoules 1398, protein 24 g, carbohydrate 4 g (sugar 0.2 g), fat 25 g (saturated fat 12 g), good source of vitamins A, B group and E, and zinc.

CALF'S LIVER WITH BALSAMIC VINEGAR

Simple liver and onions is transformed into a memorable meal by a richly flavoured sauce made with Italian balsamic vinegar, French mustard and a dash of cream, plus a sprinkling of fresh sage.

TIME: 25 MINUTES SERVES: 4

1 large Spanish onion
2 tablespoons olive oil
A small bunch of sage
4 slices calf's liver, about 125 g each
Black pepper

For the sauce:

2 tablespoons balsamic vinegar
1 tablespoon Dijon mustard
100 ml cream

1 Preheat the oven to low. Halve, peel and thinly slice the onion.
2 Heat half the olive oil in a large frying pan over high heat and fry the onion, stirring, for 1 minute. Lower the heat, cover and cook for 6 minutes, or until the onion is just tender and is beginning to brown, then transfer to a plate and keep warm.
3 Meanwhile, strip off the sage leaves and chop enough to give 1 tablespoon, then put aside.
4 Season the liver on both sides with black pepper. Add the remaining oil to the frying pan and, when very hot, fry the liver for 1–2 minutes on each side, until it changes colour. Transfer to a serving dish to keep warm.
5 To make the sauce, bring the vinegar and 2 tablespoons water to the boil in the pan, stirring and scraping up the browned residue. Reduce the heat and stir in the mustard and cream.
6 Return the liver and onions to the pan, reheat very gently in the sauce for 1–2 minutes, sprinkle with chopped sage and serve.

SERVING SUGGESTION
Serve with creamed potatoes. Put them on to cook before preparing the onion, and mash them while the liver is reheating.
VARIATION
The sauce can also be served with lamb's fry, or fried chicken or pork.

NUTRIENTS PER SERVING: kilojoules 1218, protein 25 g, carbohydrate 8 g (sugar 6 g), fat 17 g (saturated fat 5 g), good source of vitamins A, B group, C, E and folate, and iron, selenium and zinc.

COOK'S SUGGESTION

Balsamic vinegar is carefully aged in fragrant wooden barrels – a process which slowly develops a deep and distinctive sweet-sour flavour.

155

LAMB'S FRY WITH BACON AND ONIONS

*The wonderfully warm and mellow flavour and appetising fragrance of fresh sage transforms
traditional liver and bacon, while onions in a creamy sauce lend a melting richness.*

TIME: 25 MINUTES SERVES: 4

1 large onion
8 large sage leaves
2 tablespoons olive oil
4 slices lamb's fry, about 100–125 g each
2 tablespoons plain flour
Black pepper
300 ml lamb or beef stock
4 lean, rindless bacon rashers, about 150 g in total
150 ml sour cream
To garnish: small sage leaves, optional

1 Preheat the oven to low to keep
the bacon warm later. Halve, peel
and slice the onion. Shred the large
sage leaves.
2 Heat 1 tablespoon oil in a frying
pan, add the onion and fry over
moderate heat for 4–5 minutes,
until lightly browned.
3 Meanwhile, rinse the liver and
pat dry with paper towels. Put the
flour onto a plate, season well with
pepper, then coat each slice of liver
with the flour.
4 Tip the leftover flour and the
shredded sage into the onions and
cook, stirring, for 1 minute. Add the
stock and bring to the boil, stirring.
Reduce the heat; leave to simmer.
5 Heat the remaining olive oil
in a frying pan and fry the bacon
for 1–2 minutes on each side, then
remove from the pan and keep
warm in the oven. Add the liver to
the pan and fry over moderate-to-
high heat for 2 minutes each side, or
until lightly browned.
6 Return the bacon to the pan.
Add the sauce and stir, scraping up
any residue from the bottom of the
pan. Simmer for 3–4 minutes, or
until the liver is cooked but still
slightly pink in the centre.
7 Stir the sour cream into the pan
and season to taste with pepper
(because of the bacon, no salt
should be needed). Simmer for
1–2 minutes to heat the cream.
8 Transfer to a warmed serving
dish, garnish with the small sage
leaves, if using, and serve.
SERVING SUGGESTION
Accompany with plain boiled new
potatoes or mashed potatoes and
sautéed zucchini.

*NUTRIENTS PER SERVING: kilojoules 1649,
protein 26 g, carbohydrate 10 g (sugar 5 g),
fat 28 g (saturated fat 10 g), good source of
vitamins A, B group, C, E and folate, and iron,
selenium and zinc.*

LAMB CUTLETS WITH MIXED BEANS

A rustic dish of lamb cutlets fried with rosemary and accompanied by beans gets a great flavour boost from the sharp saltiness of capers simmered in a wine and cream sauce.

TIME: 30 MINUTES SERVES: 4

150 ml lamb or chicken stock
150 g small green beans
Salt and black pepper
1 tablespoon olive oil
3 tablespoons butter
1 lemon
2 sprigs rosemary
8 lamb cutlets or lean loin chops, about 100 g each
1 medium onion
2 x 300 g canned lima beans
2 cloves garlic
300 ml dry white wine
3 tablespoons thick cream
2 tablespoons capers

1 Put a kettle of water on to boil and preheat the oven to low. Put the lamb or chicken stock on to heat in a small saucepan.

2 Top and tail the green beans, then cut into 2.5-cm pieces. Put into a saucepan with a little salt, cover with boiling water and cook for 5–6 minutes, until tender.

3 Meanwhile, put the oil and 1 tablespoon butter into a frying pan and place over moderate heat. Grate the rind from the lemon into the frying pan. Add the rosemary sprigs and increase the heat.

4 Season the lamb cutlets with pepper. When the butter starts to sizzle, put them into the pan, lower the heat to moderate and fry for 4–5 minutes on each side, until golden brown and cooked but still slightly pink in the centre.

5 Meanwhile, peel and chop the onion. Melt the remaining butter in a second frying pan, add the onion to the pan and fry over moderate heat for 5 minutes, until softened.

6 Rinse the canned beans in a colander, then drain the cooked green beans into the same colander.

7 Peel the garlic, crush it into the onion and cook for 30 seconds. Add all the beans, season to taste with salt and pepper, and stir. Lower the heat and leave to heat through, stirring occasionally.

8 Remove the lamb cutlets and rosemary from the first frying pan; keep warm in the oven.

9 Pour off the fat from the pan, leaving the residue from the lamb behind. Add the wine and the juice from half the lemon and boil rapidly until reduced by half.

10 Stir the heated stock into the wine, bring to the boil, reduce to a simmer and stir in the cream. Add salt and pepper and capers and heat through gently. Do not allow the sauce to boil, or else it will curdle.

11 Return the lamb cutlets and rosemary to the pan, stirring in any juices, and heat through.

12 To serve, spoon the beans onto heated serving plates and top with the lamb cutlets and rosemary.

NUTRIENTS PER SERVING: kilojoules 4182, protein 33 g, carbohydrate 25 g (sugar 4 g), fat 74 g (saturated fat 39 g), good source of vitamins A, B group and E, and selenium and zinc.

LAMB PROVENÇALE

This lamb hotpot has a fine herby flavour and is quickly made on top of the stove with tender canned cannellini beans and tomatoes, and served with glorious onion- and garlic-flavoured mashed potatoes.

TIME: 30 MINUTES SERVES: 4

750 g floury potatoes,
such as Kennebec or Desirée

Salt and black pepper

2 tablespoons olive oil

2 medium onions

2 cloves garlic

8 lamb cutlets,
about 100 g each

4 sprigs rosemary

250 g egg tomatoes

200 ml lamb or chicken stock

445 g canned cannellini
or butter beans

Celery salt

2–3 tablespoons milk

1 Put a large pan of water on to boil. Peel and dice the potatoes and add to the boiling water with some salt. Reduce the heat, cover the pan and cook gently for 15–20 minutes, or until tender.

2 Meanwhile, heat the oil in a large frying pan or flameproof casserole. Halve, peel and slice the onions and add to the pan. Peel the garlic and crush it in. Fry over fairly high heat until the onion has softened and is well browned, then transfer to a plate and put aside.

3 Add the lamb cutlets to the pan and fry over moderately high heat for 2–3 minutes on each side, or until lightly browned.

4 While the cutlets are cooking, strip the rosemary leaves from the stems. Roughly chop the tomatoes.

5 Return half the fried onions and garlic to the lamb in the pan. Add the chopped tomatoes, lamb or chicken stock and rosemary, then increase the heat to high.

6 Drain the cannellini beans and add to the pan, along with celery salt and black pepper to taste. Bring to the boil then simmer, uncovered, for 8–10 minutes.

7 Meanwhile, drain the potatoes, mash with the milk, then stir in the remaining fried onion and garlic. Add a few extra chopped rosemary leaves to the potatoes if you like. Season to taste.

8 Serve the lamb cutlets and beans on a heated serving dish, with the potatoes on the side.

NUTRIENTS PER SERVING: kilojoules 3059, protein 39 g, carbohydrate 45 g (sugar 7 g), fat 45 g (saturated fat 18 g), good source of vitamins B group, C, E and folate, and zinc.

ORIENTAL LAMB MEDALLIONS

Succulent rounds of tender lamb are served with an assembly of stir-fried green vegetables and baby corn, brightened with the Asian flavours of fresh ginger and soy sauce.

TIME: 30 MINUTES   SERVES: 4

1-cm piece fresh root ginger
125 g broccoli florets
125 g leek
125 g watercress
125 g snow peas
125 g baby corn
500 g lamb fillet or 8 small lamb noisettes
1–2 tablespoons olive oil
Salt and black pepper
2 tablespoons peanut oil
2 tablespoons lamb or chicken stock
1 tablespoon light soy sauce

1 Peel and chop the ginger and put aside. Cut the broccoli into slices and the leek into matchstick-thin strips. Chop the watercress and top and tail the snow peas. Put them all aside, along with the baby corn.

2 If using lamb fillet, cut it into eight 2.5-cm medallions. Brush the medallions, or the noisettes, with the olive oil and season with salt and black pepper.

3 Warm a frying pan over moderate heat, add the lamb and dry-fry for 2 minutes, or until browned underneath. Turn and fry for 3–4 minutes more, until cooked but slightly pink in the centre. Cover the pan and keep warm.

4 Meanwhile, heat the peanut oil in a wok or large frying pan. Add the ginger and all the prepared vegetables; stir-fry for 3–4 minutes, until just tender.

5 Add the stock and soy sauce to the vegetables and season to taste, then cover and cook for 2 minutes more, stirring occasionally.

6 Place two lamb medallions on each plate and spoon the vegetables over and alongside them.

SERVING SUGGESTION
As an accompaniment, try the Wild Rice and Fennel Salad (page 83).

NUTRIENTS PER SERVING: kilojoules 1820, protein 30 g, carbohydrate 8 g (sugar 3 g), fat 31 g (saturated fat 10 g), good source of vitamins A, B group, C and E, and zinc.

COOK'S SUGGESTION

If lamb fillet or lamb noisettes are not readily available, cut the eye of meat from eight lamb loin chops and use these instead.

LAMB KOFTAS WITH TOMATO SALSA

Tender lean lamb is minced to a smooth paste with spices and yoghurt, then moulded around skewers to make tasty koftas, which are served with a mouthwatering fresh salsa and rice.

TIME: 30 MINUTES   SERVES: 4

3 teaspoons butter
1 medium onion
2 cups long-grain or basmati rice
Salt and black pepper
5-mm piece fresh root ginger
1 clove garlic
500 g minced lamb
A small bunch of coriander
3 teaspoons amchur (mango powder) or lemon juice
1 teaspoon garam masala
1 teaspoon ground cumin
1 teaspoon chilli powder
1 tablespoon besan
2 tablespoons natural yoghurt
1–2 tablespoons vegetable oil

For the salsa:

1 tablespoon olive oil
1 teaspoon white wine vinegar
1 large ripe tomato
1 clove garlic
1 small green or red chilli

1   Put a kettle of water on to boil. Melt the butter in a saucepan. Peel the onion, finely slice one quarter and fry gently for 3 minutes. Stir in the rice and fry for 1 minute.

2   Pour 3 cups boiling water onto the rice, add salt, cover and return to the boil. Reduce the heat and simmer for 15 minutes. Preheat the griller to high.

3   Peel and chop the ginger and garlic, roughly chop the remainder of the onion, then put all into a food processor with the lamb.

4   Chop the coriander leaves, reserving a few for a garnish. Put two-thirds aside and add the rest to the food processor with the amchur or lemon juice, garam masala, ground cumin, chilli powder, besan, yoghurt and some salt and pepper. Blend to a paste.

5   Divide the lamb mixture into eight equal portions and mould each into a sausage shape around a lightly greased metal skewer. Brush all over with the oil and grill for about 6–8 minutes, turning once.

6   To make the salsa, whisk the oil and vinegar together in a bowl. Seed and dice the tomato, peel and crush the garlic, and finely chop the chilli; add to the bowl with the remaining chopped coriander. Season with salt and black pepper.

7   Spoon the cooked rice onto serving plates, top with the koftas and spoon the salsa alongside. Garnish with coriander.

NUTRIENTS PER SERVING: kilojoules 2651, protein 36 g, carbohydrate 69 g (sugar 4 g), fat 23 g (saturated fat 4 g), good source of vitamins B group, C and E.

COOK'S SUGGESTION

Besan, also known as gram flour, is made from ground chick peas. Both besan and amchur are available from larger supermarkets and Asian grocers.

SPICED LAMB KEBABS WITH PITA BREAD

This is a delectable dish of grilled lamb cubes coated in hot spices, served on warmed pita bread with a crunchy mixed salad and topped with a traditional Greek yoghurt sauce.

TIME: 30 MINUTES   SERVES: 4

2 tablespoons olive oil
2 cloves garlic
2 teaspoons ground cumin
½ teaspoon cayenne pepper
750 g lamb fillet or lean leg steak
1 Little Gem or mignonette lettuce
4 sprigs mint
½ cucumber
4 tomatoes
1 red onion
200 g natural yoghurt
Salt and black pepper
4 large or 8 small pita breads

1   Preheat the griller to high. Put the oil into a bowl, peel the garlic and crush it into the bowl, then stir in the cumin and cayenne pepper.

2   Cut the meat into 2.5-cm cubes. Toss in the seasoned oil, thread onto metal skewers and put aside.

3   Shred the lettuce and put into a salad bowl. Chop the mint, putting a few leaves aside for a garnish. Dice the cucumber, peel and finely chop the onion, chop the tomatoes and add to the salad bowl.

4   Grill the kebabs for 6 minutes, turning once. Meanwhile, season the yoghurt with salt and pepper.

5   Remove the kebabs from the griller and put aside.

6   Cut the large pitas into four, or slit open the small ones; place, with the salad, on serving plates. Top with the kebabs and garnish with mint. Serve with the yoghurt

VARIATION

The kebabs can also be cooked on the grill rack of a hot barbecue.

NUTRIENTS PER SERVING: kilojoules 3846, protein 53 g, carbohydrate 95 g (sugar 10 g), fat 39 g (saturated fat 15 g), good source of vitamins A, B group, C, E and folate, and calcium, iron, selenium and zinc.

EASTERN PROMISE: (*top*) LAMB KOFTAS WITH TOMATO SALSA; (*bottom*) SPICED LAMB KEBABS WITH PITA BREAD.

LAMB NOISETTES WITH SPINACH

Stir-fried spinach studded with the Middle Eastern flavours of raisins and pine nuts is a great partner to lamb noisettes spread with flavoured mustard then roasted until tender.

TIME: 30 MINUTES SERVES: 4

2 tablespoons olive oil
2 tablespoons mustard (honey or herb-flavoured)
8 lamb noisettes, about 800 g in total
2 large sprigs rosemary
Salt and black pepper
½ red onion
3 cloves garlic
1 medium tomato
⅓ cup pine nuts
⅓ cup sultanas or raisins
500 g young spinach
To serve: crusty bread

1   Preheat the oven to 220°C. Use a little of the oil to grease a small baking tray.

2   Using half the mustard, spread some on top of each lamb noisette. Snip some of the rosemary leaves over the noisettes and put the tips aside for a garnish. Season with salt and pepper and put the meat aside until the oven has reached full heat.

3   Peel and thinly slice the onion and garlic; chop the tomato. Put all three aside.

4   Cook the noisettes on the top shelf of the oven for 10 minutes, then turn, spread with the rest of the mustard, scatter with more rosemary, if using, and season again. Roast for another 5–8 minutes, until cooked but still slightly pink. If you prefer the lamb well done, cook for a few minutes longer.

5   While the lamb is cooking, heat the remaining oil in a large pan. Add the onion and garlic, cover and cook over low heat for 5 minutes, or until soft but not coloured. Add the pine nuts and sultanas or raisins and fry for 3 minutes.

6   Trim the spinach, then rinse and dry thoroughly. Add the tomato to the pan and cook for 1 minute. Then add the spinach and a little salt and stir for 3–4 minutes, until the spinach wilts. If there is too much spinach in the pan to stir easily, cover for 1–2 minutes until the spinach reduces in bulk, then uncover and stir-fry.

7   Divide the spinach mixture among individual plates and arrange the lamb alongside. Garnish with the rosemary tips and serve with crusty bread to mop up the juices.

SERVING SUGGESTION
In addition, you can serve the noisettes and spinach with some oven-roasted egg tomatoes (as photographed) which can be cooked with the lamb. Cut them in half and put in the oven at the same time as you turn the noisettes.

NUTRIENTS PER SERVING: kilojoules 3034, protein 54 g, carbohydrate 48 g (sugar 14 g), fat 36 g (saturated fat 9 g), good source of vitamins A, B group, C, E and folate, and calcium, iron, selenium and zinc.

MIGHTY BURGER

This giant minced lamb and pork burger provides a spicy pizza-style base for the family's favourite vegetable toppings – you can follow these suggestions or choose your own.

TIME: 30 MINUTES SERVES: 4

Oil for greasing
300 g lean minced lamb
300 g lean minced pork, or half pork and half pork sausage meat
2 teaspoons dried Italian herb mix, or mixed herbs
1 small egg
1½ cups fresh white or brown breadcrumbs
Salt and black pepper
Worcestershire sauce
1 tablespoon olive oil
1 medium onion
1 large clove garlic
1–2 teaspoons chilli powder, optional
50 g button mushrooms
1 small red capsicum
2 tomatoes
125 g mozzarella cheese
125 g Gloucester or Cheddar cheese

1 Preheat the oven to 190°C and lightly oil a 25-cm solid-based pizza tin or a baking tray.

2 Put the lamb and pork into a bowl. Add the herbs, then stir in the egg, breadcrumbs, salt, pepper and a good splash of Worcestershire sauce. Mix well together.

3 Press the mixture evenly into the pizza tin, or put onto the baking tray and shape into a 25-cm round. Cook the burger in the oven for 15–20 minutes.

4 Meanwhile, heat the olive oil in a frying pan. Peel and chop the onion and garlic, add to the oil and fry for 5 minutes, or until soft. Stir in the chilli powder, if using, then remove from the heat.

5 Clean the mushrooms. Seed the capsicum and dice it, then slice the tomatoes and mushrooms. Cut the mozzarella into thin slices and grate the Gloucester or Cheddar.

6 Remove the burger from the oven and drain off any liquid, if necessary, then increase the oven temperature to 220°C.

7 Spread the onion mixture over the burger, add the capsicum, tomatoes and mushrooms, and sprinkle the cheese on top. Bake for 5 minutes, or until the cheese melts.

8 Serve in wedges, with crusty bread, salad and tomato sauce or a spicy relish.

VARIATION
Any combination of minced meats can be used, including poultry or venison. The herb seasoning can also be altered: an all-lamb burger could be seasoned with rosemary and mint; a pork and sausage meat burger or poultry burger with sage and parsley; a venison burger with thyme or oregano. The vegetables can include sweetcorn, olives or any other pizza topping you like.

NUTRIENTS PER SERVING: kilojoules 2637, protein 48 g, carbohydrate 23 g (sugar 6 g), fat 39 g (saturated fat 15 g), good source of vitamins A, B group, C and E, and calcium and zinc.

SPICY PORK BURGERS WITH GUACAMOLE

These hot burgers, spiked with chillies, coriander and cumin, and accompanied by a rich avocado sauce sharpened with the juice of a lemon or lime, make a fine lunch or light dinner dish.

TIME: 30 MINUTES SERVES: 4

2 tablespoons sunflower oil
2 cloves garlic
1 small onion
2 red or green chillies
1 teaspoon ground coriander
1 teaspoon ground cumin
A small bunch of coriander
500 g minced pork
1 small egg
Salt and black pepper
1 lemon or lime
1 large avocado

To serve: **corn chips or soft tortillas**

1 Heat 2 teaspoons oil in a small frying pan. Peel and crush 1 clove garlic, peel and finely chop the onion, add to the pan and fry until the onion is soft.

2 Finely chop the chillies, including the seeds. Put half aside for the guacamole and add the remainder to the onion. Stir in the ground coriander and cumin and fry gently for 3 minutes more, or until soft but not browned.

3 Roughly chop enough fresh coriander to give 2 tablespoons and add half to the reserved chillies. Put the rest of the chopped coriander into a large bowl and add the fried onion mixture, pork, egg, salt and black pepper. Finely grate the rind of the lemon or lime into the bowl and stir the mixture, which should be slightly soft.

4 Heat the remaining oil in a large frying pan. Divide the mixture into four and pat each piece into a fairly flat burger. Fry over moderate heat for 5–6 minutes on each side, until cooked through.

5 Meanwhile, make the guacamole. Squeeze the juice from half the lemon or lime and put it into a bowl with the reserved chopped chillies. Peel the remaining garlic clove and crush it in. Halve and stone the avocado (see page 53), and scoop the flesh into the bowl. Season, then mash together well.

6 Drain the burgers on paper towels. Serve on individual plates with the guacamole and corn chips or soft tortillas.

VARIATION

For a more substantial dish, fill lightly toasted buns with the burgers, sauce and a little salad.

NUTRIENTS PER SERVING: kilojoules 2838, protein 32 g, carbohydrate 33 g (sugar 2 g), fat 48 g (saturated fat 11 g), good source of vitamins B group and E, and zinc.

COOK'S SUGGESTION

Use a food processor to save time making the guacamole. Process all the coriander, remove what you need for the burgers, then add the other guacamole ingredients to the processor and blend.

GINGERED PORK ON WILTED WATERCRESS

Slices of warm potato and seared pork fillet, garnished with ribbons of omelette, make a sandwich for fresh watercress, which will wilt slightly and absorb the delicious Oriental sauce.

TIME: 30 MINUTES SERVES: 2

A bunch of watercress
250 g pork fillet
1½ teaspoons crushed ginger
250 g new waxy potatoes
Salt and black pepper
2 teaspoons sesame seeds
1 large egg
2 teaspoons sesame oil
2 tablespoons vegetable oil
½ teaspoon cornflour
2 tablespoons dry sherry
3 teaspoons soy sauce

1 Preheat the oven to low. Trim the watercress and put aside.

2 Trim any fat and tissue from the pork, then cut into 1-cm slices and place in a bowl. Stir in the ginger and put aside.

3 Scrub the potatoes, cut into 1-cm slices and put into a saucepan. Cover with cold water, add a little salt and bring to the boil. Then cover and cook for 10–12 minutes, or until tender.

4 Meanwhile, dry-fry the sesame seeds in a frying pan, shaking over moderate heat until lightly toasted, then leave to cool.

5 Lightly beat the egg in a small bowl with salt and pepper, then stir in the sesame seeds. Heat the sesame oil and 1 teaspoon vegetable oil in the frying pan. Add the egg and swirl over the base to make a thin omelette. Turn out onto a plate, roll up and slice thinly.

6 Blend the cornflour in a small bowl with 2 tablespoons cold water; stir in the sherry and soy sauce.

7 Heat the remaining vegetable oil in the pan over high heat and fry the pork slices for 1–2 minutes on each side until golden brown, then transfer to a plate and keep warm.

8 Pour the cornflour mixture into the pan and stir over moderate heat until it boils and thickens. Return the pork to the pan with any juices and heat through.

9 Drain the potatoes and arrange on two plates. Place the watercress and pork slices on top and pour over the sauce; garnish with the omelette ribbons and serve.

NUTRIENTS PER SERVING: *kilojoules 2209, protein 34 g, carbohydrate 19 g (sugar 1 g), fat 33 g (saturated fat 6 g), good source of vitamins A, B group and C, and selenium and zinc.*

PORK FILLET WITH MUSTARD SAUCE

Tender medallions of pork are served with sweet apples and a piquant sauce enhanced with apple-flavoured Calvados.

TIME: 30 MINUTES SERVES: 4

600 g pork fillet
2 small dessert apples
4 spring onions
1½ tablespoons butter
1 tablespoon plain flour
¾ cup chicken stock
1 sprig thyme
3 tablespoons wholegrain mustard
Salt and black pepper
4 tablespoons thick cream
2 tablespoons Calvados or brandy

1 Trim any fat and tissue from the pork fillet, then cut into 1-cm slices.
2 Quarter, core and slice the apples, and trim and chop the spring onions. Put both aside.
3 Melt half the butter in a large frying pan, add the pork fillet slices and fry over high heat for 1 minute on each side, or until the meat is very lightly browned. Remove from the pan and keep warm.
4 Heat the remaining butter in the pan, add the spring onions and cook for 1–2 minutes, until softened. Stir in the flour, add the stock and bring to the boil, stirring.
5 Strip the leaves from the thyme, then add to the pan with the apples, mustard, and salt and pepper to taste. Cook over moderate heat for a further 4 minutes.
6 Stir the cream into the sauce, then simmer gently for 2 minutes. Pour in the Calvados or brandy, increase the heat slightly and cook gently for a further 2 minutes. Transfer onto four heated plates and serve immediately.

SERVING SUGGESTION
Tender baby peas cooked with shredded lettuce (as photographed), and a bowl of smooth Chestnut and Celeriac Purée (page 260), make good accompaniments to this dish.

VARIATION
If you prefer, apple juice can be used instead of the alcohol.

NUTRIENTS PER SERVING: kilojoules 2260, protein 36 g, carbohydrate 11 g (sugar 9 g), fat 37 g (saturated fat 16 g), good source of vitamins A, B group and E, and selenium and zinc.

PORK WITH EGG NOODLES

The flavours of France and the Orient combine in this intriguing stir-fry of pork and vegetables, with crème fraîche and pungent wholegrain mustard providing a velvety sauce that soaks into the noodles.

TIME: 20 MINUTES   SERVES: 4

Salt and black pepper
500 g pork fillet, trimmed of any fat or tissue
8 spring onions
300 g celery
300 g small mushrooms
1 tablespoon olive oil
250 g egg noodles
2 tablespoons wholegrain mustard
200 g crème fraîche

1   Preheat the oven to low to keep the pork warm later. Put a large pan of lightly salted water on to boil.

2   Cut the pork into thin strips; season with pepper. Trim and slice the spring onions and celery; clean and slice the mushrooms.

3   Heat half the oil in a wok or frying pan over high heat and stir-fry the pork for 4–5 minutes. Remove the meat and keep warm.

4   Add the remaining oil to the wok or pan along with the celery and half the spring onions and stir-fry for 5 minutes. Add the mushrooms and cook until soft.

5   Add the noodles to the boiling water, cook for 3 minutes (or as instructed on the packet), then drain well; keep warm.

6   Stir the mustard and crème fraîche into the vegetables and bring the mixture to the boil. Add the pork, heat through, then season to taste with salt and pepper.

7   Serve the pork spooned over the noodles; sprinkle with the remaining spring onions.

VARIATION

Beef fillet or skinless chicken can be used instead of the pork.

NUTRIENTS PER SERVING: kilojoules 2812, protein 40 g, carbohydrate 48 g (sugar 4 g), fat 37 g (saturated fat 16 g), good source of vitamins B group and folate, and selenium and zinc.

PLUM-GLAZED PORK WITH SPICY CABBAGE

Plum jam and soy sauce go particularly well with pork, while the crisp cabbage gets its own spicy boost from chilli and garlic.

700 g crisp green cabbage, such as savoy
1 red chilli
2 cloves garlic
2 tablespoons good plum jam
1 tablespoon soy sauce
½ teaspoon ground allspice
½ teaspoon cayenne pepper
4 pork loin chops, about 200 g each
2 tablespoons cider vinegar
Salt and black pepper
2 tablespoons olive oil

1 Preheat the griller to high. Halve the cabbage and discard the woody centre. Coarsely chop the leaves, rinse well, then drain in a colander.
2 Halve and seed the chilli, and slice finely. Peel and roughly chop the garlic. Put them both aside.
3 Gently warm the plum jam and soy sauce in a small pan, season with the allspice and cayenne, then sieve, if necessary.
4 Trim the fat off the chops and discard the bones. Arrange the pork on the griller rack and cook for 5–7 minutes each side, basting with the glaze halfway through cooking.
5 Meanwhile, mix the cider vinegar with 2 tablespoons water and some salt and pepper.
6 Heat the oil in a large saucepan, add the chilli and garlic and fry for 30–40 seconds. Add the cabbage and toss in the oil. Stir in the diluted vinegar, cover and cook for 4 minutes.
7 Uncover the pan, raise the heat and continue to cook the cabbage until all the liquid has evaporated.
8 Serve the spicy cabbage on individual plates with the plum-glazed chops alongside.

SERVING SUGGESTION
Plain steamed rice provides the perfect foil for the richness of this dish and helps to soak up the flavoursome juices.

NUTRIENTS PER SERVING: kilojoules 2377, protein 32 g, carbohydrate 19 g (sugar 18 g), fat 41 g (saturated fat 13 g), good source of vitamins A, B group, C, E and folate, and selenium and zinc.

HAM AND LEEK PIE

An excellent casual dish, this variation on shepherd's pie pairs the smoky flavour of ham with the delicate sweetness of leeks in a mature Cheddar sauce, enhanced by juicy cherry tomatoes.

TIME: 30 MINUTES SERVES: 4

1 kg potatoes
Salt and black pepper
500 g leeks
3 tablespoons butter
500 g lean ham pieces
100 g mature Cheddar cheese
125 g cherry tomatoes
2 tablespoons plain flour
1 teaspoon mixed dried herbs
300 ml plus 1–2 tablespoons milk
To garnish: a few sprigs of parsley

1 Put a kettle of water on to boil. Peel and dice the potatoes and put into a saucepan. Add salt, cover with the boiling water and cook, covered, for 8–10 minutes until the potatoes are tender.

2 Meanwhile, slice, rinse and drain the leeks. Melt 1 tablespoon butter in a frying pan over moderate heat and fry the leeks for 6–8 minutes, stirring frequently, until softened but not browned. Preheat the griller to high.

3 Dice the ham. Melt 1 tablespoon butter in a flameproof casserole about 25 cm wide and 5 cm deep, or in a frying pan with a flameproof handle. Fry the diced ham over moderate heat for 5 minutes, stirring frequently.

4 Grate the cheese and cut the cherry tomatoes in half; put aside.

5 Stir the flour and herbs into the ham and cook for 1 minute. Add 300 ml milk and stir until it comes to the boil. Add the cheese, stir until it melts then add the leeks, season to taste and reduce the heat to low.

6 Drain and mash the potatoes with black pepper, the remaining butter and 1–2 tablespoons milk. Place large spoonfuls of potato in a circle around the top of the ham and leek mixture and place the cherry tomatoes in the centre.

7 Grill the pie for 2–3 minutes, or until the top of the mash is golden.

Strip the parsley leaves, scatter over the tomatoes and serve immediately.

SERVING SUGGESTION
Serve with a plain green vegetable, such as Brussels sprouts.

NUTRIENTS PER SERVING: kilojoules 2411, protein 37 g, carbohydrate 42 g (sugar 8 g), fat 30 g (saturated fat 18 g), good source of vitamins A, B group, C, E and folate, and calcium.

QUICK CASSOULET

These lean pork sausages are casseroled with lima and cannelini beans in a herby tomato and mustard sauce, elevating humble bangers and beans to the realms of haute cuisine.

TIME: 30 MINUTES SERVES: 4

8 large pork sausages
125 g rindless bacon rashers
1 tablespoon vegetable oil
1 large onion
2 cloves garlic
300 g canned lima beans
375 g canned cannellini beans
425 g canned tomato pieces, with their juice
1–2 teaspoons dried mixed herbs
1 tablespoon wholegrain mustard
2 tablespoons tomato paste
Salt and black pepper

1 Cut the sausages into 2.5-cm pieces, then dice the bacon. Heat the oil in a large flameproof casserole and add the sausages and bacon. Fry over moderately high heat for 8 minutes, until the sausage

pieces are golden on all sides and the diced bacon is cooked.
2 Meanwhile, halve, peel and slice the onion. Peel and crush the garlic. Rinse and drain the beans; you don't have to keep them separate.
3 Remove the sausages and bacon from the casserole, drain on paper towels and put aside. Pour away all but 2 tablespoons fat from the casserole. Add the onion and garlic and cook over moderate heat for 5 minutes, until softened.
4 Stir the tomatoes with their juice into the onion, then add the mixed herbs, mustard and tomato paste. Fill the tomato can one-third full with water, stir well, and add to the mixture. Bring to the boil, stirring, then add the drained beans.
5 Return the sausages and bacon to the casserole and season to taste.

Reduce the heat, cover and cook gently for 10 minutes, or until the sausages are cooked through.
SERVING SUGGESTION
Serve the cassoulet accompanied by a green salad and mashed potatoes, or some warm crusty bread.

NUTRIENTS PER SERVING: kilojoules 2971, protein 29 g, carbohydrate 41 g (sugar 10 g), fat 48 g (saturated fat 17 g), good source of vitamins B group, C and E.

COOK'S SUGGESTION

Lima and cannellini beans are used here, but you can use kidney or pinto beans instead if you have them in the cupboard, or you can replace one can of beans with 250 g frozen corn kernels, peas or broad beans.

HAM STEAKS WITH HOT SHERRY SAUCE

*Juicy ham steaks are quickly fried until brown then topped with a light sherry sauce
spiced with whole cloves and some Dijon mustard.*

TIME: 20 MINUTES SERVES: 4

4 ham steaks, about 1 cm thick and about 200 g each
1 tablespoon butter
3 cloves
1 cup medium-dry sherry, such as Amontillado
2 teaspoons Dijon mustard

1 Preheat the oven to low, ready to keep the ham warm later.

2 Trim any fat from the steaks. Heat the butter in a large frying pan until sizzling, add the cloves, then fry two ham steaks over fairly high heat for 3 minutes each side, until browned. Transfer to a serving dish and put in the oven to keep warm.
3 Cook the other two steaks and add them to the serving dish.
4 Pour the sherry into the frying pan and bring to the boil, scraping up the sediment from the bottom of the pan. Stir in the mustard and

boil for 2 minutes until the sauce has reduced. Discard the cloves, then pour the sauce over the ham.
SERVING SUGGESTION
Serve with rice and a vegetable such as broccoli or Celery and Apple (page 278). Or try theWild Rice and Fennel Salad (page 83).

NUTRIENTS PER SERVING: kilojoules 2712, protein 40 g, carbohydrate 4 g (sugar 4 g), fat 47 g (saturated fat 19 g), good source of vitamin B group, and zinc.

SAUSAGES WITH SPICED WINE AND APPLES

The family's favourite sausages get a delicate new flavour when they are poached in white wine and then browned in butter, and served with a sauce of apples, cinnamon and shallot.

TIME: 25 MINUTES   SERVES: 2

300 ml dry white wine
250 g good-quality pork or chicken sausages
1 shallot or ½ small onion
2 crisp dessert apples
3 tablespoons butter, at room temperature
200 ml chicken or vegetable stock
2 tablespoons brown sugar
½ teaspoon ground cinnamon

1   Bring the wine to the boil in a large frying pan and poach the sausages gently for 10 minutes.
2   Meanwhile, peel and grate the shallot or onion and peel, quarter, core and slice the apples.

3   Gently melt a small knob of the butter in a second frying pan. Remove the sausages from the first pan, reserving the wine. Discard any loose skins and fry the sausages slowly in the butter until they have browned all over.
4   Meanwhile, add the shallot or onion to the white wine in the first pan, along with the apples, chicken or vegetable stock, brown sugar, cinnamon and the remaining butter. Bring the mixture to the boil, lower the heat and simmer until the apples are tender and the liquid is reduced to a thin syrup. Serve the sausages with the apple sauce.

SERVING SUGGESTION
This is an excellent brunch dish followed by coffee and croissants.

To serve as a main meal, add some mashed potatoes, a tossed green salad and, if you like, Glazed Onions (page 278) or Sautéed Brussels Sprouts (page 261).

NUTRIENTS PER SERVING: kilojoules 3888, protein 15 g, carbohydrate 42 g (sugar 31 g), fat 69 g (saturated fat 34 g), good source of vitamins A, B group and E.

COOK'S SUGGESTION

Good-quality sausages are essential, but choose a milder variety, otherwise the flavour may clash with the apple sauce. Chicken sausages are available from most larger supermarkets and specialist poultry shops.

ITALIAN SPIRALS WITH BURST TOMATOES

Cherry tomatoes are full of flavour, and here they are cooked to bursting point on a bed of oregano, chilli and garlic to complement the spicy flavour of Italian sausage.

TIME: 30 MINUTES   SERVES: 4

500 g length of thin Italian sausage (salsiccia), peppered or spiced
2 tablespoons olive oil
2 cloves garlic
1 teaspoon dried oregano
½ teaspoon dried chilli flakes
750 g ripe cherry tomatoes
Salt and black pepper
To garnish: basil leaves

1   Preheat the griller to high. Cut the sausage into four shorter lengths and wind each into a coil. Pass a thin metal skewer horizontally through each coil to hold it in place, then arrange all four skewers on the rack of the griller tray
2   Heat the oil in a large frying pan. Peel the garlic and crush it into the oil. Then add the oregano and the chilli flakes and fry gently for about

30 seconds, without allowing the crushed garlic to change colour.
3   Spread the tomatoes in a single layer on top of the garlic and chilli; cover and cook over low heat for about 10–12 minutes, or until most of the tomatoes have burst and are half-submerged in the juices.
4   Meanwhile, grill the sausage coils for 5–6 minutes on each side, turning them about to ensure they become evenly crusty and brown on all sides.
5   Uncover the tomatoes, raise the heat to moderate and cook for a further 5 minutes, or until the juices have reduced and thickened. Press lightly occasionally with the back of a spoon to ensure that all the tomatoes have burst.
6   Season the tomato sauce to taste with salt and pepper, then pour onto four warmed serving plates and put a sausage coil in the centre

of each. Strip the basil leaves from their stems and scatter over the top.
SERVING SUGGESTION
Mashed potatoes or Polenta with Provolone (page 220) would both provide a creamy contrast to the tomato and chilli sauce.
VARIATION
Other thin spicy sausages can be used instead of salsiccia. If long lengths are unavailable in the sausage of your choice, untwist the links and smooth the sausage meat into a solid column with your fingers before winding it into coils.

NUTRIENTS PER SERVING: kilojoules 2059, protein 30 g, carbohydrate 6.5 g (sugar 6 g), fat 38 g (saturated fat 15 g), good source of vitamins B group, C and E.

SPICY SAUSAGE DISHES: (top) SAUSAGES WITH SPICED WINE AND APPLES; (bottom) ITALIAN SPIRALS WITH BURST TOMATOES.

POULTRY & GAME

Chicken, duck, turkey, quail, rabbit, kangaroo and venison all bring their own special flavours to these tempting sautées and grills, and quick-cooking roasts and casseroles.

CHICKEN WITH MUSHROOM SAUCE

Tender pan-fried breast of chicken is simmered gently in a smooth sauce of button mushrooms and spring onions laced with cream and herbs, to produce a luxurious and very satisfying dish.

TIME: 30 MINUTES SERVES: 4

1 tablespoon olive oil
1 tablespoon butter
4 boneless, skinless chicken breasts, about 185 g each
Salt and black pepper
4 spring onions
2 cloves garlic
350 g button mushrooms or oyster mushrooms
Small bunch of parsley
Few sprigs of thyme
1 tablespoon plain flour
150 ml chicken stock
150 ml cream
2 teaspoons Dijon mustard

1 Preheat the oven to low to keep the chicken warm later. Heat the oil and butter in a frying pan until sizzling. Meanwhile, season the chicken breasts with black pepper.

2 Add the chicken to the pan and cook for 2–3 minutes on each side until golden, then reduce the heat to low, cover and continue cooking for 8–10 minutes, turning once.

3 While the chicken is cooking, trim and slice the spring onions. Peel and finely chop the garlic. Clean and slice the mushrooms.

4 When the juices of the chicken run clear, transfer the breasts to a plate, cover and keep warm.

5 Add the spring onions, garlic and button mushrooms to the pan and fry over moderate heat for 3–4 minutes, or until softened.

6 Meanwhile, chop enough parsley to give 2 tablespoons, and enough thyme to give 2 teaspoons.

7 Stir the flour into the pan and cook for 1 minute, then add the stock and bring to the boil, stirring constantly. Cook the mushroom

sauce for 2–3 minutes, then reduce the heat, add the cream, parsley, thyme and mustard and stir well. Return the chicken breasts, and any juices, to the pan and heat gently for 2–3 minutes more.

8 Put the cooked chicken breasts onto warmed plates and spoon over the mushroom sauce.

SERVING SUGGESTION

New potatoes and green beans, or a refreshing salad, such as Cucumber, Radish and Melon Salad (page 103), would make a good accompaniment to the chicken.

VARIATION

This sauce also goes beautifully with escalopes of veal or pork.

NUTRIENTS PER SERVING: kilojoules 1594, protein 41 g, carbohydrate 4 g (sugar 2 g), fat 22 g (saturated fat 10 g), good source of vitamins A, B group and E.

CHICKEN BREASTS WITH TARRAGON

Tarragon, with its slight aniseed flavour, is one of the most delicate of all fresh herbs and is particularly well suited to this combination of chicken breasts and crème fraîche.

TIME: 30 MINUTES SERVES: 4

| 4 boneless, skinless chicken breasts, about 185 g each |
| 2 tablespoons plain flour |
| Salt and black pepper |
| 1 tablespoon unsalted butter |
| 1½ tablespoons sunflower oil |
| 2 shallots |
| 4 sprigs tarragon |
| 1 cup dry white wine |
| 1½ cups chicken stock |
| 4 tablespoons crème fraîche |

1 Preheat the oven to low. Trim any excess fat from the chicken and pat dry with paper towels. Dust with the flour and season lightly with salt and pepper.

2 Heat the butter and 1 tablespoon oil in a frying pan over moderate heat and cook the chicken for about 6 minutes on each side.

3 Meanwhile, peel and chop the shallots. Snip off the tip of each sprig of tarragon and reserve, then strip the leaves from the remaining stems, chop coarsely and put aside.

4 Transfer the chicken to the oven to keep warm. Add the shallots to the pan with the rest of the oil and fry, stirring, for 1 minute. Add the wine and half the chopped tarragon. Boil until the wine has reduced by half. Add the chicken stock and reduce by half again.

5 Stir in the crème fraîche and the remaining chopped tarragon, then return the chicken to the pan and warm through for 1 minute on each side. Adjust the seasoning and serve, garnished with tarragon tips.

SERVING SUGGESTION
A selection of steamed vegetables, or a plate of Grilled Chicory and Beetroot (page 265), would offset this dish beautifully.

NUTRIENTS PER SERVING: kilojoules 1737, protein 40 g, carbohydrate 5 g (sugar 1 g), fat 22 g (saturated fat 10 g), good source of vitamins B group and E, and zinc.

CHICKEN GOUJONS WITH GARLIC SAUCE

Some of the great traditional flavours of France – garlic, wine vinegar and Dijon mustard – are combined with chicken to give a full-flavoured dish served with light vermicelli noodles.

TIME: 30 MINUTES SERVES: 4

500 g boneless, skinless chicken breasts
4–6 cloves garlic
2 tablespoons Dijon mustard
1 tablespoon tomato paste
2 tablespoons wine vinegar
4 tablespoons chicken stock or water
4 spring onions
2 tablespoons olive oil
250 g egg vermicelli
Salt and black pepper
2 teaspoons cornflour
1 cup cream

1 Put a saucepan of water on to boil for the egg vermicelli. Cut the chicken breasts diagonally into long, thin strips.

2 Peel the garlic and crush it into a bowl. Stir in the mustard, tomato paste, vinegar and stock or water.

3 Holding the spring onions together firmly, slice the green parts finely and push to one side, then slice the white parts finely and keep the two separate.

4 Heat 1½ tablespoons oil in a frying pan over high heat. Stir-fry the chicken for 1–2 minutes, until it turns white.

5 Stir the garlic and vinegar into the pan and add the white parts of the spring onions. Bring to the boil, cover and simmer gently for about 5 minutes.

6 Meanwhile, add the vermicelli and some salt to the pan of boiling water. Return to the boil and cook for 3 minutes, then drain well and toss in the remaining olive oil.

7 Blend the cornflour with a little cream and stir into the chicken. Add the green parts of the spring onions, reserving some for a garnish, then add the remaining cream and season to taste. Stir over moderate heat for 2–3 minutes, until the sauce thickens.

8 Serve the chicken and sauce over the vermicelli and garnish with the reserved slices of spring onion.

SERVING SUGGESTION
Sautéed Brussels Sprouts (page 261) are a good accompaniment, as the sweetness of the diced bacon would balance the garlic and vinegar sauce.

VARIATION
A fresh pasta such as spaghetti can be substituted for the vermicelli.

NUTRIENTS PER SERVING: kilojoules 2440, protein 36 g, carbohydrate 56 g (sugar 4 g), fat 24 g (saturated fat 9 g), good source of vitamins A, B group and E.

COOK'S SUGGESTION

Goujons are very thin strips of chicken breast, usually cut on the diagonal. You can save time by buying ready-cut strips, but make sure it is breast meat, which is tender and needs very little cooking.

SPANISH-STYLE CHICKEN

Salty black olives, sweet red and yellow capsicums, spicy chorizo sausage and white wine team with pieces of tender chicken to bring a touch of the Mediterranean to an easy family casserole.

TIME: 30 MINUTES SERVES: 4

2 tablespoons olive oil
8 boneless, skinless chicken thighs, about 750 g in total
1 medium red onion
1 clove garlic
1 large red capsicum
1 large yellow capsicum
425 g canned tomato pieces
150 ml dry white wine
1 tablespoon paprika
100 g chorizo sausage
2 tablespoons pitted black olives
Salt and black pepper
A bunch of parsley
To serve: crusty white bread

1 Heat the oil in a large flameproof casserole, then cut the chicken thighs in half and fry over high heat until golden.

2 Peel and thinly slice the onion and peel and crush the garlic. Add to the chicken. Slice the capsicums (see box, right) and add to the chicken. Fry until lightly browned and slightly softened.

3 Stir in the drained tomatoes, wine and paprika and bring to the boil. Slice the chorizo thickly and add it, then simmer for 15 minutes, or until the chicken is cooked.

4 Halve the olives, add to the casserole, then season to taste with salt and pepper. Chop the parsley, scatter over the chicken and serve with some crusty bread.

NUTRIENTS PER SERVING: *kilojoules 2452, protein 44 g, carbohydrate 49 g (sugar 13 g), fat 23 g (saturated fat 5 g), good source of vitamins A, B group, C, E and folate, and selenium.*

EASY DOES IT!

To slice capsicums quickly, cut in half lengthways then cut away the stem, seeds and white membrane. Turn the halves cut side down and tap sharply on the chopping board to remove any remaining seeds. Slice shiny side down so the knife does not slip on the skin.

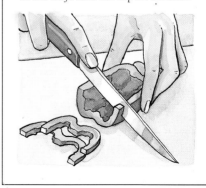

GRILLED ROSEMARY CHICKEN

*Tender grilled chicken thighs, imbued with the scent of rosemary and served with sliced new potatoes,
are perfectly finished with a warm dressing of creamy garlic-flavoured mayonnaise.*

TIME: 30 MINUTES SERVES: 4

8 sprigs rosemary, each about 5 cm long	
8 large chicken thighs, about 800 g in total	
500 g waxy new potatoes	
Salt and black pepper	
4 tablespoons olive oil	
2 large cloves garlic	
6 tablespoons mayonnaise	

1 Preheat the griller to high and put a kettle of water on to boil. Insert a sprig of rosemary under the skin on each of the chicken thighs.
2 Scrub the potatoes, put into a saucepan, cover with boiling water and add a little salt. Bring back to the boil and cook for 15 minutes, until tender.
3 Meanwhile, arrange the chicken, skin side down, on the griller rack. Brush with 1 tablespoon oil, sprinkle with salt and black pepper and cook, about 10 cm below the heat, for 10 minutes. Turn the thighs over, brush with a further 1 tablespoon oil, season with salt and pepper and cook for 10 minutes more, until the skin is golden and crisp. Turn off the griller, but leave the chicken thighs on the rack to keep warm.
4 While the chicken is cooking, put the remaining oil into a small saucepan. Peel the garlic, crush it into the oil and shake over moderate heat until beginning to sizzle; do not let it colour. Turn off the heat. Beat in the mayonnaise with 2 tablespoons hot water from the kettle until well amalgamated; cover and keep warm.
5 Drain the potatoes well, slice thickly and return to the saucepan to reheat gently.
6 Arrange the chicken thighs and potatoes on four individual plates. Spoon a little mayonnaise alongside, then sprinkle with black pepper and serve immediately.

NUTRIENTS PER SERVING: kilojoules 2352, protein 31 g, carbohydrate 19 g (sugar 2 g), fat 41 g (saturated fat 7 g), good source of vitamins B group, C and E.

RICOTTA CHICKEN WITH TOMATO SALSA

*Pesto sauce gives a wonderfully intense flavour to this dish and reveals its deep colour when the
chicken breast is sliced open, while a tomato, basil and red onion salsa adds refreshing piquancy.*

TIME: 25 MINUTES SERVES: 4

4 boneless, skinless chicken breasts, about 185 g each	
100 g ricotta cheese	
5 tablespoons pesto sauce	
2 teaspoons olive oil	
Black pepper	
2 large tomatoes	
1 small red onion	
1 clove garlic	
A small handful of basil leaves	
1 loaf crusty Italian bread	

1 Preheat the griller to moderately high. Cut a deep slit lengthways down the side of each chicken breast to make a pocket.
2 Put the ricotta cheese into a small bowl with 1 tablespoon pesto sauce and mix together. Spoon a quarter of the mixture into each breast pocket, then fold the chicken over to enclose the filling.
3 Place the breasts in an oiled griller tray, brush well with the olive oil and season with black pepper. Grill for 7–8 minutes each side, until cooked through. Put aside and keep warm.
4 Meanwhile, finely chop the tomatoes, then peel and finely chop the onion and garlic, mix together and season generously with black pepper. Put a few basil leaves aside for a garnish; tear the rest and add to the salsa.
5 Cut four slices of bread and spread with the remaining pesto. Lightly toast under the griller.
6 Arrange the chicken on the toast on individual plates. Spoon some salsa alongside and garnish with the reserved basil leaves.

VARIATION
If ricotta is not available, use cream cheese instead or, if necessary, some finely grated hard cheese, such as Gruyère or a mild Cheddar.

NUTRIENTS PER SERVING: kilojoules 1758, protein 53 g, carbohydrate 21 g (sugar 6 g), fat 21 g (saturated fat 7 g), good source of vitamins A, B group, C and E.

COOK'S SUGGESTION

Use a food processor to speed up the chopping of the tomatoes, onion and garlic, but take care to process each of them for no more than a few seconds, to leave some texture in the salsa.

TWO FROM THE GRILLER: *(top)* GRILLED ROSEMARY CHICKEN; *(bottom)* RICOTTA CHICKEN WITH TOMATO SALSA.

CHICKEN BREASTS WITH HOT SALSA

The fiery tang of a sweet roasted capsicum and chilli salsa, dressed in rich olive oil and fresh citrus juice, turns grilled chicken breasts into a fiesta of colour and taste.

TIME: 30 MINUTES SERVES: 4

| 1 red capsicum |
| 1 yellow capsicum |
| 1 green chilli |
| 4 tablespoons extra virgin olive oil |
| 2 small cloves garlic |
| 4 boneless chicken breasts, about 185 g each |
| Salt and black pepper |
| ½ lime or ½ lemon |

1 Preheat the griller to high. Quarter the capsicums, discarding the seeds, and put them, skin side up, on the griller rack. Add the chilli and grill for 15 minutes, or until the skins are blistered and brown, but not burnt. Turn the chilli over half way through.
2 Meanwhile, pour 2 teaspoons oil into a large bowl and the rest into a small salad bowl. Peel the garlic and crush 1 clove into each.
3 Add the chicken breasts to the larger bowl and turn in the oil until evenly coated. Season with pepper and put them, skin side up, on the griller rack alongside the capsicums. Grill for 7–8 minutes, until the skins are golden and blistered, then turn and cook for another 7–8 minutes.
4 When the capsicums and chilli are blistered, transfer to a bowl. Cover and put aside until cool enough to handle.
5 While the chicken finishes cooking, squeeze the juice from the half lime or lemon into the salad bowl, with salt and pepper to taste.
6 Peel the capsicums and dice the flesh finely. Peel, halve, seed and finely dice the chilli. Stir both into the dressing.

7 Serve the chicken on individual plates with the salsa alongside.
SERVING SUGGESTION
Add a vegetable side dish, such as Italian Baked Chicory (page 264).
VARIATION
The salsa also goes well with grilled fish and can be made 1–2 days ahead and stored in the refrigerator.

NUTRIENTS PER SERVING: kilojoules 1515, protein 39 g, carbohydrate 5 g (sugar 4 g), fat 21 g (saturated fat 4 g), good source of vitamins A, B group, C and E.

COOK'S SUGGESTION

Anaheim chillies, if you can get them, have a mild heat and sweet aftertaste. Fat chillies are easiest to grill as they won't slip between the bars, and grilling gives them a smoky flavour.

LIME CHICKEN WITH WATER CHESTNUTS

Scents of lime and coconut rise from this dish of spicy, stir-fried sliced chicken and crunchy water chestnuts tossed in a creamy sauce and served with rice noodles.

TIME: 25 MINUTES SERVES: 4

125 g rice noodles	
500 g boneless, skinless chicken breasts	
30 g fresh root ginger	
1 green chilli	
2 cloves garlic	
3 limes	
230 g canned water chestnuts	
1 tablespoon peanut oil	
½ teaspoon sugar	
5 spring onions	
½ cup coconut milk	
Thai fish sauce, or soy sauce	

1 Put a kettle of water on to boil. Put the rice noodles into a large bowl, cover with the boiling water and leave to stand for 10 minutes.

2 Slice the chicken into thin strips and put aside. Peel and finely chop the ginger, seed and dice the chilli, and peel and crush the garlic.

3 Finely grate the rind from two limes onto the ginger. Squeeze the juice from all three limes and put aside. Drain the water chestnuts, cut in half, and put aside.

4 Pour the oil into a lidded wok or large frying pan, add the ginger, chilli, garlic and grated lime rind and place over high heat. When very hot, add the chicken and stir-fry for 2 minutes.

5 Add the lime juice, sugar and water chestnuts to the chicken. Stir well, then cover and cook over moderate heat for 3–5 minutes, until the chicken is cooked through.

6 Meanwhile, trim and thinly slice the spring onions.

7 Drain the rice noodles well, add to the chicken with the spring onions and the coconut milk, and toss together to heat through. Add fish sauce or soy sauce to taste and serve immediately.

VARIATION

You can substitute some boneless, skinless duck breasts for the chicken, or 300 g shelled, medium-sized green prawns.

NUTRIENTS PER SERVING: kilojoules 1352, protein 30 g, carbohydrate 32 g (sugar 4 g), fat 8 g (saturated fat 2 g), good source of vitamins B group, C and E.

CHICKEN KORMA

Tender diced chicken is flavoured with gentle Indian spices, raisins and almonds and finished with smooth yoghurt and cream, to make a mild curry that will please the whole family.

TIME: 30 MINUTES SERVES: 4

| 1½ cups chicken or vegetable stock |
| 1 medium onion |
| 2 cloves garlic |
| 2 tablespoons vegetable oil |
| 2 tablespoons plain flour |
| 2 tablespoons Korma curry powder |
| 750 g boneless, skinless chicken breasts |
| A small handful of coriander |
| 2 tablespoons seedless raisins |
| ¼ cup flaked almonds |
| ½ lemon |
| 2 tablespoons natural yoghurt |
| 2 tablespoons thick cream |
| Salt and black pepper |

1 Put the stock on to boil in a small saucepan. Peel and chop the onion and garlic and fry gently in the oil in a large frying pan for about 5 minutes, until soft.
2 Mix the flour and curry powder in a large bowl, then cut the chicken into 2.5-cm cubes and toss in the mixture until evenly coated. Add the chicken and flour mixture to the pan and fry, stirring, for 3 minutes.
3 Reserve a few coriander leaves for a garnish, then chop enough to give 1 tablespoon. Add to the chicken along with the raisins and hot stock. Bring to the boil, stirring, then reduce the heat and simmer for 10 minutes.

4 Toast the almonds in a dry frying pan. Squeeze the juice from the half lemon and put aside.
5 When the chicken is cooked, remove the pan from the heat and stir in the almonds, lemon juice, yoghurt, cream and salt and pepper to taste. Reheat very gently, but do not allow to boil. Garnish with the reserved coriander leaves.

SERVING SUGGESTION
Serve the korma with rice, cooked while the chicken is simmering.

NUTRIENTS PER SERVING: kilojoules 2126, protein 46 g, carbohydrate 22 g (sugar 14 g), fat 26 g (saturated fat 8 g), good source of vitamins B group and E, and selenium.

CHICKEN AND SPINACH CURRY

This delicate chicken curry, lightly flavoured with spices and spinach, is easily made in one large saucepan and makes an ideal family meal served with hot naan bread.

TIME: 25 MINUTES SERVES: 4

2 tablespoons sunflower oil
1 small onion
1 clove garlic
2 thin slices fresh root ginger
½ teaspoon ground turmeric
½ teaspoon ground cumin
½ teaspoon ground coriander
¼ teaspoon ground chilli
¼ teaspoon garam masala
2 ripe tomatoes
4 boneless, skinless chicken breasts, about 185 g each
Salt and black pepper
150 ml thick cream
4 large naan breads
200 g baby spinach

1 Heat the oil in a large saucepan over moderate heat. Peel and chop the onion and fry in the oil. Peel and crush the garlic and stir it into the onion.

2 Peel and finely chop the ginger and stir it into the onion along with the turmeric, cumin, coriander, chilli and garam masala. Cook for a further 1 minute

3 Roughly chop the tomatoes and add to the saucepan. Fry over gentle heat for 7 minutes, until cooked down to a pulp.

4 Meanwhile, remove any tough sinews from the chicken and cut the flesh into bite-sized chunks.

5 Preheat the griller to high for the bread. When the tomatoes are ready, increase the heat to high, add the chicken and stir-fry until all the pieces have turned white. Season with salt and pepper, then pour in the cream and simmer for a further 6 minutes.

6 Put the naan under the griller to heat through. Meanwhile, rinse and dry the spinach, if necessary.

7 Add the spinach to the curry, press down and stir continuously until it wilts. Bring to the boil, then remove the pan from the heat at once. Serve with the naan.

SERVING SUGGESTION
For a dinner party, add another drier curry, such as Potato and Green Bean Curry (page 259), some Dhal (page 258), and boiled rice.

NUTRIENTS PER SERVING: kilojoules 4227, protein 55 g, carbohydrate 85 g (sugar 13 g), fat 53 g (saturated fat 14 g), good source of vitamins A, B group, C, E and folate, and selenium.

CHICKEN BREASTS WITH APPLES AND CIDER

The creamy sauce is made with sweet apples caramelised in brown sugar and imbued with the tang of dry cider.

TIME: 30 MINUTES   SERVES: 2

3 teaspoons olive oil
3 teaspoons butter
2 shallots
2 crisp, red-skinned dessert apples, about 185 g each
2 teaspoons brown sugar
2 boneless, skinless chicken breasts, about 185 g each
150 ml dry cider
1 teaspoon Worcestershire sauce
2 tablespoons crème fraîche
Salt and black pepper

1   Heat the oil and butter in a frying pan or flameproof casserole over low heat.

2   Peel and finely chop the shallots. Add to the oil and butter in the pan, increase the heat to moderate and fry for 3–4 minutes, stirring occasionally, until soft.

3   While the shallots are cooking, quarter, core and slice the apples, then add to the shallots and sprinkle with the brown sugar. Raise the heat to fairly high and fry until the mixture starts to turn a golden caramel colour.

4   Lift the shallots and apple slices from the pan with a slotted spoon and put aside.

5   Add a little more oil to the pan, if necessary. Add the chicken breasts and fry over fairly high heat for about 6 minutes, turning once, until golden brown.

6   Pour the cider over the chicken. Bring to the boil and simmer, uncovered, for about 8–10 minutes, stirring occasionally and turning the chicken once more, until cooked. The chicken is ready if the juices run clear when it is pierced with the tip of a knife.

7   Stir in the Worcestershire sauce and crème fraîche, and season to taste with salt and black pepper. Return the shallots and apple slices to the pan and warm through for another 1–2 minutes, but do not allow the sauce to boil.

SERVING SUGGESTION

Serve these succulent chicken breasts with jacket potatoes cooked in a microwave oven (see box, below), or with some boiled rice or buttered noodles and a green salad or vegetable on the side.

VARIATION

The sauce can be made with a dry white wine or richly flavoured chicken stock instead of cider, if you prefer, but you must always use red-skinned dessert apples as the green-skinned cooking apples lose their shape. This dish can also be made very successfully with tender veal escalopes instead of chicken breasts.

NUTRIENTS PER SERVING: kilojoules 2072, protein 40 g, carbohydrate 28 g (sugar 28 g), fat 23 g (saturated fat 11 g), good source of vitamins B group, C and E.

EASY DOES IT!

Jacket potatoes cooked in a microwave oven can make a speedy accompaniment to many main-course dishes. Prick the skins of two evenly sized potatoes. Place on a piece of paper towel and cook on high for 6–8 minutes, turning them over halfway through. Wrap the potatoes in foil and leave to stand for 3–4 minutes before serving.

SPICED TURKEY BURGERS

These healthy burgers have Asian flavourings of chilli, coriander, garlic and lime, enhanced with a dash of soy sauce, and are perfect for a quick family lunch.

TIME: 30 MINUTES   SERVES: 4

2 mild chillies
2 cloves garlic
A handful of coriander
2 limes
750 g raw minced turkey or chicken
2 teaspoons soy sauce
2 teaspoons sesame oil
3 teaspoons cornflour
Salt and black pepper
1 tablespoon vegetable oil
350 g snow peas
250 g bean sprouts
To serve: extra soy sauce

1 Preheat the griller to medium. Seed and finely chop the chillies and put into a large bowl. Peel and crush the garlic, then chop enough coriander to give 3 tablespoons; add both to the chillies.

2 Grate the rind from one lime and add to the garlic and coriander; reserve the other lime for a garnish.

3 Add the minced turkey, soy sauce, sesame oil, cornflour, salt and black pepper to the bowl. Work the ingredients together with your hands quickly, until well blended and compacted.

4 Divide the turkey mixture into four equal portions, shape each into a burger, then flatten on both sides using the blunt edge of a knife with a criss-cross movement. The burgers should end up about 10 cm wide.

5 Brush one side of each burger with vegetable oil, then place them, oiled side down, on the rack of the griller tray. Brush the tops with the remaining oil and cook for 10–12 minutes, turning halfway through, until golden brown.

6 Meanwhile, bring some water to the boil in a steamer, then top and tail the snow peas (see box, right) and rinse and drain the bean sprouts, if necessary.

7 When the water in the steamer has come to the boil, place the snow peas in the steamer basket and sprinkle with salt. Cover and steam for 3 minutes. Then add the bean sprouts, cover again, and steam for 1–2 minutes more. Meanwhile, cut the reserved lime into wedges.

8 Arrange the vegetables on warmed individual plates, position the burgers on top, and garnish with the lime wedges. Serve immediately, with extra soy sauce as an accompaniment.

NUTRIENTS PER SERVING: kilojoules 1222, protein 43 g, carbohydrate 9 g (sugar 4 g), fat 9 g (saturated fat 2 g), good source of vitamins B group, C, E and folate, and selenium and zinc.

EASY DOES IT!

To top and tail snow peas quickly, gather several into a bunch, tap on the work surface to even up the ends, then cut across with a pair of kitchen scissors. Turn and snip the other ends.

RED-HOT TURKEY WITH CASHEWS

Tender morsels of turkey, water chestnuts and bean sprouts are given a fiery Asian flavour and a rich honey and soy dressing, which balances well with the plain rice accompaniment.

TIME: 30 MINUTES SERVES: 4

2 cups long-grain rice
3 tablespoons plus 2 teaspoons peanut oil
Salt
8–10 dried red chillies
1 clove garlic
2 tablespoons cornflour
1 large egg white
500 g boned turkey breast
2 tablespoons honey
4 tablespoons soy sauce
2 tablespoons sake or dry sherry
230 g canned water chestnuts
8 spring onions
200 g fresh bean sprouts
100 g roasted, salted cashew nuts
2 teaspoons rice vinegar or white wine vinegar

1 Put a kettle of water on to boil. Put the rice into a saucepan and add 1 teaspoon oil, some salt and 3 cups boiling water from the kettle. Cover, bring back to the boil, then simmer for 10–15 minutes.

2 Put the chillies in a pan of water, add 1 teaspoon oil, bring to the boil and simmer for 10 minutes.

3 Peel the garlic and crush it into a bowl, then stir in the cornflour and egg white. Cut the turkey into dice, add to the egg-white mixture, coat well, then put aside.

4 Blend the honey, soy sauce and sake or sherry with 3 tablespoons water and put aside.

5 Drain, rinse and dice the water chestnuts. Trim the spring onions, cut into chunks the size of the water chestnuts and mix together. Drain the chillies. Rinse and drain the bean sprouts, if necessary.

6 Heat 2 tablespoons oil in a wok or large frying pan over high heat until smoking. Add the diced turkey and stir-fry until it begins to turn white. Add the cashews and the drained chillies and stir-fry for 30 seconds, then stir in the vinegar. Transfer the turkey to a bowl with a slotted spoon.

7 Add the remaining peanut oil to the pan, heat until smoking, then add the diced water chestnuts and the spring onions and stir-fry for a further 30 seconds.

8 Return the turkey mixture to the pan, along with the bean sprouts. Stir for 30 seconds, then pour in the honey and soy sauce mixture and stir to heat through.

9 Drain the rice, put into large individual bowls, and serve the turkey stir-fry on top.

VARIATION

You can substitute chicken breast or pork fillet for the turkey.

NUTRIENTS PER SERVING: kilojoules 3394, protein 43 g, carbohydrate 82 g (sugar 10 g), fat 34 g (saturated fat 8 g), good source of vitamins B group, C and E, and iron.

DUCK BREASTS WITH GINGER SAUCE

A wonderful sauce made with four different ginger products makes a splendid accompaniment to duck, served on a bed of lightly stir-fried leeks and finished with fruity raspberry vinegar.

TIME: 30 MINUTES SERVES: 4

4 boneless duck breasts, about 200 g each	3 tablespoons raspberry vinegar
20 g fresh root ginger	2 tablespoons stem ginger syrup
1 piece stem ginger in syrup	1 cup green ginger wine
2 medium leeks	1 cup chicken stock
	3 teaspoons butter
	Salt and black pepper

1 Preheat the oven to low to keep the duck warm later. Dry-fry the duck breasts, skin side down, in a large pan over moderate heat for about 8 minutes, then turn and cook for a further 6 minutes.

2 While the duck is cooking, peel the fresh ginger and cut into thin strips. Chop the stem ginger and put both aside.

3 Trim the leeks, cut in half lengthways, rinse and drain well, then cut into matchstick-sized strips and put aside.

4 Transfer the cooked duck to the oven to keep warm. Drain off all but about 1 tablespoon of the duck fat. Add the vinegar and bring to the boil, scraping up the brown residue, then add the fresh and stem ginger, ginger syrup, ginger wine and stock. Bring back to the boil, reduce the heat and simmer for 8–10 minutes, until the liquid has reduced by half.

5 Meanwhile, melt the butter in a small frying pan, add the leeks, season with salt and pepper and stir-fry gently for 3–4 minutes until just tender.

6 Return the duck breasts to the ginger sauce, reheat for 2 minutes, then add salt and pepper to taste.

7 Arrange the leeks on a serving dish, place the duck breasts on top and spoon over the sauce.

SERVING SUGGESTION
Sweet Potato Rösti (page 272) or potato pancakes complement the spicy flavour of the duck breasts.

VARIATION
If you would prefer a thicker sauce, dissolve 1 teaspoon arrowroot in 3 tablespoons cold water, then pour into the sauce and simmer for 2 minutes before you return the duck to the pan.

NUTRIENTS PER SERVING: kilojoules 3826, protein 27 g, carbohydrate 15 g (sugar 14 g), fat 78 g (saturated fat 23 g), good source of vitamin B group, and zinc.

DUCK BREASTS WITH BLACKBERRY SAUCE

This simple but extravagantly flavoured dish of tender duck breasts coated in exotic spices is served in a fruity wine sauce, and is perfect for a dinner party or a special celebration.

TIME: 25 MINUTES SERVES: 4

| 4 boneless duck breasts, about 200 g each |
| ¼ teaspoon Chinese five-spice powder |
| Salt and black pepper |
| 4 tablespoons crème de mure |
| 4 tablespoons red wine |
| ½ small cinnamon stick |
| 1 star anise, optional |
| 1 small orange |
| 300 g fresh blackberries |
| 2 level teaspoons arrowroot |

1 Remove any sinews from the duck and lightly score the skin into a diamond pattern. Mix the five-spice powder with some salt and pepper and rub it over the breasts.
2 Put the crème de mure, red wine, cinnamon and star anise, if using, into a small pan. Grate the rind from the orange into the pan, then bring to the boil.
3 Meanwhile, cook the duck, skin side down, in a dry frying pan over moderate heat for 4–5 minutes, until the skins have turned golden brown and enough fat has been released to cook the other sides. Turn and cook for 5–6 minutes more for medium rare, longer for well done. Spoon off excess fat.
4 While the duck is cooking, rinse the blackberries and add to the wine. Squeeze the orange. Add half the juice to the wine, return to the boil, reduce the heat and simmer gently for 5 minutes. Blend the rest of the juice with the arrowroot.
5 Strain the blackberries into a bowl and put aside. Return the liquid to the pan and stir in the blended arrowroot. Bring back to the boil, stirring, until thickened, then add the blackberries and heat through gently.
6 Slice the duck and serve on heated individual plates with the sauce spooned over the top.
SERVING SUGGESTION
For a simple vegetable side dish, cut up boiled new potatoes and mix with crème fraiche.

NUTRIENTS PER SERVING: kilojoules 3231, protein 24 g, carbohydrate 13 g (sugar 11 g), fat 65 g (saturated fat 19 g), good source of vitamins B group, C and E, and zinc.

COOK'S SUGGESTION

Crème de mure is a blackberry liqueur sold in specialist liquor stores. If it is unavailable, crème de cassis (blackcurrant liqueur) makes a very good alternative.

DUCK KEBABS WITH HONEY AND ORANGE

A classic combination, Duck à l'Orange, is given a Chinese touch in these sophisticated kebabs, infused with the flavours of orange juice, honey and soy sauce and served with scented rice.

TIME: 20 MINUTES SERVES: 2

| 1 cup white long-grain or basmati rice |
| Salt |
| 1 bay leaf or cinnamon stick |
| 2 boneless duck breasts, about 350 g in total |
| *To garnish:* onion chives or chive flowers |
| *For the sauce:* |
| 1 orange |
| 4 tablespoons thick honey |
| 2 teaspoons soy sauce |

1 Put a kettle of water on to boil and preheat the griller to high.
2 Put the rice, a pinch of salt and the bay leaf or cinnamon stick in a large saucepan and add boiling water to reach 2.5 cm above the surface of the rice. Bring the water back to the boil, cover and simmer gently for 15 minutes, or until the rice is tender.

3 Meanwhile, cut the duck breasts into cubes and thread onto two metal skewers.
4 To make the basting sauce, finely grate the rind of the orange and put into a small saucepan. Squeeze 2 tablespoons juice from the orange and add to the pan, along with the honey and soy sauce.
5 Place the kebabs on the rack of the griller tray and baste with the sauce. Grill for 4–5 minutes, then turn, baste with more sauce and any pan juices, and grill for a further 4–5 minutes. The kebabs are ready when the duck is cooked and the skin is crispy at the edges. Meanwhile, warm the remaining basting sauce.

6 Drain the rice, removing the bay leaf or cinnamon stick, and serve on warmed individual plates. Arrange the kebabs on top of the rice and garnish the plate with the chives. Pour the juices from the griller tray into the sauce, heat through quickly and transfer to a jug to accompany the kebabs.

SERVING SUGGESTION
The duck is rich and flavoursome, so a bowl of simply steamed snow peas, pattypan squash, carrots and zucchini would be ideal.

VARIATION
If you prefer, chicken breasts with the skin left on can be used instead of the duck.

NUTRIENTS PER SERVING: kilojoules 4646, protein 30 g, carbohydrate 101 g (sugar 40 g), fat 66 g (saturated fat 19 g), good source of vitamins B group and C, and zinc.

PAN-ROASTED QUAIL WITH PROSCIUTTO AND SAGE

The slight gaminess of the quail is accentuated by the addition of prosciutto and sage leaves, and further enhanced by the garlic and red wine sauce.

TIME: 30 MINUTES SERVES: 4

| 8 fresh quail |
| 8 slices prosciutto |
| 8 sage leaves |
| 2 tablespoons butter |
| 1 tablespoon olive oil |
| 4 cloves garlic |
| 1 cup red wine |
| 1 tablespoon quince paste or jelly |
| *To garnish:* sage leaves |

1 Rinse the quail inside and out under cold running water then pat dry with paper towels. Place a slice of prosciutto and a sage leaf inside each.

2 Heat the butter and oil in a large, heavy-based frying pan with a lid. Add the unpeeled garlic and the quail to the pan and sauté over moderate heat for 3–4 minutes, until the birds are golden all over and well sealed.
3 Add the red wine and quince paste or jelly to the pan and cover with the lid. Reduce the heat and simmer for 20 minutes.
4 Remove the quail from the pan and keep warm. Increase the heat under the frying pan and continue to cook, stirring, for 2–3 minutes, until the juices have reduced and thickened slightly.

5 Serve the quail with the pan juices poured over them.
SERVING SUGGESTION
These tasty birds need very simple accompaniments. They are nice served with creamy mashed potatoes and steamed asparagus.

NUTRIENTS PER SERVING: kilojoules 1363, protein 25 g, carbohydrate 5 g (sugar 5 g), fat 17 g (saturated fat 6 g), good source of vitamins A and B group, and iron.

A FLAVOURFUL DUO: *(top)* DUCK KEBABS WITH HONEY AND ORANGE; *(bottom)* PAN-ROASTED QUAIL WITH PROSCIUTTO AND SAGE.

ROASTED QUAIL WITH BITTER MARMALADE

The simplest of sauces, with the sweet tartness of the marmalade boosted by the sherry and soy, adds sparkle to the subtle flavour of the little game birds.

TIME: 30 MINUTES SERVES: 4

8 fresh quail
1 clove garlic
½ cup bitter orange marmalade or kumquat marmalade
½ cup medium dry sherry
2 tablespoons light soy sauce
2 tablespoons light olive oil
8 fresh kumquats
To garnish: 4 small sprigs watercress

1 Preheat the oven to 200°C. Rinse the quail under cold running water and pat dry with paper towels.

2 Peel and crush the garlic and combine with the marmalade, sherry, soy sauce and oil. Rub birds inside and out with this mixture.

3 Place the quail in a lightly oiled baking dish and roast for 25 minutes, basting occasionally, until the juices from the thickest part of the thigh run clear and not pink when pricked with a skewer.

4 Meanwhile, halve the kumquats and sear in a hot frying pan for no more than 15–20 seconds.

5 Arrange the quail and the kumquat halves on warmed plates.

Pour over the pan juices and garnish each plate with watercress.

SERVING SUGGESTION
To maintain the Asian influences in the basting sauce, these roasted quail are best served alongside some steamed Basmati rice rather than potatoes, with maybe a small salad of bitter greens, such as rocket and watercress, on the side.

NUTRIENTS PER SERVING: kilojoules 1325, protein 22 g, carbohydrate 21 g (sugar 21 g), fat 12 g (saturated fat 1 g), good source of vitamin B group, and iron.

CHAR-GRILLED QUAIL WITH OLIVES

Garlic, shallots and pitted green olives combine with stock to make a last-minute sauce, which is given a golden hue by a subtle touch of saffron threads.

TIME: 30 MINUTES SERVES: 4

2 cloves garlic
4 shallots
1 lemon
½ cup green olives
8 fresh quail, halved
3 tablespoons olive oil
Black pepper
1 teaspoon saffron threads
½ cup chicken stock

1 Preheat the char-grill or barbecue. Peel and chop the garlic and shallots; squeeze the juice from the lemon to give 2 tablespoons; pit the olives; put all aside.

2 Brush the quail on both sides with 2 tablespoons oil and season generously with black pepper. Grill or barbecue for about 15 minutes, until golden and tender.

3 Meanwhile, heat the remaining oil in a small frying pan and gently cook the chopped garlic and shallots over moderately low heat for about 2–3 minutes, until soft. Add the lemon juice, saffron threads and stock. Increase the heat and cook, stirring, for about 5 minutes, until reduced by half. Stir in the olives.

4 Serve the quail on individual plates and spoon over the sauce.

SERVING SUGGESTION
This dish goes well with potato wedges sautéed with fresh rosemary leaves in a little olive oil.

NUTRIENTS PER SERVING: kilojoules 1063, protein 21 g, carbohydrate 1 g (sugar 1 g), fat 17 g (saturated fat 2 g), good source of vitamins B group and folate, and iron.

RABBIT RISSOLES

Rabbit and bacon are traditional partners, and here they are teamed with aromatic vegetables, together with sage and garlic, to form tasty rissoles that all the family will enjoy.

TIME: 30 MINUTES SERVES: 4

| 2 rashers bacon |
| 1 onion |
| 1 carrot |
| 1 clove garlic |
| A few sprigs of sage |
| 2 eggs |
| 500 g minced rabbit |
| 1 teaspoon Worcestershire sauce |
| 1 cup soft white breadcrumbs |
| Black pepper |
| 4 tablespoons olive oil |

1 Remove the rind and finely chop the bacon. Peel and finely chop the onion. Peel and grate the carrot. Peel and mince the garlic. Finely chop enough sage leaves to give 1 tablespoon. Lightly beat the eggs.

2 Combine the rabbit with the bacon, onion, carrot, garlic, sage, eggs, Worcestershire sauce, half the breadcrumbs and a generous grinding of black pepper. Form into eight patties and refrigerate for about 10 minutes, to firm.

3 Heat the oil in a large, heavy-based frying pan. Coat the rissoles in the remaining breadcrumbs and cook over moderate heat for 4–5 minutes on each side, until golden brown and cooked through.

SERVING SUGGESTION
Serve with creamy mashed potatoes and some lightly sautéed tomato and zucchini.

NUTRIENTS PER SERVING: kilojoules 1888, protein 52 g, carbohydrate 13 g (sugar 2 g), fat 26 g (saturated fat 5 g), good source of vitamin B group, and selenium and zinc.

COOK'S SUGGESTION
If you have difficulty finding rabbit mince, buy 500 g boneless rabbit fillets and ask your butcher or poultry dealer to mince them for you.

MUSTARD-CRUSTED RABBIT

Mild mustard, lemon and thick yoghurt make a crisp coating for tasty pieces of grilled rabbit served with golden potatoes.

TIME: **30** MINUTES SERVES: **2**

4 medium potatoes
Salt and black pepper
2 rabbit joints, boneless or bone-in, about 200–250 g each
1 lemon
3 teaspoons vegetable oil
2 teaspoons Dijon mustard
2 tablespoons natural yoghurt
2 tablespoons olive oil
1 tablespoon butter
To garnish: 2 sprigs tarragon

1 Preheat the griller to high and put a kettle of water on to boil.

2 Scrub the potatoes and put into a pan with some salt. Cover with boiling water, bring back to the boil and cook for 8 minutes, then drain and leave to cool.

3 Meanwhile, arrange the griller so that the meat will be about 10 cm from the heat, and place the rabbit joints on the griller rack.

4 Cut the lemon in half and squeeze 1 teaspoon juice from one half; put the other half aside. Mix the vegetable oil with the mustard, yoghurt, lemon juice, salt and pepper. Brush half the mixture over the rabbit, grill for 6–7 minutes, then turn, brush with the remaining mixture and grill for a further 6–7 minutes.

5 Meanwhile, cut the cooled potatoes into 3-cm dice. Heat the oil and butter in a frying pan and fry the potatoes for 10–12 minutes over moderate heat, shaking the pan and turning frequently until golden. Drain on paper towels.

6 Cut the unsqueezed lemon half into wedges.

7 Transfer the cooked rabbit onto serving plates and garnish with tarragon sprigs. Serve with the fried potatoes and wedges of lemon.

SERVING SUGGESTION
If you wish to serve a vegetable with this dish, some lightly steamed green peas go well.

NUTRIENTS PER SERVING: kilojoules 3030, protein 41 g, carbohydrate 49 g (sugar 6 g), fat 42 g (saturated fat 16 g), good source of vitamins A, B group, C, E and folate.

197

KANGAROO BURGERS

Kangaroo mince, complemented by the addition of some chopped parsley, a dash of hot mustard and a generous grind of black pepper, comes to the table as burgers fit for a feast.

TIME: 25 MINUTES SERVES: 4

1 onion
A small bunch of parsley
400 g minced kangaroo rump
2 egg yolks
1 cup soft white breadcrumbs
1 teaspoon English mustard
Black pepper
1 bunch rocket
2 tomatoes
4 focaccia buns
4 tablespoons olive oil
1–2 tablespoons butter
½ cup tomato relish
To serve: oven-baked potato wedges

1 Peel and finely chop the onion. Finely chop enough parsley to give 2 tablespoons. Combine both with the kangaroo mince, egg yolks, breadcrumbs, mustard and a generous grinding of pepper; mix well. Form into four patties and refrigerate for about 10 minutes.
2 Trim the rocket leaves and put aside. Slice the tomatoes and put aside. Cut the focaccia buns in half.
3 Heat the oil in a large, heavy-based frying pan. Add the patties and cook over moderate heat for 4–5 minutes on each side, until golden brown and cooked through.
4 While the patties are cooking, lightly grill the focaccia halves then spread with the butter.
5 Serve the patties on the buns, along with the rocket leaves, tomato slices and tomato relish. Accompany with the potato wedges.

NUTRIENTS PER SERVING: kilojoules 3688, protein 60 g, carbohydrate 65 g (sugar 16 g), fat 42 g (saturated fat 17 g), good source of vitamin B group, and iron, zinc and calcium.

COOK'S SUGGESTION
Lean, tender and richly flavoured, several cuts of kangaroo meat are sold all year round in specialist butchers, some delicatessens and most larger supermarkets. The meat is normally sold vacuum-packed, and should always be cooked as soon as possible after opening.

KANGAROO FILLET WITH PINK AND NATIVE PEPPERCORNS

The indigenous flavours of the bush – succulent kangaroo and native peppercorns – are combined with garlic, thyme and rosemary, then bathed in a reduction of port and stock.

TIME: 25 MINUTES SERVES: 4

1 tablespoon dried pink peppercorns
1 tablespoon native peppercorns
A few sprigs of thyme
A few sprigs of rosemary
2 cloves garlic
1 kangaroo loin fillet, about 800 g in total
2 tablespoons olive oil
½ cup port
1 cup beef stock
2 tablespoons bitter orange marmalade or kumquat marmalade
To garnish: 4 small sprigs rosemary

1 Preheat the oven to 180°C. Coarsely grind the pink and native peppercorns. Finely chop the thyme leaves and rosemary leaves to give 1 tablespoon of each. Peel and crush the garlic. Combine on a plate.
2 Roll the fillet in the peppercorn mixture and press on well.
3 Heat the oil in a baking dish on top of the stove, then add the fillet and sear for 2–3 minutes, until sealed on all sides.
4 Add the port and stock to the baking dish. Transfer the dish to the oven and cook the fillet for a further 12 minutes.
5 Transfer the baking dish back to the stove top and remove the meat. Place on a heatproof plate and return to the turned-off oven to keep warm. Add the marmalade to the baking dish and cook over moderate heat, stirring often, for 4–5 minutes, until the liquid has reduced and thickened slightly.
6 Slice the fillet on the diagonal, arrange the slices on heated serving plates and spoon over the sauce. Garnish with the rosemary.

SERVING SUGGESTION
This peppery kangaroo fillet teams well with mashed sweet potato.
VARIATION
Venison fillet can be substituted if kangaroo is difficult to find.

NUTRIENTS PER SERVING: kilojoules 1644, protein 32 g, carbohydrate 13 g (sugar 12 g), fat 12 g (saturated fat 2 g), good source of vitamin B group, and iron and zinc.

COOK'S SUGGESTION
Dried pink peppercorns can be found in specialist food stores and larger supermarkets, while native peppercorns are available from bush food suppliers.

BUSH FOOD BONANZA: *(top)* KANGAROO BURGERS; *(bottom)* KANGAROO FILLET WITH PINK AND NATIVE PEPPERCORNS.

GLAZED VENISON STEAKS

Venison steaks are given a fruity coating of port-flavoured sauce and sprinkled with crushed allspice and juniper berries before being grilled and served with a delicious root vegetable purée.

TIME: 30 MINUTES SERVES: 4

500 g large carrots
500 g swede
Salt and black pepper
3 tablespoons cranberry sauce
1 tablespoon port or red wine
1 tablespoon olive oil
4 venison steaks, about 125 g each
1 teaspoon allspice berries
10 juniper berries
2 tablespoons butter
To garnish: a handful of parsley, preferably flat-leaf

1 Put a kettle of water on to boil. Peel the carrots and swede and cut into small chunks. Put into a saucepan, cover with boiling water and add some salt. Bring back to the boil, then cover and simmer for 12 minutes or until tender.

2 Meanwhile, preheat the griller to high. Put 4 sprigs parsley aside for a garnish, then chop the rest.

3 Mix the cranberry sauce, port or wine and the oil. Place the venison steaks on the rack of the griller tray and brush half the mixture over the steaks, reserving the rest.

4 Put the allspice and juniper berries into a polythene bag and coarsely crush with a rolling pin. Sprinkle half over the steaks, then season the meat with pepper.

5 Grill the steaks for 7–8 minutes, sprinkling with salt after 5 minutes. Turn the steaks, spread with the rest of the cranberry mixture and sprinkle with the remaining spices and more black pepper. Grill for 5 minutes more, then sprinkle again with salt.

6 Drain the vegetables and return to the pan over low heat. Shake to dry off excess water, then mash with the butter and season with black pepper.

7 Serve the purée on individual plates and scatter over the chopped parsley. Add steak and garnish each plate with a parsley sprig.

SERVING SUGGESTION
This meal is complete in its own right but, if you like, you could serve a simple green vegetable, such as steamed broccoli, on the side.

NUTRIENTS PER SERVING: kilojoules 1398, protein 27 g, carbohydrate 19 g (sugar 18 g), fat 16 g (saturated fat 8 g), good source of vitamins A, B group, C and E, and iron and zinc.

VENISON SAUSAGES WITH STILTON MASH

An old favourite with a distinctive new flavour: game bangers and a designer mash of celeriac, potatoes and blue cheese are just the thing, with a bottle of hearty red wine, for a warming dinner.

TIME: 30 MINUTES SERVES: 4

| 750 g floury potatoes, such as Desirée or Kennebec |
| 400 g celeriac |
| Salt and black pepper |
| 1 tablespoon olive oil |
| 8 venison sausages, about 75 g each |
| 2 tablespoons milk |
| 2 tablespoons butter |
| 50 g Stilton cheese |
| A pinch of ground mace |
| *To serve:* mixed mustards, chutneys and pickles |

1 Put a kettle of water on to boil; preheat the oven to low. Peel the potatoes and the celeriac, cut into small chunks and put into separate saucepans. Cover both with boiling water, add salt and cook gently for 15 minutes, or until soft.

2 Meanwhile, heat the oil over moderate heat and fry the sausages for 10 minutes, turning frequently to brown well, then transfer to the oven to keep warm.

3 Drain the celeriac and purée with the milk in a blender, or by hand. Drain the potatoes, add the butter and mash by hand. Combine the celeriac and potato purées, then crumble in the Stilton cheese; season with salt, pepper and mace, and mash again.

4 Pile the purée into a warm dish and arrange the sausages around the mash or on top of it. Serve with a selection of hot and mild mustards, and chutneys and pickles.

NUTRIENTS PER SERVING: kilojoules 2139, protein 29 g, carbohydrate 41 g (sugar 4 g), fat 58 g (saturated fat 27 g), good source of vitamins A, B group, C, E and folate.

VENISON TERIYAKI WITH SWEET POTATO

Serve steak and chips with a difference! Lean, ginger-coated venison steaks are simmered in a dark, sweet-and-sour rice wine sauce and accompanied by chunky sweet potato chips.

TIME: 30 MINUTES SERVES: 4

5-cm piece fresh root ginger
1 teaspoon sea salt
4 well-trimmed venison steaks, about 125 g each
600 g sweet potatoes
Cooking oil for deep frying
2 tablespoons sake
2 tablespoons mirin (sweet sake) or sweet sherry
1½ tablespoons dark soy sauce

1 Preheat the oven to low to keep the venison warm later. Peel and grate the ginger and mix with the salt. Smear the mixture over one side of each venison steak and leave to marinate for 10 minutes.

2 Meanwhile, thinly peel the sweet potatoes and cut lengthways into long, fat chips.

3 Half fill a deep frying pan or large wok with cooking oil and heat to a temperature of 170°C on a frying thermometer, or until the oil is hot enough to brown a small cube of bread in about 45 seconds (sweet potatoes need to be fried over gentler heat than you would use for ordinary potato chips). Add the sweet potato chips and deep-fry for 12 minutes.

4 While the chips are cooking, smear another frying pan with a little cooking oil and heat until a faint haze rises from the pan. Add the venison steaks and fry for 2 minutes on each side, then remove from the pan and transfer to the oven to keep warm.

5 Pour the sake, mirin or sherry, and soy sauce into the pan and stir over the heat until the liquid

bubbles, scraping up the pan juices. Return the steaks to the pan and cook for 3 minutes on each side.

6 Drain the chips. Arrange the venison on warmed plates, pour the sauce over or alongside the steak, and serve with the chips.

NUTRIENTS PER SERVING: kilojoules 2080, protein 28 g, carbohydrate 33 g (sugar 2 g), fat 27 g (saturated fat 4 g), good source of vitamin B group, and iron and zinc.

COOK'S SUGGESTION

Bottles of sake and mirin are available from Asian food stores and many supermarkets. If you do not have them to hand, eliminate the soy sauce as well and use commercially bottled teriyaki sauce in this recipe.

PEPPERED VENISON STEAKS

Lean venison steaks with a peppery coating are served with a rich and sumptuous flambéed sauce of brandy, port and cream, spiked with aromatic juniper berries for extra flavour.

TIME: 20 MINUTES SERVES: 4

1 tablespoon black peppercorns
¼ cup plain flour
Salt
2 tablespoons olive oil
4 venison steaks, about 150 g each
6 juniper berries
2 tablespoons brandy
150 ml port
150 ml thick cream

1 Preheat the oven to low. Put the peppercorns into a polythene bag and coarsely crush with a rolling pin. Tip onto a plate, add the flour and a little salt, and mix together.
2 Heat the olive oil in a frying pan. Lightly coat the venison steaks with the seasoned flour, pressing the peppercorns firmly into the flesh. As soon as the oil is hot, fry the steaks briskly over high heat for 2½–4 minutes on each side, depending on whether you like them rare or well done.
3 Meanwhile, crush the juniper berries using the same method that you used for the peppercorns, and measure out the brandy.
4 When the steaks are done, reduce the heat, pour in the brandy and set it alight carefully, standing well back. When the flames die down, remove the steaks from the pan, put them onto a plate, then cover and keep warm in the oven.
5 Pour the port into the pan, add the juniper berries and bring to the boil, stirring and scraping up the brown residue from the bottom of the pan. Continue boiling until the sauce is reduced by half, then lower the heat; stir in the cream and cook for another 2 minutes.
6 Transfer the steaks to heated plates and serve with the sauce.

SERVING SUGGESTION
Simple accompaniments, such as new potatoes sprinkled with sea salt, and runner beans, are ideal.

NUTRIENTS PER SERVING: kilojoules 1996, protein 35 g, carbohydrate 10 g (sugar 6 g), fat 26 g (saturated fat 13 g), good source of vitamins A, B group and E, and iron and zinc.

COOK'S SUGGESTION

Most venison sold in supermarkets is farmed, and is more tender than wild venison. You can cook farmed venison steaks as you would lean beef steaks, but they are best served rare.

PASTA &
GRAINS

*Simple bases of pasta and noodles, rice, burghul,
polenta and couscous are transformed in minutes into
a feast of memorable dishes from all over the world.*

FETTUCCINE WITH BROCCOLI

A buttery Dijon mustard sauce, flavoured with basil and parsley, makes an unusual spicy dressing for ribbons of fresh egg pasta, crunchy green florets of fresh broccoli and juicy cherry tomatoes.

TIME: 20 MINUTES SERVES: 4

10 basil leaves
3 sprigs parsley
2 spring onions
2 small cloves garlic
2 tablespoons Dijon mustard
125 g softened butter
2 large heads broccoli, to give 600 g florets
2 teaspoons olive oil
Salt and black pepper
500 g fresh fettuccine or tagliatelle
To garnish: 10 cherry tomatoes

1 Put a large saucepan of water on to boil for the pasta. Finely chop the basil and parsley. Trim the spring onions; finely slice the green tops and put aside, then slice the rest. Peel and crush the garlic.

2 Blend the mustard and butter in a bowl then stir in the herbs, white spring onion and garlic, crushing them against the bottom of the bowl to release their flavours. Put aside.

3 Trim the broccoli into florets. Add the oil, salt, pasta and broccoli to the boiling water, return to the boil and cook for 4 minutes, or until the pasta is al dente. Meanwhile, halve the cherry tomatoes.

4 Thoroughly drain the pasta and broccoli. Quickly melt the flavoured butter in the pasta pan. Return the pasta and broccoli to the pan and toss gently in the butter over moderate heat until the pasta is well coated, but do not allow it to fry.

5 Transfer the pasta to a heated serving platter, season with salt and black pepper to taste, and garnish with the green spring onion tops and the tomatoes.

NUTRIENTS PER SERVING: kilojoules 1842, protein 12 g, carbohydrate 32 g (sugar 5 g), fat 30 g (saturated fat 18 g), good source of vitamins A, B group, C, E and folate.

206

PAPPARDELLE WITH CHICKEN LIVERS AND PORT

The powerful flavours of chicken livers, sage and port are combined in this rich sauce served on ribbon noodles.

TIME: 25 MINUTES SERVES: 4 AS A STARTER, 2 AS A MAIN COURSE

2 tablespoons olive oil
1 small onion
2 cloves garlic
2 large sprigs parsley
1 sage leaf
500 g fresh chicken livers
250 g fresh pappardelle or tagliatelle, or 185 g dried pasta
Salt and black pepper
2 teaspoons vegetable oil
4 tablespoons port
1 tablespoon butter

1 Bring a large saucepan of water to the boil and preheat the oven to low. Heat the olive oil in a frying pan over low heat. Peel and chop the onion and add to the oil. Peel the garlic and crush it into the pan, then leave to fry gently.
2 Chop the parsley and sage leaf and add to the frying pan.
3 Cut away any discoloured areas and tough sinews from the chicken livers, then slice into large pieces and put aside.
4 Add the pasta, some salt and the vegetable oil to the boiling water, then return to the boil and cook fresh pasta for about 3 minutes, dried for 10–12 minutes, or until al dente. Drain and keep warm.
5 Meanwhile, raise the heat under the onion, add the chicken livers and stir-fry until nicely browned. Then pour in the port and boil vigorously until the liquid has reduced by half.
6 Stir in the butter and season with salt and black pepper. Add the chicken livers to the pasta, toss gently together and serve.

SERVING SUGGESTION
For a main-course meal, serve the dish with a large green salad.

VARIATION
Duck livers can be used instead of chicken livers, and Marsala instead of the port.

NUTRIENTS PER SERVING, WHEN SERVING 4: kilojoules 1817, protein 28 g, carbohydrate 31 g (sugar 4 g), fat 21 g (saturated fat 6 g), good source of vitamins A, B group, C, E and folate, and iron and zinc.

FARFALLE WITH PESTO AND BACON

This nourishing mixture of pasta, potatoes and peas is flavoured with bacon, fried onion and pesto and given a creamy flourish with a choice of sour cream or yoghurt.

TIME: 30 MINUTES SERVES: 4

500 g boiling potatoes, such as Sebago or Pontiac
300 g smoked bacon, in one piece
1 medium onion
250 g dried farfalle (bow ties) or other small pasta shapes
Salt and black pepper
175 g frozen peas
1 tablespoon olive oil
90 g pesto
300 ml sour cream or 300 g natural yoghurt
50 g Parmesan cheese
To garnish: basil leaves

1 Bring a large saucepan of water to the boil for the pasta, and a medium one for the potatoes.

2 Peel the potatoes and cut into 1-cm dice. Discard the rind and fat, then cut the bacon into 1-cm dice. Peel and finely chop the onion.

3 Add the pasta and some salt to the large pan and cook, uncovered, for 6–10 minutes, then add the peas and cook for 4 minutes, until the pasta is al dente.

4 Add salt to the medium-sized saucepan and cook the potatoes, partially covered, over moderate heat for 7 minutes or until tender. Drain and keep hot.

5 Meanwhile, heat half the olive oil in a pan and fry the bacon over high heat, stirring frequently, for 2–3 minutes, until cooked. Transfer to a plate and put aside.

6 Heat the remaining oil in the same pan, add the onion and cook gently for 5 minutes, until soft but not brown. Return the bacon to the pan and stir in the pesto and sour cream or yoghurt. Season well with pepper, then cover and keep warm.

7 Drain the pasta and peas and return to their pan. Add the potatoes and gently stir in the bacon and pesto mixture.

8 Grate the Parmesan cheese. Serve the pasta on individual warmed plates, garnished with the basil leaves and sprinkled with the grated Parmesan.

NUTRIENTS PER SERVING: *kilojoules 3579, protein 33 g, carbohydrate 75 g (sugar 14 g), fat 48 g (saturated fat 21 g), good source of vitamins A, B group, C, E and folate, and calcium and zinc.*

COOK'S SUGGESTION

If you find it difficult to buy bacon in a piece, you can substitute smoked ham or ham steaks. Cut the ham into 1-cm dice as directed; eliminate Step 5, and add the ham to the onions in Step 6 to heat through gently.

PASTA WITH RUSTIC SAUCE

Children will love this simple family meal of chunky pasta shapes, peas, tomatoes and pork sausage meat — a fast, filling and inexpensive alternative to spaghetti bolognese.

TIME: 25 MINUTES SERVES: 4

1 medium onion
1 clove garlic
1 tablespoon olive oil
500 g lean pork sausages
2 tablespoons brandy, white wine or chicken stock
425 g canned tomato pieces, with their juice
Salt and black pepper
500 g fresh penne or 350 g dried penne
150 g frozen peas
To garnish: a small bunch of chives
To serve: Parmesan cheese

1 Bring a large saucepan of water to the boil for the pasta. Peel and coarsely chop the onion and peel and crush the garlic. Heat the oil in a large frying pan. Add the onion and garlic and cook over moderate heat for about 4 minutes, stirring occasionally, until the onion is soft.

2 Coarsely chop the sausages, or remove the skins and break up the meat with a fork. Add the sausages to the frying pan and stir over high heat for 7 minutes, or until well browned all over.

3 Add the brandy, wine or stock and the tomatoes with their juice, and season to taste with salt and pepper. Bring to the boil, reduce the heat and simmer for 10 minutes, stirring occasionally.

4 When the water comes to the boil, add the fresh pasta, peas and some salt, bring back to the boil and cook for 4–5 minutes, or until the pasta is al dente. If using dried pasta, cook for 6–7 minutes before adding the peas.

5 Meanwhile, trim and snip or chop the chives.

6 Drain the pasta and peas and toss in the tomato sauce. Taste and adjust the seasoning, garnish with the chives, and serve with freshly grated Parmesan.

NUTRIENTS PER SERVING: kilojoules 2812, protein 36 g, carbohydrate 80 g (sugar 7 g), fat 23 g (saturated fat 8 g), good source of vitamins B group, C and E, and calcium and zinc.

COOK'S SUGGESTION

The choice of sausage is crucial to the success of this dish. Use a really meaty, coarse-cut variety, or a very high-quality sausage meat from an Italian butcher.

SPAGHETTI ALLA VONGOLE

Canned clams, briefly heated in a simple tomato and white wine sauce, make a light and refreshing alternative to the heavier meat and cheese sauces for spaghetti.

TIME: 30 MINUTES   SERVES: 4–6

1½ tablespoons olive oil
1 large clove garlic
425 g canned tomato pieces, with their juice
290 g canned clams (vongole)
3 tablespoons dry white wine
350 g dried spaghetti
Salt and black pepper
To garnish: parsley, optional

1 Bring a large saucepan of water to the boil for the pasta. Meanwhile, heat the olive oil in a saucepan. Peel the garlic and crush it into the oil, sizzle briefly, then add the canned tomatoes and their juice.

2 Drain the clams, reserving the liquid. Put the clams aside. Add half the liquid to the tomatoes, along with the wine; cook over moderate heat, stirring occasionally, for 20 minutes, or until the mixture is reduced to a thick sauce.

3 When the saucepan of water comes to the boil, add the spaghetti, some salt, and the remaining liquid from the clams, if you wish. Return to the boil and cook the spaghetti, uncovered, for 10–12 minutes, until al dente.

4 While the pasta is cooking, chop enough parsley, if using, to give about 2 tablespoons.

5 Stir the clams into the thickened tomato sauce and heat through gently, without allowing the sauce to boil. Season to taste with salt and black pepper.

6 Drain the spaghetti, transfer to a serving bowl or individual plates and spoon the clam sauce on top. Sprinkle with parsley, if using. It is not usual to serve grated cheese with fish sauces for pasta.

VARIATION
If you prefer, canned tuna or peeled prawns could be added to the sauce instead of clams.

NUTRIENTS PER SERVING, WHEN SERVING 4: kilojoules 1737, protein 18 g, carbohydrate 70 g (sugar 6 g), fat 8 g (saturated fat 1 g), good source of vitamins B group, C and E, and iron.

FUSILLI WITH HAM AND GORGONZOLA

A scattering of crunchy poppy seeds tops a powerful smoked ham and blue cheese sauce that is softened with button mushrooms and freshly grated nutmeg and swirled over pretty pasta spirals.

TIME: 25 MINUTES   SERVES: 4

200 g thickly sliced smoked ham
250 g button mushrooms
1 cup thick cream
¼ teaspoon freshly grated nutmeg
Salt and black pepper
500 g fresh fusilli (twists) or other small pasta shapes
60 g Gorgonzola cheese
A few sprigs of flat-leaf parsley
1½ teaspoons poppy seeds

EASY DOES IT!

Grating fresh nutmeg straight into a dish gives the food far more flavour than using the ready-ground variety.

1 Bring a large saucepan of water to the boil. Trim off and discard any excess fat and rind from the ham, then cut the meat into small cubes or lardons.

2 Clean and slice the mushrooms. Put into a heavy, medium-sized saucepan with the cream, nutmeg and some black pepper. Bring to the boil, reduce the heat to moderate and cook, stirring frequently, until the cream starts to thicken.

3 Add the pasta and some salt to the saucepan of boiling water, then bring back to the boil and cook gently, uncovered, for 3–5 minutes, until al dente.

4 Meanwhile, crumble the cheese into small pieces and finely chop the parsley.

5 When the cream has thickened enough to coat the back of a spoon, remove the pan from the heat, add the cheese and stir until it melts.

6 Add the ham to the sauce, then return the pan to the heat and warm through gently. Stir in the chopped parsley and put the sauce aside to keep warm.

7 Drain the pasta, transfer to a serving bowl and sprinkle with the poppy seeds. Pour over the sauce, toss gently and serve.

NUTRIENTS PER SERVING: kilojoules 2733, protein 25 g, carbohydrate 56 g (sugar 3 g), fat 39 g (saturated fat 22 g), good source of vitamins A, B group and E.

TWO EASY PASTA DISHES: (*top*) SPAGHETTI ALLA VONGOLE; (*bottom*) FUSILLI WITH HAM AND GORGONZOLA.

PAGLIA E FIENO WITH SMOKED SALMON

Italians call this combination of yellow and green pasta 'straw and hay' because of its colours.
It looks especially pretty served with richly flavoured smoked salmon in a wine sauce.

TIME: 25 MINUTES SERVES: 6 AS A
STARTER, 4 AS A MAIN COURSE

1 small onion
6 tablespoons white wine or dry vermouth
375 g fresh paglia e fieno or other narrow yellow and green pasta such as linguine or fettuccine, or 300 g dried yellow and green pasta
Salt and black pepper
350 g smoked salmon or smoked salmon trimmings
4 large sprigs dill
2 teaspoons capers

1 Bring a large saucepan of water to the boil for the pasta. Peel and finely chop the onion and put aside.
2 Bring the wine or vermouth to the boil in a frying pan and boil for 1–2 minutes, until the liquid has reduced by half. Stir in the chopped onion and cook until softened, then reduce the heat to very low.
3 Add the pasta and some salt to the saucepan of boiling water. Return to the boil, then cook the fresh pasta for 4–5 minutes, or the dried pasta for 10–12 minutes, until al dente.
4 While the pasta is cooking, cut the smoked salmon into small strips. Add to the onion and wine mixture in the frying pan and heat through very gently.
5 Chop the dill. Rinse, dry and roughly chop the capers. Stir into the onion and salmon mixture in the frying pan.
6 As soon as the pasta is cooked, drain well and transfer to a large serving bowl.

7 Season the salmon mixture with black pepper to taste (it won't need any salt), then spoon over the pasta. Stir gently and serve.

VARIATION
If you cannot find fresh dill, use mint or flat-leaf parsley instead, while diced green olives or gherkins would make an agreeable substitute for the capers.

SERVING SUGGESTION
Serve the pasta as a starter, or turn it into a substantial main course by adding a mixed green side salad or a plate of thinly sliced tomatoes with fennel, black olives and lemon and olive oil dressing.

NUTRIENTS PER SERVING, WHEN SERVING 6:
kilojoules 1042, protein 21 g, carbohydrate 31 g (sugar 1 g), fat 4 g (saturated fat 0.8 g), good source of vitamin B group.

FETTUCINE WITH CRAB AND FRESH ASPARAGUS

Creamy crab meat and crisp chunks of green asparagus are added to chopped parsley and sage and tossed through a pot of freshly cooked, steaming pasta.

TIME: 30 MINUTES SERVES: 4–6

75 g Parmesan cheese	
A bunch of flat-leaf parsley	
A few sprigs of sage	
500 g fresh fettucine	
Salt and black pepper	
2 bunches asparagus	
200 g fresh cooked crab meat	
3 tablespoons olive oil	

1 Put both a kettle of water and a large saucepan of water on to boil. Shave the Parmesan and put aside. Finely chop enough parsley to give ½ cup and enough sage leaves to give 1 tablespoon; put both aside.
2 Add the fettucine and some salt to the saucepan of boiling water. Return to the boil and cook for 2–3 minutes, until al dente.
3 Meanwhile, trim and halve the asparagus, cut diagonally into 7-cm lengths and blanch for 3 minutes in boiling water from the kettle. Drain and put aside.
4 When the pasta is ready, drain and return to the cooking pot. Add the asparagus, crab meat, oil, parsley and sage; toss well.
5 Spoon the pasta into heated bowls and top with the shaved Parmesan and a generous grinding of black pepper.

NUTRIENTS PER SERVING, WHEN SERVING 4:
kilojoules 1635, protein 21 g, carbohydrate 33 g (sugar 2 g), fat 20 g (saturated fat 6 g), good source of vitamins B group and C, and calcium, iron, potassium and iodine.

COOK'S SUGGESTION

Dried pasta can be used if fresh is difficult to find. Allow two to three times the cooking time, and start taste-testing after 5 minutes.

PASTA WITH BROAD BEANS, ARTICHOKES AND SPINACH

Small pasta shapes and a tasty selection of assorted vegetables make this sturdy casserole perfect for a family dinner.

TIME: 30 MINUTES SERVES: 4

2 tablespoons olive oil
1 medium onion
1 large clove garlic
1 medium red capsicum
200 g dried pasta shapes (bow ties, shells or rigatoni)
Salt and black pepper
425 g canned tomato pieces, with their juice
A pinch of dried oregano
½ teaspoon brown sugar
250 g frozen broad beans
350 g young spinach or silverbeet
400 g canned artichoke hearts

To serve: Parmesan cheese, crusty Italian bread loaf

1 Bring a large saucepan of water to the boil, and preheat the oven to its lowest setting. Heat the oil in another large saucepan. Peel and roughly chop the onion, then peel and crush the garlic. Add both to the oil and fry gently for 5 minutes, until soft.

2 Halve, seed and slice the capsicum. Add to the onion and fry for a further 2 minutes.

3 Add the pasta and some salt to the boiling water. Return to the boil and cook for 10–12 minutes, until the pasta is al dente.

4 Stir the tomatoes, oregano, sugar and some black pepper into the onion, garlic and red capsicum. Bring to the boil, then partially cover and simmer the sauce for about 10 minutes.

5 Put the bread loaf into the oven to heat through. Add the broad beans to the tomato sauce, return to the boil and simmer for 3 minutes.

6 Rinse and drain the spinach or silverbeet, then remove any tough stalks and add the leaves to the sauce; cook for 1 more minute.

7 Drain and quarter the artichoke hearts. Drain the pasta. Add both to the sauce and heat through for another 1–2 minutes.

8 Turn the pasta and sauce into a warm serving bowl, grate or shave some Parmesan cheese over the top and serve with the hot bread.

NUTRIENTS PER SERVING: kilojoules 3185, protein 26 g, carbohydrate 92 g (sugar 16 g), fat 32 g (saturated fat 6 g), good source of vitamins A, B group, C, E and folate, and calcium.

COOK'S SUGGESTION

You can use canned artichoke bottoms (fonds d'artichaut), the nutty-tasting chunk from the bottom of the artichoke that has no leaves attached, instead of artichoke hearts, if you prefer. Cut them into slices instead of into quarters and add to the casserole as before.

TAGLIATELLE WITH BREADCRUMBS

Pine nuts and freshly toasted breadcrumbs provide a tasty crunch in this extraordinarily frugal pasta combination.

TIME: 30 MINUTES SERVES: 4

350 g crusty white bread
A bunch of flat-leaf parsley
A few sprigs of oregano
A few chives
½ cup extra virgin olive oil
3 cloves garlic
⅓ cup pine nuts
Salt and black pepper
500 g fresh tagliatelle
To serve: 60 g Parmesan cheese

1 Bring a saucepan of water to the boil for the pasta. Remove and discard the crusts from the bread, break into pieces and reduce to crumbs in a food processor.

2 Chop enough parsley to give 4 tablespoons and enough oregano and chives to give 1½ tablespoons of each. Add to the breadcrumbs and process briefly to combine well.

3 Heat 3 tablespoons oil in a frying pan over moderate heat. Peel the garlic and crush it into the oil. Add the pine nuts and stir in the breadcrumb mixture. Season to taste and stir for 5–6 minutes, until the breadcrumbs are lightly browned but still quite soft, then remove the pan from the heat and keep warm.

4 Meanwhile, add the pasta and some salt to the pan of boiling water. Return to the boil and cook for 3–4 minutes, or until al dente. Grate the Parmesan into a serving dish and put aside.

5 Drain the pasta thoroughly and place in a large serving bowl with the remaining oil. Toss well, then add the breadcrumb mixture and toss again. Serve accompanied by the Parmesan, either scattered on top or in a separate bowl.

SERVING SUGGESTION
A simple tomato salad seasoned with black pepper and scattered with torn basil leaves would go well with this dish.

NUTRIENTS PER SERVING: kilojoules 4089, protein 29 g, carbohydrate 106 g (sugar 4 g), fat 52 g (saturated fat 9 g), good source of vitamins B group and E, and calcium, selenium and zinc.

DUCK CHOW MEIN

Chow mein, which means fried noodles, makes the perfect base for fresh vegetables and fresh or cooked meat. Stir-fried duck and slightly sweet hoisin sauce give this version a rich flavour.

TIME: 30 MINUTES SERVES: 4

1 cup vegetable or chicken stock
250 g Chinese noodles
3–4 duck breast fillets, about 400 g in total
2 tablespoons soy sauce
1 clove garlic
3 large spring onions
300 g mixed vegetables, such as Chinese cabbage, carrots, broccoli, red capsicum and leeks
2 tablespoons peanut oil
125 g baby corn
2 tablespoons hoisin sauce
1 teaspoon cornflour
50 g bean sprouts

1 Put a kettle of water on to boil. Put the stock on to heat and preheat the oven to low.

2 Put the noodles into a bowl, cover with boiling water and leave to soak for 6 minutes, or cook according to the packet instructions.
3 Remove the duck skin and cut the flesh into 1-cm x 7.5-cm strips. Put into a bowl with 1 tablespoon soy sauce and mix.
4 Peel and chop the garlic, trim and slice the spring onions; put aside. Trim and slice the mixed vegetables into matchstick-sized strips. Drain and rinse the noodles.
5 Heat half the oil in a large wok or frying pan. Add the duck and stir-fry for 4–5 minutes. Transfer to a dish and keep warm in the oven.
6 Heat the remaining oil in the wok or frying pan. Add the garlic and spring onions, mixed vegetables and corn, and stir-fry for 15 seconds

in the wok, or for 30 seconds in the frying pan.
7 Return the duck to the pan, add the hoisin sauce and the hot stock and simmer for a few minutes.
8 Blend the cornflour with 1 teaspoon cold water and stir into the pan, along with the bean sprouts. Cook for 1–2 minutes, then add the noodles and the remaining soy sauce. Toss well, reheat for 3–5 minutes, then serve.
VARIATION
Chicken breast fillets, or a mixture of beef and chicken strips, can be used instead of the duck.

NUTRIENTS PER SERVING: kilojoules 3202, protein 25 g, carbohydrate 59 g (sugar 8 g), fat 50 g (saturated fat 13 g), good source of vitamins A, B group, C, E and folate, and zinc.

217

VEGETABLE COUSCOUS

Sweet winter vegetables and chick peas, mingled with dried apricots and Middle Eastern spices, make a warm and comforting topping to serve with the grains of couscous.

TIME: 30 MINUTES   SERVES: 2

1 small onion
3 teaspoons butter
3 teaspoons olive oil
2 small carrots
½ small swede
1 medium parsnip
A pinch of cayenne pepper
A pinch of ground turmeric
½ teaspoon ground ginger
½ teaspoon ground cinnamon
A pinch of saffron threads, optional
Salt and black pepper
½ cup dried apricots
⅓ cup frozen baby peas
⅓ cup canned chick peas
⅔ cup couscous
To garnish: 2 sprigs coriander

1 Put a kettle of water on to boil. Peel and chop the onion. Heat the butter and olive oil in a large, heavy flameproof casserole. Add the onion and fry gently until soft.

2 Meanwhile, peel the carrots, swede and parsnip. Cut into 1-cm chunks and add to the onions. Stir in the cayenne, turmeric, ginger, cinnamon and the saffron threads, if using, and season to taste with salt and black pepper.

3 Chop the apricots and add them, along with the baby peas. Drain, rinse and add the chick peas. Add 300 ml boiling water and bring back to the boil. Reduce the heat, cover and simmer for 15 minutes.

4 Meanwhile, pour 1 cup boiling water into a saucepan, add the couscous and stir, then turn off the heat and leave to stand, covered, until the vegetables are ready.

5 When the vegetables are cooked, season the couscous to taste with salt and pepper. Break up with a fork and transfer to a serving dish. Spoon the vegetables over the top, garnish with coriander and serve.

VARIATION

Other fresh root vegetables, such as celeriac, potatoes or turnips, make excellent substitutes for the carrots, swede or parsnip.

NUTRIENTS PER SERVING: kilojoules 2511, protein 20 g, carbohydrate 95 g (sugar 37 g), fat 17 g (saturated fat 5 g), good source of vitamins A, B group, C, E and folate, and calcium and iron.

COUSCOUS WITH PRAWNS AND MINT

Couscous is a wonderfully useful basis for any number of quick meals, because while it is soaking you have time to cook some little delicacies, such as these fresh prawns, to serve with it.

TIME: 25 MINUTES SERVES: 4

1 ¾ cups fish or chicken stock
2 shallots
1 clove garlic
350 g small zucchini
2 tablespoons olive oil
Salt and black pepper
1 ¼ cups couscous
A handful of mint
250 g peeled cooked prawns
To serve: harissa, optional

1 Bring the stock to the boil in a saucepan. Peel and chop the shallots and the garlic. Trim and thinly slice the zucchini.
2 Heat 1 ½ tablespoons oil in a frying pan, add the shallots, garlic and zucchini, stir to coat with oil, then fry for 4 minutes until slightly softened. Season to taste with salt and black pepper.
3 Add the boiling stock, return to the boil then stir in the couscous. Remove from the heat, cover and leave to stand for 10 minutes, until the stock is absorbed.
4 Chop the mint and put aside. Heat the remaining olive oil in a small frying pan. Stir in the prawns and heat through gently.
5 Add the prawns and mint to the couscous, stir and season to taste with salt and black pepper. Serve accompanied by a side dish of harissa, if using.

NUTRIENTS PER SERVING: kilojoules 1168, protein 18 g, carbohydrate 31 g (sugar 2 g), fat 10 g (saturated fat 1 g), good source of vitamins B group, C, E and folate, and iron.

COOK'S SUGGESTION

If you like spicy food, you will enjoy harissa, a fiery sauce made with red chillies, garlic and olive oil. Harissa can be found in Middle Eastern food shops, some Asian grocers, and larger supermarkets.

POLENTA AND TOMATO TART

Polenta and Parmesan are made to go together; here the mix is topped with slices of succulent tomatoes, shredded basil and crisply cooked prosciutto.

TIME: 30 MINUTES SERVES: 4–6

3 cups chicken stock
1 cup coarse polenta
50 g Parmesan cheese
3 tablespoons unsalted butter
¼ cup virgin olive oil
6 vine-ripened tomatoes
A small bunch of basil
Black pepper
1 tablespoon caster sugar
4 slices prosciutto

1 Preheat the griller. Bring the stock to the boil in a large saucepan then gradually stir in the polenta. Cook over low heat for about 10 minutes, stirring constantly, until the polenta is smooth and thick. Remove from the heat.

2 Grate the Parmesan cheese to give 3 tablespoons. Add, along with the butter, to the polenta and press the mixture into a lightly oiled 23-cm flan dish. Brush the top with a little olive oil and refrigerate for 10 minutes.

3 Finely slice the tomatoes and shred enough basil leaves to give about 4 tablespoons. Put aside.

4 When the polenta has firmed, place the flan dish under the griller and cook for 7 minutes, until golden. Remove the flan dish but leave the griller on.

5 Arrange the tomatoes on top of the polenta and scatter over the basil. Season the tomatoes with pepper, sprinkle with sugar, drizzle over the remaining oil and top with the prosciutto. Put the tart back under the griller for 5 minutes, until the prosciutto is crisp. Cut into wedges and serve immediately.

SERVING SUGGESTION
This tart is superb served on its own for a light meal. It also teams well with a plainly grilled steak.

NUTRIENTS PER SERVING, WHEN SERVING 4: kilojoules 1925, protein 12 g, carbohydrate 34 g (sugar 8 g), fat 30 g (saturated fat 12 g), good source of vitamins B group and C.

COOK'S SUGGESTION

Good-quality, coarsely ground polenta should be used; 'instant' polenta will not give the same result.

POLENTA WITH PROVOLONE

In this versatile, colourful and substantial version of an Italian favourite, the creamy grains are given the extra flavours of cheese and olives, along with your choice of herbs and crushed peppercorns.

TIME: 20 MINUTES SERVES: 4

1 ⅓ cups instant polenta
A small bunch of sage, oregano, basil or parsley
200 g Provolone or Gruyère cheese
2 teaspoons black or mixed peppercorns
1 teaspoon salt
8 – 10 pitted black olives

1 Put the polenta into a saucepan with 3½ cups water. Place over high heat, bring to the boil, then reduce the heat and simmer for 10 minutes, stirring frequently with a large wooden spoon or paddle to remove any lumps.

2 Meanwhile, strip the leaves from the sage, oregano, basil or parsley, and chop finely. Grate or dice the cheese and crush the peppercorns. Finely chop the black olives.

3 When the polenta becomes thick and starts to stiffen, stir in the herb, grated cheese, peppercorns, salt and the olives. Beat vigorously until the cheese is incorporated and the mixture begins to leave the sides of the saucepan when stirred.

4 Serve immediately, or leave to stand for 5–10 minutes to stiffen further. It will remain hot.

SERVING SUGGESTION
While the polenta is standing, make a green leaf salad (as photographed) or steam vegetables such as snow peas or fennel, to serve alongside. For a vegetarian feast, serve with Spinach and Baby Corn Salad (page 105), Italian Baked Chicory (page 264) and roasted vegetables.

NUTRIENTS PER SERVING: kilojoules 1096, protein 9 g, carbohydrate 46 g (sugar 10 g), fat 2 g (saturated fat 1 g), good source of vitamins B group and E.

EASY DOES IT!

For everyday meals, the polenta can be served straight from the saucepan into a serving dish. For a more stylish presentation, you can mould it into rounded quenelle shapes, using two large metal spoons.

A PERFECT POLENTA PAIR: *(top)* POLENTA AND TOMATO TART; *(bottom)* POLENTA WITH PROVOLONE.

SUMMER SQUASH WITH POLENTA

This colourful and adaptable stew is an excellent way to deal with a glut of ripe summer vegetables.

1 ½ cups instant polenta
2 tablespoons olive oil
1 small onion
1 clove garlic
500 g mixed yellow and green pattypan squash and/or young green and yellow zucchini
4 sprigs thyme
Salt and black pepper
200 g Cheshire or Cheddar cheese
1 tablespoon butter
2 large tomatoes
1 lemon
A few sprigs of parsley

1 Put the polenta into a saucepan with 3 cups water. Bring to the boil, reduce the heat and simmer for 8 minutes. Stir occasionally to remove any lumps.

2 Slowly heat the olive oil in a shallow pan over moderate heat. Halve, peel and finely chop the onion, peel and crush the garlic and cook for 5–8 minutes, until soft.

3 Meanwhile, top and tail the squash and/or the zuchini. Cut the squash into quarters, the zucchini into rounds, and add to the onions. Add the thyme, salt and pepper, and cook for 10 minutes.

4 When the polenta comes away cleanly from the sides of the pan, remove from the heat. Grate the cheese and beat it into the polenta along with the butter, then season to taste, cover and keep warm.

5 Dice the tomatoes and add to the other vegetables.

6 Finely grate the lemon rind and finely chop the parsley. Add both to the vegetables. Remove and discard the thyme.

7 Serve the stewed vegetables on individual plates, with a portion of polenta on the side.

VARIATION

For extra flavour, add eggplants or red and yellow capsicums, or enrich the stew with a little crème fraîche.

NUTRIENTS PER SERVING: kilojoules 2030, protein 18 g, carbohydrate 39 g (sugar 15 g), fat 29 g (saturated fat 14 g), good source of vitamins A, B group, C, E and folate, and calcium.

222

BURGHUL PILAF WITH MUSHROOMS

A bed of healthy grains simmered in stock is mixed with a selection of fresh mushrooms, nuts and parsley for a sustaining dish that can also be served as an accompaniment.

TIME: 30 MINUTES SERVES: 4

| 1 onion |
| 125 g butter |
| 350 g burghul |
| 3 ½ cups vegetable stock |
| 250 g mixed mushrooms, such as button, oyster and shiitake |
| A small bunch of parsley |
| 3 teaspoons olive oil |
| Salt and black pepper |
| ⅓ cup flaked almonds |
| ⅓ cup chopped hazelnuts |

1 Halve, peel and finely chop the onion. Heat half the butter in a flameproof casserole, add the onion and fry until translucent.
2 Add the burghul to the casserole and cook, stirring frequently, for 3 minutes. Add the stock, bring to the boil, then reduce the heat, cover the casserole and simmer gently for about 10–15 minutes, until all the stock has been absorbed.
3 Meanwhile, clean and finely slice the mushrooms. Finely chop the parsley and put aside.
4 Heat the oil in a frying pan, add the sliced mushrooms and fry until softened. Season with salt and black pepper. Pour the mushrooms and any juices on top of the partially cooked burghul, cover the casserole again and leave to continue cooking.
5 Add the flaked almonds to the frying pan and shake over moderate heat for 1–2 minutes, then add the chopped hazelnuts and cook both until lightly browned.

6 When the stock is absorbed and the burghul cooked, stir in the remaining butter, the toasted nuts and the parsley. Taste for seasoning, adding more salt and pepper if necessary, and serve the pilaf straight from the casserole.

NUTRIENTS PER SERVING: kilojoules 3064, protein 15 g, carbohydrate 73 g (sugar 3 g), fat 44 g (saturated fat 17 g), good source of vitamins A, B group and E, and iron.

COOK'S SUGGESTION

Burghul, traditionally used in Middle Eastern dishes such as tabbouleh, is hulled, parboiled cracked wheat. It is also sold as bulgar and bulgur.

SAFFRON PILAF WITH RAISINS AND NUTS

This delicately scented Eastern pilaf provides the perfect base for tender broad beans doused in spicy chilli oil and served with a thick sauce of creamy yoghurt spiked with fresh coriander.

TIME: 30 MINUTES SERVES: 4–6

2 cups long-grain rice
2 tablespoons butter
1 medium red onion
2 cloves garlic
1 teaspoon ground coriander
2 teaspoons ground cumin
1 cinnamon stick
A pinch of saffron threads
⅓ cup seedless raisins
Salt and black pepper
500 g frozen broad beans
½ cup flaked almonds
150 g natural yoghurt
A few sprigs of coriander
1–2 tablespoons chilli-flavoured olive oil, optional

1 Put a kettle of water on to boil. Put the rice into a bowl, cover with cold water and leave to soak, to remove some of the starch.

2 Melt the butter in a heavy-based saucepan over very low heat. Peel and chop the onion and garlic and add to the pan. Increase the heat and fry for 1–2 minutes or until the onion softens. Stir in the ground coriander and cumin and reduce the heat to very low.

3 Pour the rice into a sieve and rinse. Add to the onion and stir in 1½ cups boiling water. Add the cinnamon stick, saffron threads, raisins, salt and pepper.

4 Bring the water to a fast boil, then reduce the heat until barely simmering. Cover and cook the rice for 15 minutes; do not lift the lid.

5 Meanwhile, put the broad beans into a saucepan, cover with boiling water and bring back to the boil. Reduce the heat, cover and simmer for 5–6 minutes.

6 Lightly toast the almonds and put aside. Put the yoghurt into a bowl, chop the coriander, then stir it into the yoghurt.

7 Drain the broad beans and drizzle with the oil, if using.

8 Remove the rice from the heat and leave to stand, still covered, for 3 minutes. Then add the almonds and broad beans and fluff up with a fork. Serve the rice accompanied by the bowl of yoghurt.

NUTRIENTS PER SERVING, WHEN SERVING 4: kilojoules 2704, protein 18 g, carbohydrate 84 g (sugar 16 g), fat 27 g (saturated fat 9 g), good source of vitamins B group, C, E and folate.

EGG-TOPPED KEDGEREE

For brunch with a touch of the Raj, poached eggs add a melting richness to the rice, smoked fish and prawns in this famous colonial dish.

TIME: 30 MINUTES SERVES: 4

2 cups long-grain rice
Salt and black pepper
3 tablespoons butter
1 small onion
250 g skinned smoked haddock fillet
1 tablespoon Indian curry powder
A few sprigs of parsley
1 tablespoon white wine vinegar
4 large eggs
8 anchovy fillets
20 capers
½ lemon
125 g peeled cooked prawns

1 Put a kettle of water on to boil. Put the rice into a saucepan, add salt and enough boiling water to cover well. Return to the boil, cover and cook gently for 15 minutes.

2 Meanwhile, melt the butter in a large saucepan. Peel and chop the onion and fry in the butter for a few minutes until soft.

3 Place the haddock in a shallow dish and cover with boiling water. Leave to stand for 2–3 minutes, then drain well. Flake the fish into chunks, removing any bones, then add to the onion, along with the curry powder. Cook for 5 minutes. Chop the parsley and put aside.

4 Fill a frying pan with about 6 cm water, add the vinegar, and heat until boiling gently. Poach the eggs for about 3 minutes, or until set but still soft in the centres.

5 While the eggs are poaching, chop the anchovy fillets and capers, and squeeze 1 tablespoon juice from the half lemon.

6 Drain the rice, stir it into the fish, add the prawns and heat through gently. Season to taste with salt and pepper, then spoon out the kedgeree onto individual plates or shallow bowls.

7 Sprinkle the rice with the parsley, anchovies, capers and lemon juice. Make a hollow in each serving and top with a poached egg.

NUTRIENTS PER SERVING: kilojoules 2394, protein 33 g, carbohydrate 58 g (sugar 1 g), fat 23 g (saturated fat 11 g), good source of vitamins A, B group and E.

ONE-DISH RICE MEALS: *(top)* SAFFRON PILAF WITH RAISINS AND NUTS; *(bottom)* EGG-TOPPED KEDGEREE.

PRAWN PILAF

Finely spiced rice, turned a tempting golden colour with threads of fragrant saffron, needs only a handful of swiftly cooked prawns and some fresh herbs to become a memorable dish.

TIME: 30 MINUTES SERVES: 4

3 cups fish stock
1 small onion
1 tablespoon butter
1½ tablespoons olive oil
1 clove garlic
2 dried red chillies
1½ cups long-grain rice, such as basmati
A pinch of saffron threads
3 bay leaves
500 g peeled green prawns
Salt and black pepper
To garnish: a few sprigs of flat-leaf parsley or dill

1 Bring the stock to the boil in a saucepan. Peel and thinly slice the onion. Heat the butter and oil in a large saucepan, then add the onion.
2 Peel and slice the garlic, crumble the chillies, add to the pan and stir-fry for a few minutes. Then add the rice and stir to coat in the oil.
3 Add the saffron and fish stock to the pan, return to the boil, then add the bay leaves, prawns and some salt. Cover, reduce the heat and simmer for 10 minutes, then remove from the heat and stand, covered, for 4 minutes.
4 Chop the parsley or dill. Spoon the prawn pilaf onto a serving dish,

season with salt and pepper to taste, and garnish with the chopped parsley or dill.

NUTRIENTS PER SERVING: kilojoules 1674, protein 27 g, carbohydrate 46 g (sugar 1 g), fat 12 g (saturated fat 4 g), good source of vitamins B group and E, and iodine.

COOK'S SUGGESTION

Saffron threads are expensive, but only a very few are needed to infuse a dish with its superb colour and aroma. Stored in a dry, dark place, saffron threads will never go off.

EGG FRIED RICE

The inspiration for this recipe comes from one of the most popular Cantonese dishes and, as the vegetables can be varied endlessly according to the season, it is always fresh and different.

TIME: 30 MINUTES SERVES: 4

2 cups long-grain rice, such as basmati
Salt
2 tablespoons vegetable oil
4 medium eggs
250 g rindless bacon rashers
3 medium carrots
8 spring onions
2 cloves garlic
200 g frozen baby peas
200 g bean sprouts
250 g peeled cooked prawns
3 tablespoons soy sauce
3 tablespoons sake or dry sherry
3 tablespoons mirin (sweet sake) or 1 teaspoon honey
1 tablespoon sesame seed oil

1 Put a kettle of water on to boil. Put the rice into a pan with a little salt, add 3 cups boiling water and 1 teaspoon vegetable oil. Bring back to the boil, reduce the heat, cover the pan and simmer the rice for 10–15 minutes.

2 While the rice is cooking, heat 1 tablespoon vegetable oil in a wok or large frying pan. Beat the eggs lightly and pour into the pan or wok, tipping the mixture to make a thin omelette. Cook the eggs over moderate heat until set, then turn the omelette onto a plate to cool.

3 Trim the bacon rashers, discarding the fat, and cut the meat into strips. Add the remaining oil to the pan and fry the bacon over moderate heat until crisp.

4 Peel and dice the carrots, add to the bacon, reduce the heat and leave to fry gently. Trim the spring onions, slice into rounds and add to the pan. Peel the garlic and crush it in, and stir in the baby peas.

5 Rinse and drain the bean sprouts and add to the pan. Turn up the heat, stir-fry for 1 minute, then add the prawns.

6 Transfer half the mixture to another wok or large frying pan. Drain the rice and slice the omelette into thin strips; divide both equally between the two pans.

7 Add half the soy sauce, half the sake or sherry and half the mirin or honey to each pan. Then add half the sesame oil to each. Mix together thoroughly and stir-fry over high heat for 5 minutes, or until the mixture is dry. Serve immediately.

VARIATION

For a vegetarian version, use water chestnuts and bamboo shoots instead of bacon and prawns.

NUTRIENTS PER SERVING: *kilojoules 3081, protein 44 g, carbohydrate 68 g (sugar 7 g), fat 28 g (saturated fat 5.5 g), good source of vitamins A, B group and folate, and iron, selenium and zinc.*

COOK'S SUGGESTION

While dividing the rice between two woks or frying pans may seem to complicate the procedure, you'll find that doing so prevents the mixture from steaming instead of frying and – as an extra bonus – also shortens the cooking time.

SPANISH RICE WITH CHORIZO AND SAGE

Turmeric gives a golden glow to this hearty dish, where the rice, vegetables and sausage are all cooked in one pan.

TIME: 30 MINUTES   SERVES: 4

1¼ cups chicken stock
2 tablespoons olive oil
1 medium red onion
1 clove garlic
1 medium red capsicum
1⅓ cups long-grain rice
1 teaspoon turmeric
425 g canned tomato pieces, with their juice
Salt and black pepper
200 g chorizo sausage
A small bunch of sage
200 g frozen peas

1 Put the chicken stock on to heat in a small saucepan. Heat the olive oil in a wide frying pan.
2 Peel and chop the onion and garlic, add to the frying pan and cook over fairly high heat for about 3 minutes, stirring frequently, until the onion is soft.
3 While the onion and garlic are frying, halve, seed and roughly chop the capsicum. Add to the pan, along with the rice and turmeric, and stir-fry for 3 minutes.
4 Add the heated stock, the canned tomatoes with their juice, and season to taste with salt and black pepper. Bring to the boil, reduce the heat, cover the pan and simmer, stirring occasionally, for about 5 minutes.
5 Cut the chorizo into fairly thick chunks, then stir into the rice and cook for another 5 minutes.
6 Roughly chop the sage and add to the rice, along with the peas. Return to the boil, then reduce the heat and simmer for 5 minutes until the rice is tender and has absorbed most of the liquid. If the mixture dries out before the rice is cooked, add a little more stock, or some dry white wine. Serve the rice hot, straight from the cooking pan.

VARIATION
Kabanos, or a spicy salami cut into thick slices, can be used instead of chorizo, if you wish.

NUTRIENTS PER SERVING: kilojoules 1745, protein 15 g, carbohydrate 53 g (sugar 7 g), fat 14 g (saturated fat 4 g), good source of vitamins A, B group, C, E and folate.

EMERALD RISOTTO

Young tender leaves of baby spinach have a vivid colour and an extra-fresh flavour that is packed with goodness. Try this risotto for a healthy meal that requires little from the cook except stirring.

TIME: 30 MINUTES   SERVES: 4

5 cups vegetable stock or 5 cups water and 3 tablespoons vegetable stock powder
4 tablespoons white wine
250 g baby spinach
3 tablespoons virgin olive oil
1 small onion
2 cloves garlic
2 cups risotto rice (arborio, carnaroli or vialone)
Salt and black pepper
Whole nutmeg for grating

1 Bring the stock to the boil in a saucepan, or bring the water to the boil and stir in the stock powder. Add the wine, reduce the heat and leave to simmer.

2 Rinse the spinach leaves, chop roughly and put aside.

3 Heat the oil in a large saucepan or wok. Peel and finely chop the onion and garlic and fry gently for 2–3 minutes, until soft but not brown. Then add the rice and stir-fry until the grains are translucent and coated with oil.

4 Add a ladleful of stock, adjust the heat to maintain a gentle boil, and stir until most of the liquid has been absorbed. Keep adding stock, a ladleful at a time, and stir constantly for about 15 minutes, until the rice is almost cooked.

5 Add the spinach and more stock and stir until the rice is cooked – risotto rice should retain a bite, but the mixture should be of a soft, dropping consistency.

6 Season to taste with salt, pepper and grated nutmeg (see page 210). Serve straight from the pan.

SERVING SUGGESTION
Add a mixed-leaf salad and some walnut or olive bread.

VARIATION
Emerald Risotto is a vegan meal, but for a non-vegan dish you can add 2–3 tablespoons freshly grated Parmesan cheese before serving.

NUTRIENTS PER SERVING: kilojoules 1875, protein 8 g, carbohydrate 73 g (sugar 2 g), fat 14 g (saturated fat 2 g), good source of vitamins A, B group, C, E and folate.

COOK'S SUGGESTION

Italian risotto rice is a fat grain which absorbs the cooking liquid. Never wash the rice before cooking, because it is the starch in the grains that gives risotto its lovely creamy texture.

MEATLESS
MAIN DISHES

Explore the dazzling variety of fresh vegetables now available, used imaginatively in fabulous omelettes, gratins, fritters, pizzas and tarts – all designed to please the palate.

VEGETABLE PRIMAVERA

The secret of this dish lies in the light cooking of a mixture of fine spring vegetables, which gives them a crisp texture and fresh flavour, and contrasts agreeably with the stuffed pasta.

TIME: 30 MINUTES SERVES: 4

200 g baby carrots
150 g baby corn cobs
200 g small green beans
Salt and black pepper
250 g small zucchini
A small handful of parsley
or chervil
400 g fresh ricotta
and spinach tortellini
3 teaspoons olive oil
½ lemon
1 tablespoon wholegrain mustard

1 Put a large saucepan of water and a kettle of water on to boil. Preheat the oven to low.
2 Trim the carrots, corn and beans and cut into short lengths if large. Plunge the vegetables into the saucepan of boiling water, add salt, bring back to the boil, then simmer

for 4–5 minutes, until cooked but still slightly crisp.
3 Meanwhile, trim and slice the zucchini and put aside. Chop the parsley or chervil.
4 Lift the cooked vegetables from the boiling water with a slotted spoon, put into a bowl and keep warm in the oven. Bring the vegetable water back to the boil, topping up with more from the kettle if necessary. Add the pasta and cook gently for 5–6 minutes.
5 Meanwhile, heat the olive oil in a large saucepan, add the zucchini slices and fry, stirring continuously, for 2–3 minutes.
6 Squeeze the juice from the half lemon into the zucchini, then add the drained vegetables, mustard, salt and pepper to taste. Toss gently.
7 Drain the pasta and mix into the vegetables. Transfer to a warmed

serving dish, add a sprinkling of parsley or chervil, and serve hot.
VARIATION
You can substitute thin young asparagus for the green beans and, for a creamy finish, stir in 1–2 tablespoons sour cream or natural yoghurt just before serving.

NUTRIENTS PER SERVING: kilojoules 1674, protein 18 g, carbohydrate 55 g (sugar 8 g), fat 12 g (saturated fat 5 g), good source of vitamins A, B group, C, E and folate.

COOK'S SUGGESTION
You can use any of the wide variety of stuffed pastas to make this dish, such as agnolotti, cappelletti, ravioli or tortellini, but the pasta you choose should be fresh rather than dried to complement the fresh vegetables.

ONION AND FETA CHEESE FLAN

The flan case for this recipe is quickly made using a scone-style dough, and the subtle flavour of fresh thyme makes an ideal accompaniment to the creamy texture of the Greek cheese filling.

TIME: 30 MINUTES SERVES: 4

1½ cups plain flour
1 teaspoon baking powder
4 tablespoons butter, at room temperature
150 ml sour cream
500 g onions
2 sprigs thyme
3 tablespoons olive oil
125 g button mushrooms
250 g feta cheese
Black pepper
To garnish: a few chives

1 Preheat the oven to 220°C. Sift the flour and baking powder into a bowl, then rub in 2½ tablespoons butter. Add 4 tablespoons sour cream and mix to a soft dough.
2 Roll out the dough on a floured surface into a circle about 28 cm in diameter, and fit into a 25-cm loose-based flan or sandwich tin. Trim the edge, prick the base, line with greaseproof paper and fill with baking beans or small balls of scrunched-up cooking foil. Bake blind for 10 minutes.
3 Meanwhile, halve, peel and thinly slice the onions, then strip the thyme leaves from the stems and chop finely. Heat the oil in a large frying pan, add the onions and thyme and fry over moderate heat until the onions are soft and golden.
4 Melt the remaining butter in another frying pan. Clean and halve the mushrooms and fry until lightly browned, then stir in the rest of the sour cream and keep warm.
5 Remove the paper and baking beans or foil from the flan case, then return to the oven for a few minutes until the pastry is golden.
6 Snip the chives. Crumble the feta cheese into the onions. Heat for 1 minute then season to taste with pepper. Spoon the mixture into the flan case and spoon the mushrooms over the top. Sprinkle with chives and more pepper and serve.

VARIATION
You can add extra colour to this flan by using red onions; you can also use a variety of mushrooms, rather than just the one.

NUTRIENTS PER SERVING: kilojoules 2821, protein 17 g, carbohydrate 46 g (sugar 10 g), fat 48 g (saturated fat 26 g), good source of vitamins A, B group, E and folate, and calcium.

THREE EGGS OVER EASY

INDIAN SCRAMBLED EGGS

Flavoured with herbs and spices from the East, these eggs are topped with a crisp garnish of fried onion.

TIME: 25 MINUTES SERVES: 2

Oil for deep frying
1 large onion
2 tablespoons butter
2.5-cm piece fresh root ginger
1–2 green chillies
A small bunch of coriander
6 large eggs
1 teaspoon ground turmeric
Salt and black pepper
To serve: pappadams or naan bread

1 Heat 5 cm oil in a small saucepan. Peel the onion and halve lengthways. Finely slice one half and deep fry over low–medium heat until crisp and brown. Drain on paper towels.
2 Melt the butter in another small saucepan. Finely chop the other half of the onion and fry gently over low heat for 6–7 minutes until softened, stirring frequently.
3 Meanwhile, peel and grate the ginger and halve, seed and finely slice the chillies. Stir into the onion and cook for another 1 minute, then remove from the heat.
4 Heat the naan in the oven, if using. Put aside a few sprigs of coriander for a garnish, then chop enough to give 2 tablespoons.
5 Break the eggs into a bowl, then add the turmeric, salt and pepper, and beat lightly. Stir into the onion mixture and cook over low heat, stirring, until thick but not dry.
6 Stir in the chopped coriander and serve the eggs sprinkled with the fried onions, garnished with coriander sprigs and accompanied by pappadams or the naan.

NUTRIENTS PER SERVING: kilojoules 3358, protein 29 g, carbohydrate 15 g (sugar 4 g), fat 60 g (saturated fat 22 g), good source of vitamins A, B group, E and folate, and iron.

SPEEDY EGGS FLORENTINE

A blend of mayonnaise, cream and horseradish makes a quick but luxurious sauce.

TIME: 15 MINUTES SERVES: 2

A few sprigs each of basil, parsley and thyme
A few chives
½ cup mayonnaise
½ cup thick cream
1 teaspoon horseradish cream
½ bunch spinach
2 muffins
4 large eggs
Salt and black pepper

1 Put a kettle of water on to boil and preheat the griller to high. Chop the basil, parsley and thyme leaves and snip the chives.
2 Combine the herbs in a small saucepan with the mayonnaise, cream and horseradish, and heat gently until just hot. Move the pan aside and keep warm.
3 Blanch the spinach leaves in boiling water for 2–3 minutes, then squeeze out the excess moisture.
4 Meanwhile, halve the muffins and toast on both sides under the griller. Turn off the heat, put a serving of spinach leaves on each muffin half and leave under the warm griller.
5 Bring some water and a dash of vinegar to simmering point in a shallow frying pan. Poach the eggs for 2–3 minutes, or until the whites are set. Carefully remove the eggs with a slotted spoon and drain on paper towels.
6 Put two muffin halves on each plate and place the poached eggs on top of the spinach. Spoon over the warm sauce and add a grinding of pepper, if liked.

NUTRIENTS PER SERVING: kilojoules 3297, protein 23 g, carbohydrate 45 g (sugar 13 g), fat 58 g (saturated fat 27 g), good source of vitamins A, B group and folate, and calcium.

BAKED EGGS WITH CRAB

Baked and served in individual dishes, these eggs on a layer of crab meat make a rich but simple meal.

TIME: 30 MINUTES SERVES: 2

Butter for greasing
170 g canned crab meat
2 teaspoons brandy
4 large eggs
Salt and black pepper
4 tablespoons cream
Cayenne pepper
4 slices bread
1–2 tablespoons butter
To garnish: a few sprigs of chervil

1 Preheat the oven to 190°C. Lightly grease two gratin or other ovenproof dishes. Put half the crab into each dish and sprinkle with the brandy.
2 Break 2 eggs carefully into each dish. Season with salt and pepper, then spoon the cream over the top. Dust lightly with cayenne pepper.
3 Put the dishes on a baking tray and bake for 20–25 minutes, until the whites of the eggs are set but the yolks are still soft.
4 Meanwhile, toast and butter the bread and cut on the diagonal.
5 Garnish the eggs with the chervil and serve with the toast.

VARIATION
Strips of smoked salmon and a dash of sherry can be used instead of the crab and brandy, or you could use 2 chopped anchovy fillets with a very little chopped thyme and a sprinkling of brandy.

NUTRIENTS PER SERVING: kilojoules 1126, protein 19 g, carbohydrate 25 g (sugar 2 g), fat 13 g (saturated fat 5 g), good source of vitamins A, B group and E, and selenium.

A TRIO OF EGGS: *(top right)* INDIAN SCRAMBLED EGGS; *(centre left)* BAKED EGGS WITH CRAB; *(bottom)* SPEEDY EGGS FLORENTINE.

NUTTY SPINACH AND MUSHROOM FRITTATA

This hearty omelette, packed with crunchy nuts, ribbons of spinach and tender mushrooms, can be served hot or cold.

TIME: 25 MINUTES SERVES: 4

250 g young spinach leaves
A small bunch of parsley
2 tablespoons olive oil
1 small onion
350 g closed button mushrooms
⅔ cup roasted cashew nuts
5 eggs
Salt and black pepper
100 g Cheddar or Parmesan cheese

1 Preheat the griller to high. Rinse and dry the spinach and put aside; chop enough parsley to give about 2 tablespoons and put aside.

2 Heat the oil in a large frying pan. Halve, peel and finely chop the onion. Fry the onion over moderate heat for 3–4 minutes, stirring, until soft but not browned.

3 Clean and quarter the button mushrooms, add to the chopped onion and fry, stirring frequently, for a further 3–4 minutes.

4 Add the spinach and cook over fairly high heat, stirring frequently, for 3–4 minutes, until the leaves have wilted and the excess liquid has evaporated. Stir in the cashews and reduce the heat to low.

5 Break the eggs into a bowl, then add 2 tablespoons cold water and the chopped parsley. Add salt and pepper and beat together.

6 Pour the egg mixture into the spinach and cook for 5 minutes, until the egg is set and golden.

7 Grate the cheese and sprinkle over the top. Place under the griller and grill for 2–3 minutes, until the fritatta is set and the top is golden. Alternatively, place the frittata on a baking tray under the griller.

SERVING SUGGESTION
Serve the frittata, hot or cold, with crusty bread and a tomato salad.

VARIATION
You can make the frittata with vegetarian cheese, if you prefer.

NUTRIENTS PER SERVING: kilojoules 1737, protein 22 g, carbohydrate 6 g (sugar 3 g), fat 34 g (saturated fat 10 g), good source of vitamins A, B group, C, E and folate, and calcium, iron, selenium and zinc.

CHEESY CHICK PEA ENCHILADAS

Spicy chick peas stuffed into flaky tortilla pancakes and topped with bubbling cheese make a filling dish for an informal meal. Serve with yoghurt or sour cream for a cooling contrast.

TIME: 30 MINUTES SERVES: 4

1 medium red onion
1 tablespoon vegetable oil
1 clove garlic
1 small red chilli
500 g tomatoes
425 g canned chick peas
1 teaspoon ground cumin
Salt and black pepper
100 g mature Cheddar cheese
1 small iceberg lettuce
4 soft flour tortillas, 18–20 cm in diameter
To serve: thick natural yoghurt or sour cream

1 Preheat the griller to high. Peel and thinly slice the onion. Heat the vegetable oil in a frying pan and cook the sliced onion over fairly high heat, stirring, until softened and lightly browned.

2 Peel and crush the garlic, then seed and slice the chilli. Chop the tomatoes and drain and rinse the chick peas.

3 Stir the cumin into the onion, then add the garlic, chilli, chopped tomatoes and chick peas. Cook the mixture over moderate heat, stirring occasionally, for 5–8 minutes, until most of the liquid has evaporated, then season the filling with salt and pepper to taste.

4 Coarsely grate the cheese. Rinse, dry and shred the lettuce.

5 Place the tortillas flat and divide the lettuce among them. Spoon the chick pea mixture down the centre of each, fold the sides over and place in a flameproof dish. Sprinkle with the cheese and put under the griller until the cheese melts.

6 Serve the enchiladas with the yoghurt or sour cream.

VARIATION
You can use ordinary pancakes as a substitute for the tortillas.

NUTRIENTS PER SERVING: kilojoules 2285, protein 27 g, carbohydrate 61 g (sugar 18 g), fat 23 g (saturated fat 7 g), good source of vitamins B group, C, E and folate.

COOK'S SUGGESTION

Enchiladas, a Mexican dish of soft tortillas stuffed with beans, meat or cheese and topped with a hot sauce, are traditionally baked, but grilling is faster.

ORIGINAL OMELETTES

Whether you use added ingredients to introduce an exciting new flavour or a contrasting texture, filling an omelette is an easy way to transform a handful of eggs into a delicious meatless meal in a matter of minutes.

Omelettes do not have to be filled, but there is usually a benefit. A filling can add flavour, such as mushrooms in rich truffled cream, or a generous scattering of fresh herbs. It can build in substance, with cheese melting through diced potato. Or it can offer the chance to use up leftovers in a new context – a spoonful or two of warm ratatouille, a cushion of well-seasoned spinach, or a little smoked haddock with herb cream.

There are no fixed rules for filling omelettes, except not to overdo it. The filling should not dominate, and it should not need further cooking once added to the omelette.

Each of the following fillings will make enough for two 2–3-egg omelettes. Prepare the fillings while you cook the omelette, so both are ready at the same time.

FINES HERBES

This is the classic French way to flavour an omelette. Trim and finely shred a spring onion and mix it with about 2 teaspoons each chopped fresh chervil, chives and parsley, and 1–2 teaspoons fresh tarragon.

The chopped herbs can either be beaten into the eggs before the omelettes are made, or they can be stirred into 2 tablespoons warmed thick cream, seasoned to taste with salt and pepper, and added to the omelette as a filling in the usual way.

PEAS IN HERB BUTTER

Melt 2 tablespoons butter in a pan with 3 torn mint leaves or some chopped tarragon, then add 4 tablespoons cooked fresh or frozen peas to warm through; season to taste with a little salt and pepper.

MAKING A PERFECT OMELETTE

For perfect results every time – where the egg is light, layered and slightly runny – always make the omelettes individually, using a 15–18-cm omelette pan.

1 For two people, break 4–6 eggs into a large measuring jug, season lightly with salt and black pepper, and beat together.
2 Put 3 teaspoons butter into the omelette pan, or a small frying pan, over high heat. When the butter is sizzling, pour in half the beaten egg mixture and stir quickly with a fork.
3 Draw the set mixture into the centre and tilt the pan to allow the uncooked egg to run underneath. Cook until the omelette is golden brown underneath but still very moist on top.
4 Remove the pan from the heat, spoon on half the chosen filling slightly off-centre of the middle of the omelette, then fold the rest of the omelette over to enclose the filling as you roll it from the pan onto the plate.
5 Serve immediately, or cover the omelette with foil and keep warm in the oven while you make the second one.

POTATO, ONION AND TASTY CHEESE

Peel and slice 1 medium onion, dice 1 cooked potato, then add ½ cup grated hard cheese – Gruyère gives the best results, but Cheddar is a good alternative. Soften the onion in 2 tablespoons oil over low heat, add the potato and cook gently, stirring occasionally, until heated through. Season with salt and black pepper, then divide the filling between the omelettes while still very hot and sprinkle over the cheese before you fold the omelette.

CREAMY TOMATO AND CORIANDER

Peel and finely chop ½ onion and fry in 1 tablespoon butter until softened. Add 2 chopped tomatoes, 2 teaspoons chopped coriander, and salt and pepper. Simmer until the mixture is thick and pulpy. Divide the filling between the omelettes and sprinkle each with 50 g softened cream cheese, cut into small dice, before folding.

MUSHROOMS IN TRUFFLED CREAM

Cook 150 g thinly sliced button mushrooms in 1 tablespoon butter, then stir in 2 tablespoons crème fraîche or sour cream and 1 teaspoon truffle oil. Season to taste with salt and black pepper.

SMOKED HADDOCK IN PARSLEY CREAM

Skin, bone and flake 100 g cooked smoked haddock. Warm the fish through in 3 tablespoons thick cream, stir in 1 tablespoon chopped parsley and plenty of black pepper.

For a little touch of luxury, you could use other smoked or cooked fish for this creamy filling, particularly salmon or trout.

CLASSIC EGG DISH:
OMELETTE FINES HERBES.

SPICY BROCCOLI AND CAULIFLOWER

Spicy and crisp, this delicious combination of broccoli and cauliflower with capers and pickled green peppercorns is finished off with a tasty cheese and breadcrumb topping.

TIME: 25 MINUTES   SERVES: 4

5 cloves garlic
1 green chilli
1½ tablespoons olive oil
500 g broccoli florets
500 g cauliflower florets
Salt and black pepper
50 g Gruyère cheese
50 g Parmesan cheese
3 tablespoons dried breadcrumbs
2 tablespoons capers
1–2 tablespoons green peppercorns in brine

1 Preheat the griller and put a kettle of water on to boil.

2 Peel and thinly slice the garlic, then seed and chop the chilli.

3 Heat the oil in a frying pan or large wok with a lid. Add the garlic and chilli, stir in the broccoli and cauliflower florets, sprinkle with salt and black pepper and add 150 ml boiling water. Cover the pan and cook the vegetables over high heat for 4–5 minutes, or until tender. Stir or toss halfway through the cooking time.

4 Meanwhile, grate the Gruyère and Parmesan cheeses and mix with the breadcrumbs.

5 Stir the capers and peppercorns into the vegetables. Transfer to a shallow flameproof dish, sprinkle the cheese and breadcrumb mixture over the top, and place the dish under the griller until the cheese melts and the topping turns golden. Serve hot.

SERVING SUGGESTION

For a complete vegetarian meal, serve these vegetables with some rice, potatoes, or Burghul Pilaf with Mushrooms (page 223).

NUTRIENTS PER SERVING: kilojoules 1197, protein 20 g, carbohydrate 16 g (sugar 6 g), fat 16 g (saturated fat 6 g), good source of vitamins A, B group, C, E and folate, and calcium and zinc.

GRILLED VEGETABLE BRUSCHETTA

Grilling brings out all the sweet flavours of an assortment of Mediterranean vegetables, which are then piled on top of crusty bread that has been rubbed with garlic and tomato to give it extra zest.

TIME: 30 MINUTES SERVES: 4

1 medium red capsicum
1 medium yellow capsicum
2 small zucchini
1 medium head fennel
1 red onion
4 tablespoons olive oil
2 cloves garlic
1 small tomato
1 loaf ciabatta bread or 1 baguette
Salt and black pepper
6 large basil leaves

1 Preheat the griller to high. Cut the capsicums lengthways into eight, then remove the stems and any seeds. Trim the zucchini and slice diagonally. Trim the fennel, then cut lengthways into thin slices. Peel the onion and slice into rings.

2 Cover the griller rack with a single layer of the vegetables, positioning the capsicums skin side down. Brush with some of the olive oil and grill, on one side only, until lightly browned but still slightly firm. If necessary, cook the vegetables in batches and keep the first batch warm in the oven.

3 Meanwhile, peel and halve the cloves of garlic and halve the tomato. Cut four thick slices of bread and toast on both sides.

4 Rub the top of each bread slice with the cut garlic and tomato, then pile the grilled vegetables on top. Trickle over the remaining olive oil and season the bruschetta with salt and pepper to taste. Tear the basil leaves and scatter over the top; serve while still warm.

NUTRIENTS PER SERVING: kilojoules 1238, protein 11 g, carbohydrate 26 g (sugar 10 g), fat 16 g (saturated fat 2 g), good source of vitamins A, B group, C, E and folate.

COOK'S SUGGESTION

Bruschetta, in its purest form, is an ideal accompaniment to many meals, especially those of Mediterranean origin. It is made with slices of crusty bread that are grilled or toasted, then rubbed with garlic, sprinkled with pepper and salt, and drizzled with extra virgin olive oil. It should be served as soon as possible.

LEEK AND CHEDDAR CHEESE TART

*Ready-made puff pastry lets you turn leeks, cheese and a dash
of mustard into a dish that looks as pretty as a picture.*

TIME: 30 MINUTES SERVES: 4

7–8 slim leeks, about 1 kg in total
Salt and black pepper
250 g puff pastry
1 tablespoon Dijon mustard
1 medium egg
50 g Cheddar cheese

1 Preheat the oven to 230°C. Put a kettle of water on to boil.
2 Trim the leeks to a length of about 18 cm and rinse well. Arrange in a single layer in a wide saucepan or frying pan, pour on the boiling water from the kettle, add a pinch of salt, return to the boil, reduce the heat and simmer, covered, for 6–8 minutes.
3 While the leeks are cooking, roll out the puff pastry on a lightly floured surface to a 25-cm square, then carefully transfer the pastry to a baking tray.
4 Cut a 1-cm strip of pastry from each of the four sides. Dampen the area round the edge of the square with water and trim the pastry strips to fit flat on top of the edges, to resemble a picture frame; press lightly into place.
5 Drain the leeks and cool under cold running water. Drain again, then wrap in a folded tea towel and press gently with your hands to remove any remaining moisture.
6 Arrange the leeks inside the pastry case and brush with the mustard. Break the egg into a small bowl and beat lightly, then brush over the border of the tart. Grate the Cheddar cheese and sprinkle it evenly over the top of the leeks.
7 Position the baking tray on the top shelf of the oven and bake the tart for 15 minutes, or until the pastry is risen and golden and the cheese has melted and is bubbling.
8 Remove the tray from the oven and cut the tart into quarters with a serrated-edged knife. Serve the portions hot or warm.
SERVING SUGGESTION
Try a leafy salad to accompany this dish, such as Frisée, Cucumber and Red Onion Salad (page 100).

NUTRIENTS PER SERVING: kilojoules 1683, protein 11 g, carbohydrate 31 g (sugar 3 g), fat 26 g (saturated fat 3 g), good source of vitamins A, B group, C, E and folate.

COOK'S SUGGESTION

When you shop for this recipe, buy the well-trimmed leeks that are now available in many supermarkets. This will cut down on your preparation time.

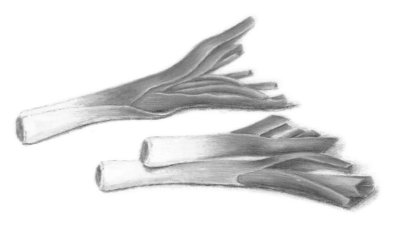

HOT POTATO SALAD

Tiny new potatoes and spicy vegetarian sausages, garnished with cheese, gain additional flavour from a dressing made with garlic and French mustard.

TIME: 30 MINUTES SERVES: 4

650 g baby new potatoes
Salt and black pepper
500 g spicy vegetarian sausages
2 tablespoons vegetable oil
1 shallot
1 large clove garlic
A small bunch of parsley
A small bunch of garlic chives
1 teaspoon Dijon mustard
3 teaspoons plain flour
½ lemon
2 tablespoons white wine vinegar
4 tablespoons olive oil
3 teaspoons caster sugar
100 g Cheshire or Cheddar cheese

1 Preheat the griller to high. Scrub the new potatoes and boil in salted water for 15–20 minutes.

2 Meanwhile, grill the sausages for about 10 minutes, or according to the manufacturer's instructions, turning often until they are cooked through and browned.

3 Heat the vegetable oil in a small saucepan. Peel and chop the shallot and the garlic, add to the pan and cook for 3 minutes, until soft and just turning brown.

4 Chop the parsley and chives. Add to the pan, with the mustard and flour, and cook for 1 minute.

5 Remove the pan from the heat. Squeeze 1 tablespoon juice from the half lemon and add to the pan with the vinegar, olive oil and sugar. Return the pan to the heat and bring the mixture slowly to the boil, stirring, until smooth and thick. Add salt and pepper to taste, then take the pan off the heat.

6 Drain the potatoes and put into a serving dish. Slice the sausages and mix with the potatoes, then pour over the hot dressing. Crumble the cheese over the top and serve.

VARIATION
The vegetarian sausages can be omitted if you like, and the salad served as a side dish.

NUTRIENTS PER SERVING: kilojoules 2917, protein 25 g, carbohydrate 43 g (sugar 10 g), fat 48 g (saturated fat 17 g), good source of vitamins B group, C and E.

COOK'S SUGGESTION

Garlic chives add a stronger, much more garlicky flavour to the salad, but if they are difficult to find you can use ordinary chives instead.

WARM LIMA BEAN AND CHARRED VEGETABLE SALAD

*Balsamic vinegar enhances the strong flavours of the vegetables
in this piquant salad, excellent served as a light lunch.*

TIME: 20 MINUTES SERVES: 4

1 red capsicum
1 yellow capsicum
1 medium onion
2 medium zucchini
2 tablespoons olive oil
500 g canned lima beans
500 g canned lentils
2 large sprigs basil
2 medium tomatoes
2 tablespoons crushed sun-dried tomatoes in oil
1 tablespoon balsamic vinegar
Salt and black pepper
To garnish: 12 large black olives

1 Seed and roughly chop the capsicums. Peel and slice the onion. Trim and thinly slice the zucchini.
2 Heat the oil in a large frying pan and brown the capsicums, onion and zucchini over high heat, stirring occasionally.
3 Meanwhile, drain and rinse the canned lima beans and lentils. Tear the basil leaves and roughly chop the fresh tomatoes.
4 Add the beans and lentils to the pan, stir gently, then add the basil, fresh tomatoes, sun-dried tomatoes and vinegar.
5 Season the mixture with salt and pepper, then heat through, stirring well. Turn into a warm dish, garnish with the olives and serve immediately.

SERVING SUGGESTION
Some crusty wholemeal rolls, warmed in the oven while the salad is heating through, are all you need for a nourishing meal.

VARIATION
Balsamic vinegar has the best flavour, but you can use a good wine or cider vinegar instead.

NUTRIENTS PER SERVING: kilojoules 1716, protein 21 g, carbohydrate 52 g (sugar 9 g), fat 13 g (saturated fat 1 g), good source of vitamins A, B group, C and E.

COOK'S SUGGESTION
*Greek Kalamata olives, already pitted, have an excellent flavour.
To pit olives easily, use a cherry pitter.*

PITA PIZZAS

When there's no time to make pizza dough, try these zesty little alternatives made with pita bread topped with chilli and tomato sauce, three different cheeses and a mixture of tasty vegetables.

TIME: 27 MINUTES SERVES: 2

Oil for greasing
2 wholemeal pita breads
2 tablespoons tomato sauce
½ teaspoon Tabasco sauce
50 g mozzarella cheese
50 g mature Cheddar cheese
50 g Taleggio, Fontina or Chaumes cheese
1 medium red onion
2 medium tomatoes
½ large red or green capsicum
1 clove garlic
1 tablespoon olive oil
4 black olives
A few sprigs of basil
A few sprigs of marjoram
¼ cup grated Parmesan cheese

1 Preheat the oven to 190°C. Lightly grease a baking tray and split the pita breads in half.
2 Mix the tomato sauce with the Tabasco sauce. Spread on each pita half and arrange on the baking tray.
3 Grate the mozzarella and the Cheddar cheeses together and sprinkle over the pitas.
4 Thinly slice or dice the Taleggio, Fontina or Chaumes cheese and spread over the grated cheese.
5 Peel the onion and cut into thin wedges. Slice the tomatoes and finely chop the half capsicum. Arrange the onion and tomato over the cheese; scatter with capsicum.
6 Peel and crush the garlic, mix with the olive oil and drizzle over

the pizzas. Place an olive in the centre of each and bake on the top shelf of the oven for 10 minutes.
7 Meanwhile, strip off the basil and marjoram leaves and put into a bowl. Mix in the Parmesan.
8 Remove the pizzas from the oven, sprinkle with the herb and Parmesan mixture, and serve hot.
VARIATION
Instead of wholemeal pitas, you can use white pita bread which has a crunchier texture when baked.

NUTRIENTS PER SERVING: kilojoules 2671, protein 27 g, carbohydrate 53 g (sugar 16 g), fat 37 g (saturated fat 13 g), good source of vitamins A, B group, C, E and folate, and calcium and zinc.

HASTY PIZZA

You can enjoy a great pizza topping even without the pizza if you take a herb and tomato sauce, add a capsicum and artichoke garnish, top with plenty of cheese and pile it onto toasted crusty bread.

TIME: 30 MINUTES SERVES: 4

2 tablespoons olive oil
1 medium onion
1 medium green capsicum
1 medium red capsicum
400 g canned artichoke hearts
425 g canned tomato pieces
1 clove garlic
1 teaspoon dried basil
1 teaspoon dried mixed herbs
Salt and black pepper
½ teaspoon sugar
1 small wholemeal or cob loaf
200 g Cheddar or mozzarella cheese, or a mixture of the two
16 black olives
To garnish: sprigs of basil

1 Heat 1 tablespoon oil in a frying pan over moderate heat. Peel and chop the onion and fry gently for about 3–4 minutes, until soft.

2 Seed and finely slice the capsicums into rings. Drain the artichoke hearts and cut in half, then put aside.

3 Drain the canned tomatoes and put into a bowl. Peel the garlic and crush it into the tomatoes, then add the fried onions, dried basil, dried mixed herbs, salt and black pepper to taste, and sugar. Mix together and put aside.

4 Preheat the griller to high. Heat the remaining oil in the pan, then add the capsicum rings and stir-fry for 5 minutes.

5 Meanwhile, slice the round top off the bread and cut the rest across into four 1-cm slices and grill on one side. Grate the Cheddar and dice the mozzarella.

6 Turn the bread over on the griller rack and spread the tomato mixture evenly over the untoasted side of each slice. Arrange the fried capsicum and the artichokes on top of the tomato, sprinkle with the cheese and dot with the olives.

7 Grill the slices for 4–5 minutes, or until the cheese is melted and golden. Garnish the pizzas with the basil and serve immediately.

VARIATION
Sliced mushrooms or avocados could be used in place of artichoke hearts. Meat eaters could add ham or salami, prawns or anchovy fillets.

NUTRIENTS PER SERVING: kilojoules 4315, protein 34 g, carbohydrate 104 g (sugar 14 g), fat 56 g (saturated fat 15 g), good source of vitamins A, B group, C, E and folate, and calcium, iron and zinc.

BEAN AND MUSHROOM BURGERS

These hearty, lightly spiced vegetarian burgers, made with wholesome ingredients and topped with a sweet red onion relish, make a satisfying family meal at any time.

TIME: 30 MINUTES SERVES: 4

425 g canned red kidney beans
3 tablespoons olive oil
2 medium red onions, about 200 g in total
2 tablespoons red wine vinegar
2 tablespoons brown sugar
200 g cup mushrooms
1 clove garlic
1 tablespoon garam masala
2 tablespoons wholemeal flour
A small bunch of mint
Salt and black pepper
To serve: 4 pita breads

1 Rinse the beans well and spread on a clean tea towel to drain.

2 To make the red onion relish, heat 1 tablespoon olive oil in a saucepan. Peel the onions, thinly slice one and add to the pan with the vinegar and sugar. Bring to the boil, stirring, then reduce the heat and simmer the onions, uncovered, for 15–20 minutes, stirring occasionally, or until softened and slightly sticky. Remove the pan from the heat and keep warm.

3 Meanwhile, quarter the other onion and put into a food processor. Clean the mushrooms, add to the onion and process until finely chopped. Alternatively, chop both finely by hand.

4 Heat 1 tablespoon olive oil in a frying pan, add the onion and mushroom mixture and cook over fairly high heat for 5–8 minutes, stirring occasionally, until golden and dry.

5 Peel the garlic, crush it into the mushroom mixture, stir in the garam masala and flour and cook for 1 minute. Chop enough mint to give 2 tablespoons. Remove the pan from the heat, add the mint and season well with salt and pepper.

6 Dry the kidney beans and tip into a deep plate. Mash firmly with a potato masher, then stir in the cooled mushroom mixture.

7 Divide the mixture into four and, with lightly floured hands, shape each portion into a burger.

8 Heat the remaining oil in a large frying pan, add the burgers and cook over fairly high heat for 6–8 minutes, turning carefully once, until browned. Meanwhile, warm the pita breads.

9 Arrange the burgers on a warm dish or individual plates and spoon some onion relish over the top of each. Serve with the warm pitas.

SERVING SUGGESTION
A simple mixed green salad with a scattering of whole baby radishes is an ideal accompaniment.

NUTRIENTS PER SERVING: kilojoules 1930, protein 15 g, carbohydrate 73 g (sugar 15 g), fat 13 g (saturated fat 2 g), good source of vitamins B group, E and folate.

COOK'S SUGGESTION

It is important to dry the kidney beans thoroughly before adding them to the mushroom mixture. If the beans retain too much liquid, the burgers will be difficult to handle.

SPICED CARROT AND CHICK PEA FRITTERS

Vividly coloured carrots and chick peas are whizzed together in a food processor with fresh herbs and strong spices to produce a fresh-tasting variation on the commercial vegeburger.

TIME: 20 MINUTES SERVES: 4

350 g carrots
1 clove garlic
A large bunch of coriander
425 g canned chick peas
1½ teaspoons ground cumin
1½ teaspoons ground coriander
1 large egg
2 tablespoons plain flour
1–2 tablespoons vegetable oil
To serve: hamburger buns and salad of your choice

1 Peel the carrots, grate coarsely and put aside. Peel and roughly chop the garlic, then chop enough coriander to give 4 tablespoons.

2 Drain and rinse the chick peas and put into a food processor with the garlic, fresh coriander, ground cumin and ground coriander. Process to a rough paste then add the carrot, egg and flour and process briefly, until evenly mixed but still slightly chunky.

3 Heat the oil in a frying pan and divide the mixture into eight flat fritters. Fry in two batches for 2–3 minutes on each side, until golden, then drain on paper towels. Serve in the buns, with salad.

VARIATION
The fritters can be made smaller and served as a snack or as an entrée or party dish, accompanied by some red onion relish (see the recipe above), or with your own favourite chutney.

NUTRIENTS PER SERVING: kilojoules 1942, protein 21 g, carbohydrate 66 g (sugar 12 g), fat 14 g (saturated fat 2 g), good source of vitamins A, B group and E.

HEALTHY VEGEBURGERS: *(top)* BEAN AND MUSHROOM BURGERS; *(bottom)* SPICED CARROT AND CHICK PEA FRITTERS.

TOFU AND VEGETABLES WITH TAHINI SAUCE

Cubes of tofu, or bean curd, add body and flavour to these grilled vegetables served with a creamy tahini sauce.

TIME: 30 MINUTES SERVES: 2

3 tablespoons soy sauce
3 tablespoons olive oil
350 g small firm zucchini, or a mixture of zucchini and baby eggplants
125 g medium cup mushrooms
250 g firm tofu

For the sauce:
A small bunch of parsley
3 tablespoons light tahini paste
1 large clove garlic
½ teaspoon sesame seed oil
1 teaspoon Dijon mustard
Salt and black pepper

1 Preheat the griller to moderate. Blend the soy sauce and olive oil thoroughly in a large bowl.

2 Trim the zucchini and slice into thin rounds. Trim and slice the eggplants, if using (there is no need to peel the little ones). Clean and thickly slice the mushrooms, then cut the tofu into bite-sized pieces.

3 Add the vegetables and tofu to the soy sauce and oil and stir gently until well coated.

4 Spread in a single layer in the griller tray or on a baking tray. Grill for 20 minutes, until cooked and browned, shaking the vegetables occasionally to prevent sticking.

5 Meanwhile, make the sauce. Chop enough parsley to give 2 tablespoons; put aside. Pour the tahini into a jug, peel the garlic and crush it into the jug, then briskly stir in just enough water to give the sauce the consistency of pouring cream. Stir in the chopped parsley, sesame oil and Dijon mustard, and season to taste with salt and pepper.

6 When the vegetables and tofu are cooked, transfer to a warm serving plate and pour over the tahini sauce. Serve hot or warm.

NUTRIENTS PER SERVING: kilojoules 2453, protein 29 g, carbohydrate 8 g (sugar 4 g), fat 49 g (saturated fat 9 g), good source of vitamins A, B group, C, E and folate, and calcium, iron and zinc.

TOFU STIR-FRY WITH CASHEWS

*Tofu soaks up the flavour of a tangy marinade of soy sauce and dry sherry and
is then stir-fried with a crisp mixture of vegetables and cashew nuts and served with noodles.*

TIME: 30 MINUTES SERVES: 4

300 g fresh tofu
1-cm piece fresh root ginger
150 g snow peas
100 g shiitake mushrooms
1 large red or yellow capsicum
400 g Chinese cabbage or cos lettuce
1 bunch spring onions
2 tablespoons peanut oil
250 g fine egg noodles
Salt
100 g roasted cashew nuts

For the marinade:

2 cloves garlic
1 tablespoon Japanese soy sauce
1½ tablespoons dry sherry
1½ teaspoons sesame seed oil
1 teaspoon brown sugar
Black pepper

1 Preheat the oven to low and put a kettle of water on to boil. To make the marinade, peel the garlic and crush it into a bowl. Add the soy sauce, sherry, sesame oil, sugar and pepper, then stir.

2 Drain the tofu and cut into oblongs 1 cm thick, add to the marinade and leave to soak.

3 Peel and finely chop the ginger. Top and tail the snow peas. Clean the mushrooms and slice thinly. Quarter and seed the capsicum, stack the pieces and slice into long strips. Put them all aside.

4 Remove any damaged outer leaves from the cabbage or lettuce, then cut across into 1-cm slices. Trim and slice the spring onions.

5 Heat 1 tablespoon peanut oil in a frying pan over moderate heat. Drain the tofu, reserving the marinade, stir-fry for 3 minutes, then remove and keep warm.

6 Heat the remaining oil in the pan. Add the ginger, snow peas and mushrooms and stir-fry for 2 minutes. Then add the capsicum, stir-fry for 2 minutes more, and add the cabbage or lettuce and the spring onions and stir-fry for a further 2 minutes.

7 Put the noodles into a bowl, add salt and cover with boiling water. Stir gently, cover and put aside for as long as instructed on the packet.

8 While the noodles are soaking, pour the reserved marinade into the vegetables, add the cashew nuts and stir for 1–2 minutes until hot.

9 Stir the tofu into the vegetable mixture and keep warm. Drain the noodles. Mix with the vegetables and serve immediately.

NUTRIENTS PER SERVING: kilojoules 2402, protein 24 g, carbohydrate 58 g (sugar 10 g), fat 30 g (saturated fat 7 g), good source of vitamins A, B group, C, E and folate, and calcium and zinc.

251

TOMATOES WITH A SPINACH STUFFING

A generous filling of fresh spinach enriched with pine nuts and Parmesan cheese gives an Italian flavour to the tomatoes in this dish, which is equally delicious served hot or cold.

TIME: 30 MINUTES SERVES: 2

1 tablespoon olive oil
250 g spinach
4 large tomatoes, about 250 g each
125 g pine nuts
1 clove garlic
125 g Parmesan cheese
Salt and black pepper

1 Preheat the oven to 220°C. Use a little of the oil to lightly grease a baking tray. Rinse and dry the spinach, discarding the stalks.
2 Heat the rest of the oil in a saucepan and add the spinach; cover and cook for 2 minutes. Uncover, stir, and cook for 1 minute. Drain off the liquid, transfer the spinach to a bowl and put aside.

3 Slice off and reserve the tomato tops. Scoop out the centres.
4 Lightly toast the pine nuts (see box, right), then add to the spinach. Peel the garlic and crush it in, then grate over the Parmesan, season to taste with salt and pepper, and mix.
5 Press the spinach mixture into the tomatoes, piling it up, then balance the tomato tops on the stuffing. Bake on the top shelf of the oven for 12–15 minutes.
SERVING SUGGESTION
A mixed leaf salad on the side is a refreshing accompaniment.

NUTRIENTS PER SERVING: kilojoules 4011, protein 40 g, carbohydrate 19 g (sugar 18 g), fat 81 g (saturated fat 18 g), good source of vitamins A, B group, C, E and folate, and calcium, iron and zinc.

EASY DOES IT!

Pine nuts have a wonderful flavour which is enhanced by toasting. Simply place them in a dry frying pan over low heat and cook, stirring and turning constantly, until golden brown.

ASPARAGUS PIPERADE

In this well-travelled Spanish dish, fresh asparagus, capsicums, chunks of chopped tomatoes and just enough chilli to tantalise the palate are temptingly combined with fluffy scrambled eggs.

TIME: 30 MINUTES SERVES: 4

1 large onion
1 green chilli
1 large red capsicum
1 large green capsicum
2 tablespoons olive oil
3 cloves garlic
Salt and black pepper
500 g asparagus
425 g canned tomato pieces
8 slices crusty bread
Extra olive oil for brushing
4 large eggs
To garnish: a few sprigs of chervil

1 Peel and slice the onion; seed and dice the chilli, then seed and slice the capsicums.
2 Heat the oil in a large frying pan or a wok with a lid. Peel the garlic, crush it into the oil and add the onion, chilli and capsicum, with salt and pepper to taste. Stir-fry for 1 minute, then cover and cook over high heat for 3–4 minutes, shaking the pan occasionally.
3 Trim the woody ends from the asparagus, then cut each of the spears into four pieces. Add the asparagus to the onions, cover the pan and cook for 7–8 minutes, stirring occasionally. Preheat the griller to high.
4 Stir the drained tomatoes into the pan, increase the heat and bring the mixture to simmering point; cook, uncovered, for 2 minutes.
5 Meanwhile, brush one side of each bread slice with a little oil and toast under the griller.
6 Lightly beat the eggs, then add to the vegetables and cook over moderate heat, stirring, until the eggs are just set.

7 Serve the piperade on individual plates alongside the toast, and garnish with the sprigs of chervil.
SERVING SUGGESTION
To make a more substantial meal, you could serve the piperade with sautéed potatoes instead of the toasted bread.
VARIATION
Sliced button or oyster mushrooms can replace the asparagus; cook with the onions for 1–2 minutes before the tomatoes are added.

NUTRIENTS PER SERVING: kilojoules 2730, protein 20 g, carbohydrate 50 g (sugar 14 g), fat 43 g (saturated fat 20 g), good source of vitamins A, B group, C, E and folate, and selenium and zinc.

TEMPTING VEGETARIAN DUO:
(top) TOMATOES WITH A SPINACH STUFFING; *(bottom)* ASPARAGUS PIPERADE.

VEGETABLE
SIDE DISHES

Delicious and unusual accompaniments, from leek and carrot stir-fry to curried parsnip purée, sweet potato rösti to baked chicory, provide a wealth of partners for the main course.

EGGPLANT PARMAGIANA

In this simple variation on an Italian classic, slices of eggplant are layered with a thick tomato sauce and creamy mozzarella cheese, and finished with a topping of grated Parmesan.

TIME: 25 MINUTES SERVES: 4

500 g eggplants
4–8 tablespoons olive oil
125 g mozzarella cheese
A small bunch of basil or oregano
200 ml tomato passata
Salt and black pepper
30 g Parmesan cheese

1 Trim the eggplants and slice into thin rounds.

2 Heat 1 tablespoon oil in a large frying pan, or two smaller pans, and fry the eggplant in batches over fairly high heat, turning once, until golden brown. Add more oil to the pan as necessary.

3 Meanwhile, preheat the griller to high. Thinly slice the mozzarella. Chop enough basil or oregano to give 2 tablespoons. Put aside.

4 When the eggplant is ready, arrange in layers in a wide, shallow, flameproof dish. Alternate with layers of mozzarella, tomato passata, basil or oregano, salt and pepper.

5 Grate the Parmesan over the top layer, then grill for 4–5 minutes, or until golden brown and bubbling.

SERVING SUGGESTION
Serve with grilled meats, such as lamb cutlets or steak, with simply cooked white fish, or alongside a vegetarian risotto.

NUTRIENTS PER SERVING: kilojoules 1352, protein 12 g, carbohydrate 5 g (sugar 5 g), fat 28 g (saturated fat 8 g), good source of vitamins B group and E, and calcium.

COOK'S SUGGESTION

Passata is a thick, sieved tomato juice which adds a rich tomato flavour to a dish. If you buy a brand with added garlic and herbs, omit the herbs and seasoning when making this dish. If passata is unavailable, purée enough drained canned tomato pieces to make 200 ml.

EGGPLANT WITH TAHINI DRESSING

Lightly steamed eggplant slices spiked with spring onions and sun-dried tomatoes are served in a Middle Eastern dressing of sesame-based tahini – an unusual alternative to cream or butter sauces.

TIME: 25 MINUTES SERVES: 4

400 g eggplants
4 spring onions
¼ cup sun-dried tomatoes in oil
To garnish: a few sprigs of dill

For the dressing:
1 clove garlic
1 lemon
3 teaspoons tahini paste
2 tablespoons olive oil
Salt and black pepper

1 Fill a steamer with water and bring it to the boil.
2 Trim the eggplants. Halve lengthways if large, then cut across into slices about 5 mm thick. Put into the steamer, cover and cook for 6–8 minutes, or until softened.
3 To make the dressing, peel the garlic and crush it into a small bowl, then squeeze 2 tablespoons juice from the lemon and add to the garlic. Add the tahini paste and olive oil, season to taste with salt and black pepper, and mix.
4 Trim and thinly slice the spring onions, and drain and chop the sun-dried tomatoes; put both aside.
5 Transfer the cooked eggplant to a colander and press down firmly with a spoon to remove as much liquid as possible – do not worry if the slices break up. Then transfer to a serving bowl and stir in the spring onions and the sun-dried tomatoes.
6 Pour over the tahini dressing and toss well. Chop enough dill to give 1 tablespoon and scatter it over the eggplant. Leave to cool for 5 minutes to let the flavour develop.

SERVING SUGGESTION
This unusual dish goes particularly well with simple grilled lamb or chicken. It can also be served as a starter, accompanied by some hot crusty bread.

NUTRIENTS PER SERVING: kilojoules 1005, protein 2 g, carbohydrate 4 g (sugar 2 g), fat 13 g (saturated fat 2 g), good source of vitamins B group, C and E.

DHAL

Indian cookery uses a wide variety of lentils and split peas which are simmered with spices and served with curries.

| 350 g split red lentils |
| 1 teaspoon ground turmeric |
| ½ teaspoon chilli powder |
| 1-cm piece fresh root ginger |
| 2 cloves garlic |
| ½ teaspoon garam masala |
| Salt |
| 1 tablespoon butter |
| A pinch of ground cumin |
| 1 small onion |

1 Put a kettle of water on to boil. Pick over the lentils and remove any small pieces of grit, then put into a sieve and rinse under cold running water.

2 Put the lentils into a saucepan and cover with 5 cups boiling water from the kettle. Add the turmeric and chilli powder, cover and bring to the boil.

3 Meanwhile, peel the ginger, cut into thin slices and add to the lentils. Peel the garlic and crush it into the saucepan. As soon as the water reaches boiling point, reduce the heat and gently simmer for 10 minutes, or until the lentils are soft and almost all the liquid has been absorbed.

4 Stir in the garam masala, then add some salt to taste and cook the dhal for a further 5 minutes, leaving the pan uncovered if the mixture is still soupy.

5 Meanwhile, heat the butter and cumin in a small frying pan. Peel and dice the onion and fry gently in the spiced butter until soft.

6 Transfer the dhal to a heated serving dish, stir in the fried onion and serve hot.

NUTRIENTS PER SERVING: kilojoules 1394, protein 21 g, carbohydrate 51 g (sugar 3 g), fat 6 g (saturated fat 4 g), good source of vitamins B group and E, and iron and zinc.

COOK'S SUGGESTION

Many pulses require soaking in cold water followed by a long period of boiling, but split red lentils are ideal for meals in a hurry. They do not need soaking and cook very quickly.

POTATO AND GREEN BEAN CURRY

*Sliced new potatoes and fine green beans are cooked in an aromatic mixture of butter and delicate
spices, and can be served as a light meal with naan bread, or as a side dish with other curries.*

TIME: 30 MINUTES SERVES: 4

500 g small new potatoes
250 g small green beans
3 teaspoons butter
2 tablespoons sunflower oil
2 small green chillies
½ teaspoon cumin seeds
½ teaspoon ground turmeric
¼ teaspoon garam masala
1 clove garlic
Salt

1 Scrub the potatoes and cut into
thick slices. Top and tail the green
beans, then cut into 2.5 cm lengths;
put aside.

2 Heat the butter and oil in a
wide, shallow saucepan or frying
pan, over high heat. When it begins
to sizzle, stir in the whole green
chillies, the cumin seeds, turmeric
and garam masala. Peel the garlic
and crush it into the pan; stir and
fry for 30 seconds.

3 Add the potatoes to the pan and
season with some salt. Stir until
coated with the butter and oil.

4 Stir in the beans, cover the pan,
then reduce the heat to moderate
and cook for 15 minutes, stirring
occasionally. The curry is ready to
serve as soon as the potatoes are
cooked through.

SERVING SUGGESTION
These lightly spiced vegetables go
beautifully with Chicken and
Spinach Curry (page 185) and Dhal
(page 258). Serve some steamed or
boiled rice on the side.

*NUTRIENTS PER SERVING: kilojoules 825,
protein 3 g, carbohydrate 20 g (sugar 3 g),
fat 12 g (saturated fat 3 g), good source of
vitamins B group, C, E and folate.*

CHESTNUT AND CELERIAC PURÉE

This velvety purée of celeriac and chestnuts, cooked in vegetable stock, is perfect on a cold night as a comforting accompaniment to roast meat or game dishes.

TIME: 30 MINUTES SERVES: 4

300 ml vegetable stock
1 bouquet garni
500 g celeriac
500 g whole cooked chestnuts
A small bunch of chives
1 tablespoon butter
2 tablespoons crème fraîche or natural fromage frais, optional
Salt and black pepper

1 Pour the vegetable stock into a large saucepan, add the bouquet garni and bring to the boil. Reduce the heat, cover the pan and leave the stock to simmer

2 Peel the celeriac, cut into small (1 cm) dice and add to the stock.

Cover and cook for 10 minutes, or until softened.

3 Drain the chestnuts, if canned, add to the celeriac and simmer for 3–4 minutes more. Meanwhile, chop or snip the chives.

4 When the chestnuts and celeriac are cooked, strain and reserve the stock. Remove the bouquet garni and purée or blend the vegetables. Return the purée to the saucepan, add the butter and place over low heat until the butter has melted.

5 Stir in the crème fraîche or fromage frais, if using, 1 tablespoon at a time so the purée does not become too thin. If it is still too thick, add a little of the reserved stock, or some more crème fraîche or fromage frais, to thin it slightly.

6 Taste, season with salt and black pepper, then turn into a serving dish and sprinkle with the chives.

NUTRIENTS PER SERVING: kilojoules 1201, protein 4 g, carbohydrate 48 g (sugar 1 g), fat 9 g (saturated fat 3 g), good source of vitamins B group, C and E.

COOK'S SUGGESTION

To quickly cook fresh chestnuts, score the outer skin, place on a glass plate and cook in a microwave oven on high for 5 minutes, turning often. As soon as they are cool enough to handle, remove the outer and inner skins from the kernels. If you are using canned chestnuts for this dish, make sure they are unsweetened.

SAUTÉED BRUSSELS SPROUTS

Lightly fried Brussels sprouts mingle with crisp morsels of bacon and water chestnuts in this crunchy dish, while wholegrain mustard and a hint of orange add an aromatic touch and enhance the flavour.

TIME: 25 MINUTES SERVES: 4

3 teaspoons vegetable oil

100 g thick rindless bacon

500 g small Brussels sprouts

1 orange

3 tablespoons butter

2 teaspoons wholegrain mustard

125 g canned whole
water chestnuts

Salt and black pepper

1 Heat the vegetable oil in a frying pan, then dice the bacon and fry for 2–3 minutes, until golden brown.
2 Trim the Brussels sprouts, if necessary, and cut in half. Grate the rind from the orange into the frying pan with the bacon and add the butter, wholegrain mustard and sprouts. Cook over moderately high heat for 5 minutes, stirring, until the sprouts are crisp.

3 Meanwhile, drain and chop the water chestnuts, stir into the sprouts and cook for 3–4 minutes, until the sprouts are golden and the chestnuts are heated through. Add salt and black pepper to taste and serve.

NUTRIENTS PER SERVING: kilojoules 938, protein 8 g, carbohydrate 7 g (sugar 5 g), fat 20 g (saturated fat 9 g), good source of vitamins B group, C, E, and folate.

A TRIO OF FRESH FLAVOURS

LEEK AND CARROT STIR-FRY

Two favourite winter vegetables team with tarragon in this refreshing combination, stir-fried in minutes.

TIME: 20 MINUTES SERVES: 4

750 g leeks
250 g carrots
2 tablespoons olive oil
1 large sprig tarragon
Salt and black pepper

1 Discard the tough outer leaves and two-thirds of the green tops from the leeks, then slice thinly, widthways. Place in a colander and rinse under cold running water, then drain well.
2 Peel and grate the carrots.
3 Heat the oil in a wok or large frying pan over moderate heat. Chop the tarragon.
4 Add the leeks to the hot oil and fry for about 2 minutes, or until just beginning to wilt.
5 Stir in the grated carrots and add salt, pepper and the chopped tarragon. Continue to cook for a further 2 minutes, then serve.

VARIATION
You can vary the choice of fresh herb to suit your own taste, or use whatever herb is available.

NUTRIENTS PER SERVING: kilojoules 373, protein 2 g, carbohydrate 7 g (sugar 6 g), fat 8 g (saturated fat 1 g), good source of vitamins A, B group, C, E and folate.

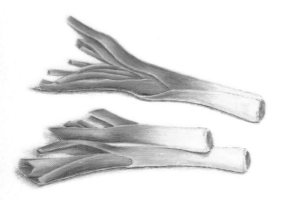

ORANGE AND SESAME CARROTS

The natural crunch and sweet taste of baby carrots is enhanced by the simple addition of butter and some fresh orange juice.

TIME: 25 MINUTES SERVES: 4

500 g small carrots
1 medium orange
3 teaspoons butter or sunflower oil
Salt and black pepper
1 tablespoon sesame seeds

1 Trim and peel the carrots, if necessary. If they are very small, leave whole; otherwise, cut them in half lengthways.
2 Remove the rind from the orange with a zester and squeeze out the juice. Put both into a large saucepan, then add the butter or sunflower oil and bring to the boil over moderate heat.
3 Add the carrots to the saucepan, then season to taste with salt and black pepper. Bring back to the boil, reduce the heat to moderate, cover the saucepan and simmer for 10–12 minutes, shaking the pan occasionally, until the carrots are tender but not soft.
4 Meanwhile, put the sesame seeds into a small frying pan and dry-fry over fairly high heat for about 2 minutes, shaking the pan, until the seeds are golden.
5 Stir the sesame seeds into the carrots and serve.

SERVING SUGGESTION
Serve with plainly grilled chicken, lamb, veal or beef.

VARIATION
If baby carrots are not in season, you can use larger, older ones, but they will need to be sliced thinly.

NUTRIENTS PER SERVING: kilojoules 364, protein 2 g, carbohydrate 8 g (sugar 7 g), fat 6 g (saturated fat 2 g), good source of vitamins A, B group and E.

CURRIED PARSNIP PURÉE

Sweet-tasting parsnips are complemented by the addition of curry powder to make a warmly substantial purée.

TIME: 20 MINUTES SERVES: 4

650 g parsnips
Salt and black pepper
3–4 sprigs parsley
1 tablespoon butter
1 tablespoon medium or hot curry powder
4 tablespoons sour cream

1 Put a kettle of water on to boil. Peel the parsnips, cut into small chunks and put into a saucepan with a little salt. Cover with boiling water and return to the boil, then reduce the heat and simmer for 8–10 minutes, or until tender.
2 While the parsnips are cooking, chop the parsley and put aside.
3 Drain the parsnips thoroughly, then return to the saucepan and mash coarsely.
4 Add the butter, curry powder and sour cream, season well with black pepper, and beat until the parsnips are puréed.
5 Transfer the purée to a heated serving dish. Sprinkle the chopped parsley over the top.

SERVING SUGGESTION
Serve with grilled pork chops or crumbed lamb cutlets.

VARIATION
You can make this purée with a mixture of parsnips and freshly cooked or leftover mashed potatoes.

NUTRIENTS PER SERVING: kilojoules 678, protein 3 g, carbohydrate 16 g (sugar 7 g), fat 10 g (saturated fat 6 g), good source of vitamins B group, C, E and folate.

FRESH AND EASY ACCOMPANIMENTS:
(top) LEEK AND CARROT STIR-FRY; *(bottom left)* ORANGE AND SESAME CARROTS; *(right)* CURRIED PARSNIP PURÉE.

ITALIAN BAKED CHICORY

Plump heads of chicory, married to the intense Mediterranean flavours of sun-dried tomatoes, lemon juice and black olives, are baked beneath a crunchy crust of Parmesan cheese and breadcrumbs.

TIME: 30 MINUTES SERVES: 4

1 medium slice day-old bread or ¼ cup fresh white breadcrumbs

40 g Parmesan cheese

6 sun-dried tomatoes in oil

4 large heads chicory, about 150–175 g each

½ lemon

2 tablespoons olive oil

Black pepper

16 pitted black olives

1 Preheat the oven to 200°C. Remove and discard the crusts from the slice of bread, if using, and grind into breadcrumbs in a food processor. Grate the Parmesan cheese into the breadcrumbs, mix together and put aside.

2 Drain the sun-dried tomatoes on paper towels, then snip or chop and put aside.

3 Remove any blemished outer leaves from the chicory heads, neaten the bases and cut each head into quarters lengthways.

4 Squeeze the lemon half and measure 1 tablespoon juice into a large, shallow, ovenproof dish. Then stir in 1 tablespoon olive oil.

5 Arrange the quartered chicory, cut side up, in the ovenproof dish. Drizzle over the remaining olive oil, then season with black pepper.

6 Scatter the sun-dried tomatoes over the chicory, followed by the black olives, then sprinkle the cheese and breadcrumb mixture over the top. Put the dish into the oven and bake for 15 minutes, until the topping is golden brown.

NUTRIENTS PER SERVING: kilojoules 791, protein 5 g, carbohydrate 7 g (sugar 1 g), fat 16 g (saturated fat 4 g), good source of vitamins B group and E.

GRILLED CHICORY AND BEETROOT

This colourful combination of grilled chicory teamed with whole beetroot in an orange juice and wholegrain mustard dressing can be served either warm or cold with hot or cold cuts of meat.

TIME: 25 MINUTES SERVES: 4

4 large heads white chicory, about 150–175 g each

3 tablespoons olive oil

250 g cooked baby beetroot

For the dressing:

1 orange

2 tablespoons mayonnaise

2 teaspoons wholegrain mustard

To garnish: chives, optional

1 Preheat the griller to medium-high. Trim the chicory and cut the heads in half, lengthways.
2 Put the chicory halves on the griller rack, cut side down, brush with half the olive oil and grill for 5 minutes, about 10 cm from the heat. Turn the chicory, brush with the remaining oil, and grill for a further 3 minutes, or until the edges begin to char.
3 Meanwhile, make the dressing. Squeeze 1 tablespoon juice from the orange and stir into the mayonnaise, then stir in the wholegrain mustard.
4 Remove the chicory from the griller. Arrange, cut side up, in a serving bowl with the beetroot alongside. Drizzle the orange and mustard dressing over the top and garnish with the chives, if using.

NUTRIENTS PER SERVING: kilojoules 933, protein 2 g, carbohydrate 10 g (sugar 7 g), fat 21 g (saturated fat 3 g), good source of vitamins B group, E and folate.

ZUCCHINI, APPLES AND PERSILLADE

Persillade, a wonderfully scented combination of chopped parsley and garlic, contributes a classic French flavouring to this fruity dish of fried zucchini, tomato, onion and apple.

TIME: 25 MINUTES   SERVES: 4

1 red or white onion
3 tablespoons olive oil
1 medium apple
1 medium tomato
500 g small zucchini
Salt and black pepper
A medium bunch of parsley
1 clove garlic

1 Peel and thinly slice the onion. Heat 2 tablespoons oil in a frying pan, add the onion and cook over low heat for 7–8 minutes, until the onion has softened.

2 Core the apple, chop into cubes, then cube the tomato. When the onion is soft, stir in the apple and tomato and cook over low heat for 5 minutes, stirring occasionally.

3 Trim the zucchini, slice into thin strips, then cut the strips into 5-cm batons. Sprinkle with salt and toss well. Heat the remaining oil in another frying pan and fry the zucchini strips over moderate heat until they release their moisture.

Increase the heat and cooking until the liquid has evaporated, shaking the pan to make sure the zucchini does not burn.

4 Reduce the heat, then add the apple, tomato and onion mixture and simmer for 5–6 minutes.

5 While the mixture is simmering, chop enough parsley to give 4 tablespoons, then peel and crush the garlic and mix with the parsley to make the persillade.

6 Stir the persillade into the frying pan with the vegetables. Simmer for

a few minutes to cook the garlic, then grind in some black pepper and add more salt if necessary. Serve the vegetables immediately.

SERVING SUGGESTION

This is a wonderful dish to serve with pan-fried or grilled pork chops or steaks.

VARIATION

This vegetable dish can be turned into a light main course by stirring 250 g chopped cooked ham into the mixture and heating gentle until just warmed through, before adding the persillade.

NUTRIENTS PER SERVING: kilojoules 628, protein 3 g, carbohydrate 9 g (sugar 8 g), fat 12 g (saturated fat 2 g), good source of vitamins B group, C, E and folate.

LEMON ZUCCHINI

Thinly sliced zucchini seasoned with lemon zest, flaky sea salt and black pepper makes a simple but refreshing dish.

TIME: 15 MINUTES SERVES: 4

| 500 g small zucchini |
| 1 tablespoon olive oil |
| 1 lemon |
| **Flaky sea salt and black pepper** |

1 Trim the zucchini and slice very thinly on the diagonal.

2 Heat the oil in a large frying pan, then add the zucchini and fry, stirring frequently, until tender.

3 Meanwhile, finely grate the rind of the lemon. When the zucchini is cooked, sprinkle over the lemon rind and season well with flaky sea salt and black pepper.

SERVING SUGGESTION

This lightly flavoured vegetable is a delicious accompaniment to many main course dishes, especially Chicken Breasts with Apples and Cider (page 186). Try it, also, with plainly grilled fish.

NUTRIENTS PER SERVING: kilojoules 234, protein 2 g, carbohydrate 2 g (sugar 2 g), fat 4 g (saturated fat 1 g), good source of vitamins B group, C and E.

PARSNIP AND APPLE CREAM

The tart flavour of cooking apple balances the smooth sweetness of parsnips in this luxurious vegetable dish, perfect to offer with plain roasts or grills.

TIME: 20 MINUTES SERVES: 4

500 g parsnips
2 tablespoons olive oil
1 cooking apple, preferably Granny Smith
Salt and black pepper
½ lemon
3 sprigs thyme
⅓ cup thick cream

1 Peel and coarsely grate the parsnips. If they are old, cut into quarters and remove and discard the woody cores before grating.
2 Heat the olive oil in a large, shallow saucepan, add the parsnips and cook over moderate heat.

3 Meanwhile, peel and coarsely grate the apple. Stir into the pan, season with salt and black pepper, then squeeze in 1 teaspoon juice from the half lemon.
4 Strip the thyme leaves from the stems (see box, right) and add to the pan. Cook for 3–5 minutes more, until parsnips are tender.
5 Pour the cream into the pan and stir until the mixture is heated through. Spoon into a warmed serving dish.

NUTRIENTS PER SERVING: kilojoules 887, protein 2 g, carbohydrate 17 g (sugar 11 g), fat 18 g (saturated fat 7 g), good source of vitamins B group, C, E and folate.

EASY DOES IT!

To strip the thyme, hold by the tip and run thumb and forefinger down the stem, pushing off the leaves as you go.

MIXED BEANS WITH PANCETTA

Fresh and canned beans mixed with cubes of bacon and simmered in a herby sauce go well with any meat or firm fish dish, especially chicken, rabbit or salmon.

TIME: 30 MINUTES SERVES: 4

1 cup chicken stock or white wine
1 bouquet garni
350 g small green beans
400 g canned cannellini beans
250 g pancetta or rindless, dry-cured smoked bacon
1 medium red or white onion
A few sprigs of tarragon or parsley
1 tablespoon crème fraîche
Salt and black pepper

1 Put the stock or white wine into a small saucepan with the bouquet garni, bring to the boil then simmer until the liquid has reduced by half.

2 Top and tail the green beans, cut into 2.5-cm lengths and put aside. Drain and rinse the canned beans and put aside.

3 Cut the pancetta or bacon into small cubes. Fry in a large frying pan for 1–2 minutes until crisp, then drain on paper towels.

4 Peel and chop the onion and fry in the remaining fat in the pan over medium heat until golden.

5 Add both lots of beans and the reduced stock or wine to the frying pan. Bring to the boil, cover, then reduce the heat and simmer for about 10 minutes, until the green beans are tender. To test, cool a bean under cold running water, then bite into it. When the beans are ready, there should be almost no liquid left in the pan.

6 Meanwhile, chop the tarragon or parsley. Add the crème fraîche to the beans, warm through, then add the pancetta or bacon, the herb, and salt and pepper to taste. Warm through again, then serve.

NUTRIENTS PER SERVING: kilojoules 1348, protein 20 g, carbohydrate 19 g (sugar 4 g), fat 19 g (saturated fat 2 g), good source of vitamins B group, C, E and folate.

BABY VEGETABLES WITH SOUR CREAM

This warm quartet of steamed vegetables makes an excellent accompaniment to grilled fish or meat dishes.

TIME: 20 MINUTES SERVES: 4

175 g baby carrots
250 g baby zucchini
1 baby cauliflower
250 g young asparagus spears, green or white
¾ cup sour cream
2 teaspoons wholegrain or Dijon mustard
2–3 teaspoons butter, at room temperature
Black pepper

1 Prepare a steamer by half filling the bottom pan with water and putting it on to boil.
2 Meanwhile, peel and trim the carrots and cut any large ones in half lengthways. Trim the zucchini and halve lengthways, quarter the cauliflower and trim the asparagus.
3 Put the carrots into the steamer, cover and steam for 5 minutes. Then layer the zucchini over the carrots, the cauliflower over the zucchini, and the asparagus over the cauliflower. Replace the cover and steam for 5 minutes.
4 While the vegetables are in the steamer, put the sour cream into a saucepan and stir in the mustard. Heat the mixture very gently until just warmed through.
5 Put the vegetables into a warmed serving bowl and stir in the butter

EASY DOES IT!

You can use a conventional steamer or a Chinese bamboo steamer set over a large wok of boiling water for the vegetables. If you do not have either, you can successfully compromise with a metal sieve and a saucepan. Ensure the sieve sits above the level of the water so that the steam circulates all round.

and some black pepper. Pour on the dressing and serve at once.
VARIATION
If asparagus is not in season, replace with small green beans. You can also use small florets of cauliflower or broccoli.

NUTRIENTS PER SERVING: kilojoules 712, protein 5 g, carbohydrate 7 g (sugar 6 g), fat 14 g (saturated fat 8 g), good source of vitamins A, B group, C, E and folate.

270

SWEET POTATO RÖSTI

Grated potato cakes make a crunchy accompaniment to grilled meat or roasted game.
Here they are given a fresh appeal by using succulent sweet potatoes.

TIME: 30 MINUTES SERVES: 4

650 g sweet potatoes
Salt and black pepper
2 tablespoons sunflower oil
1 tablespoon butter

1 Preheat the oven to its lowest setting. Line a baking tray with a double thickness of paper towels and put aside.

2 Peel and coarsely grate the sweet potatoes, then put into a mixing bowl. Season with salt and black pepper and mix well.

3 Heat half the sunflower oil in a large, nonstick frying pan and add half the butter.

4 Take half the potato mixture and divide it into four, then shape each portion into a round patty about 1 cm thick and press together firmly. As soon as the butter and oil begins to sizzle, carefully place the patties in the pan.

5 Cook the rösti over moderate heat for 5 minutes, or until crisp and golden brown underneath, then turn carefully with a fish slice and cook for a further 5 minutes (do not worry if the patties break up as you turn them over – simply pat back into shape). While they are cooking, shape the remaining mixture into four more cakes.

6 When the first batch is cooked, transfer to the lined baking tray and drain for 1–2 minutes. Keep warm in the oven.

7 Add the rest of the sunflower oil and butter to the pan, heat until sizzling and fry the remaining rösti.

VARIATION
The rösti can also be cooked in one large cake and divided into eight portions at the table. You can add finely chopped bacon or ham for extra flavour.

NUTRIENTS PER SERVING: *kilojoules 975, protein 2 g, carbohydrate 28 g (sugar 7 g), fat 14 g (saturated fat 5 g), good source of vitamins A, B group, C and E.*

COOK'S SUGGESTION
The skins of sweet potatoes range from white and pink to reddish brown, their flesh from white to orange. The white-fleshed variety discolours very quickly when peeled and should be kept in cold water until ready to cook.

ROAST NEW POTATOES WITH ROSEMARY

Tiny new potatoes, delicately scented with lemon and flavoured with fresh rosemary, are roasted to golden perfection in this tasty dish that takes very little time to prepare.

TIME: 30 MINUTES SERVES: 4

600 g even-sized baby new potatoes
2 tablespoons olive oil
1 lemon
2–3 large sprigs rosemary
Salt and black pepper

1 Preheat the oven to 230°C and put a kettle of water on to boil.

2 Scrub the potatoes and put into a large saucepan. Cover with boiling water, bring back to the boil and cook gently for 5 minutes.

3 Meanwhile, pour the olive oil into a large, shallow baking dish and put into the oven to heat.

4 Finely grate the lemon rind or remove with a zester. Strip the rosemary leaves from the stems.

5 Drain the potatoes. Put into the hot oil and stir well to coat evenly. Sprinkle the lemon rind, rosemary leaves and some salt and black pepper over them. Make sure the oil is really hot before you begin roasting – the potatoes should start to sizzle as soon as you put them into the baking dish.

6 Roast the potatoes on the top shelf of the oven for 20 minutes, until golden.

NUTRIENTS PER SERVING: kilojoules 745, protein 3 g, carbohydrate 25 g (sugar 2 g), fat 8 g (saturated fat 1 g), good source of vitamins B group, C and E.

COOK'S SUGGESTION
Choose tiny new potatoes, about the size of a marble, for this elegant dish. If larger, cut into halves or quarters.

CABBAGE WITH CREAM AND STILTON

White cabbage, with a rich dressing of cream and blue vein cheese, goes particularly well with roast lamb.

TIME: 20 MINUTES SERVES: 4

1 tablespoon olive oil
1 large onion
1 small savoy cabbage, about 450 g
125 g Stilton cheese
200 ml cream
Black pepper

1 Heat the olive oil in a saucepan. Peel and finely chop the onion. Add to the oil and cook gently.
2 Meanwhile, trim off and discard any tough or bruised outer leaves from the cabbage. Halve, remove the core, and finely shred the leaves.
3 Add the cabbage to the saucepan and stir, then cover and cook over moderate heat for 6–8 minutes, shaking the pan frequently. You do not need to add salt as the cheese will contribute enough.
4 While the cabbage is cooking, cut the Stilton into small cubes. Remove the pan from the heat, add the cream, Stilton and a generous grinding of black pepper, then return to the heat. Stir until the cheese has melted, but do not allow it to boil. The melted cheese will thicken the cream.

NUTRIENTS PER SERVING: kilojoules 1189, protein 10 g, carbohydrate 10 g (sugar 8 g), fat 25 g (saturated fat 13 g), good source of vitamins A, B group, C, E and folate.

STIR-FRIED CABBAGE AND CASHEWS

White and green cabbage combine in this easy stir-fry, while cashew nuts and celery add extra crunch.

TIME: 20 MINUTES SERVES: 4–6

350 g white cabbage
350 g green cabbage
2 cloves garlic
2-cm piece fresh root ginger
2 stalks celery
4 spring onions
2 tablespoons sesame oil
⅓ cup unsalted cashew nuts
To serve: light soy sauce

1 Trim and shred the cabbages. Peel and chop the garlic, peel and grate the ginger, and trim and slice the celery and spring onions.
2 Heat the sesame oil in a large frying pan and fry the cashew nuts for 30 seconds, until just beginning to turn brown.
3 Add the garlic, ginger, celery and spring onions; cook for 30 seconds, being careful not to burn the garlic.
4 Add the shredded cabbage; stir-fry for 3–5 minutes, until just softened but not wilted.
5 Serve sprinkled with soy sauce.
SERVING SUGGESTION
This vegetable dish can accompany plainly grilled pork chops; it also teams well as part of an Asian meal.

NUTRIENTS PER SERVING, WHEN SERVING 4: kilojoules 762, protein 7 g, carbohydrate 10 g (sugar 7 g), fat 13 g (saturated fat 2 g), good source of vitamins A, B group, C and folate, and calcium.

CREATIVE CABBAGE DISHES: *(top)* CABBAGE WITH CREAM AND STILTON; *(bottom)* STIR-FRIED CABBAGE AND CASHEWS.

MIXED MUSHROOMS WITH BRANDY

A harmonious mixture of dried and fresh mushrooms, cooked in olive oil and their own juices with onion, garlic, fresh parsley and a splash of brandy, makes an indulgent side dish.

TIME: 30 MINUTES SERVES: 4

A small bunch of parsley
30 g dried morels or ceps
1 tablespoon butter
1 tablespoon olive oil
2 cloves garlic
1 medium onion
200 g Swiss brown mushrooms
200 g open cup mushrooms
150 g oyster mushrooms
1–2 tablespoons brandy
Salt and black pepper

1 Put a kettle of water on to boil. Chop enough parsley to give 3 tablespoons. Put the morels or ceps into a bowl, cover with 200 ml boiling water and leave to soak.

2 Meanwhile, heat the butter and olive oil in a large frying pan over moderate heat. Peel and crush the garlic and put aside. Peel and finely chop the onion, add to the pan and fry over moderate heat while preparing the fresh mushrooms.

3 Clean all the mushrooms then halve the Swiss brown mushrooms, slice the open cup mushrooms, and cut the oyster mushrooms into strips, removing the stalks if tough.

4 Raise the heat under the pan and add the garlic and mushrooms. Stir-fry for 5 minutes, until the mushrooms are just softened.

5 Meanwhile, line a sieve with paper towels and place it over a bowl. Pour the soaked mushrooms into it, so the paper catches any grit and the soaking water drains into the bowl. Reserve this liquid. Rinse and chop the drained mushrooms.

6 With a slotted spoon, lift the fried onions and mushrooms from the frying pan and put into a bowl, leaving the juices in the pan.

7 Add the drained mushrooms and their soaking water to the pan. Boil rapidly until the liquid has a syrupy consistency.

8 Stir in the brandy. Return the mushrooms to the pan, season to taste with salt and black pepper, stir in the chopped parsley and reheat. Transfer to a warm dish to serve.

SERVING SUGGESTION
This mushroom dish goes well with succulent grilled steaks.

NUTRIENTS PER SERVING: kilojoules 527, protein 5 g, carbohydrate 4 g (sugar 3 g), fat 11 g (saturated fat 4 g), good source of vitamins B group, E and folate, and selenium.

PUNJABI POTATO PATTIES

In India, these aromatic and scrumptiously spicy potato patties, known as aloo tiki, are eaten hot or cold as a tea-time snack with mint chutney, tomato sauce or sweet tamarind relish.

TIME: 30 MINUTES SERVES: 4

500 g potatoes
Salt
1 medium onion
¼ teaspoon chilli powder
1 teaspoon garam masala
½ lemon
A handful of coriander
2 tablespoons vegetable oil
3 teaspoons butter

1 Peel and dice the potatoes, put into a pan and cover with cold salted water. Cover, bring to the boil and cook gently for 10 minutes, until tender but not disintegrating.
2 Peel and roughly grate the onion onto a double thickness of paper towels. Squeeze out any juice then put it into a bowl. Add the chilli, garam masala and a pinch of salt.
3 Squeeze 2 teaspoons juice from the half lemon into the onion. Reserve a few sprigs of coriander for a garnish, then chop the remaining leaves and add to the bowl.
4 Drain the potatoes, add to the onions and mash roughly together. Shape into eight patties, each about 5 cm wide.
5 Heat the oil and butter in a large frying pan until sizzling, then fry the patties for 2–3 minutes on each side, until crisp and golden.
6 Drain the patties on paper towels and serve hot, garnished with the reserved coriander.

SERVING SUGGESTION
These patties are an unusual but very successful accompaniment to plainly cooked fish or grilled veal. They can also be served as part of a curry meal.

NUTRIENTS PER SERVING: kilojoules 812, protein 3 g, carbohydrate 21 g (sugar 3 g), fat 12 g (saturated fat 3 g), good source of vitamins B group and C.

COOK'S SUGGESTION

The patties can also be made from leftover potatoes and can be mixed and shaped in advance, then kept chilled in the refrigerator until needed.

VEGETABLES WITH FLAIR

CELERY AND APPLE

Crisp celery and apples are delicious when combined with wine, herbs and capers.

TIME: 30 MINUTES   SERVES: 4

1 head young celery
3 medium-sized red dessert apples
2 tablespoons olive oil
12 sage leaves
1 large clove garlic
1 bay leaf
½–¾ cup dry white wine
1 tablespoon capers, optional
Salt and black pepper

1   Trim off the leaves and the root end of the celery. Slice the stalks diagonally into thin semicircles, cutting across the entire head, then put aside.
2   Core the apples but do not peel. Slice finely and put aside.
3   Generously cover the bottom of a large frying pan with olive oil, and heat until it shows a haze. Snip the sage leaves into the pan. Peel the garlic and crush it in. Allow the sage and garlic to sizzle for a few seconds, then quickly add the celery, apples and bay leaf and stir well.
4   After 1 minute, pour in enough white wine to cover the mixture. Continue cooking over high heat for 2–3 minutes, stirring occasionally, until the celery is cooked but still crunchy. If the mixture dries out before the celery is cooked, add a little more wine.
5   When the celery is done to your liking, stir in the capers, if using, and heat through quickly. Season the dish with salt and black pepper to taste, discard the bay leaf and serve immediately.

NUTRIENTS PER SERVING: kilojoules 590, protein 1 g, carbohydrate 13 g (sugar 12 g), fat 7 g (saturated fat 1 g), good source of vitamins B group and E.

SKIRLIE TOMATOES

Skirlie is a meaty-flavoured oatmeal garnish often served in Scotland with game and poultry dishes or scattered over mashed potatoes. In this recipe it enhances baked tomatoes.

TIME: 30 MINUTES   SERVES: 4

4 large tomatoes, about 200 g each
Salt and black pepper
1 medium onion
50 g shredded beef suet or 2 tablespoons butter
125 g medium oatmeal
A small bunch of parsley

1   Preheat the oven to 200°C . Halve the tomatoes across their middles and make deep, criss-cross slashes over the cut sides. Place, cut side up, on a baking tray, add salt and pepper to taste, then bake for 20 minutes.
2   While the tomatoes are baking, peel and finely chop the onion, mix with the suet or butter in a frying pan and cook over low heat, stirring frequently, for 15 minutes.
3   When the onion is soft and begins to brown, stir in the oatmeal and add more salt and pepper. Raise the heat to moderate and cook for a further 5–10 minutes, stirring, until the oatmeal is toasted.
4   Chop enough parsley to give 2 tablespoons. Pile the skirlie onto the tomatoes and sprinkle with the chopped parsley.

NUTRIENTS PER SERVING: kilojoules 1155, protein 6 g, carbohydrate 33 g (sugar 8 g), fat 14 g (saturated fat 6 g), good source of vitamins A, B group, C, E and folate.

COOK'S SUGGESTION

This recipe is made with oatmeal rather than the rolled oats sold for porridge. Beef suet is available from most butchers and some larger supermarkets.

GLAZED ONIONS

Whole baby onions glow in a golden glaze flavoured with soy sauce, mustard and rosemary.

TIME: 30 MINUTES   SERVES: 4–6

500 g pickling onions
½–1 teaspoon dried rosemary
1 tablespoon butter
2 teaspoons treacle or 3 teaspoons honey
2 teaspoons Dijon mustard
3 teaspoons soy sauce
To garnish: 1 sprig rosemary

1   Put a kettle of water on to boil. Put the onions into a saucepan, cover with the boiling water and cook over moderate heat for 5 minutes. Pour into a colander and put under cold running water. When the onions are cool enough to handle, drain well and peel .
2   Crush the rosemary as finely as possible, using a pestle and mortar or the end of a rolling pin.
3   Melt the butter gently in a large frying pan over moderate heat. Add the crushed rosemary, treacle or honey, Dijon mustard and soy sauce and mix well to form an emulsion.
4   Stir in the onions and cook gently, stirring and basting with the sauce, for 10–15 minutes, until the glaze has thickened and the onions are tender. Watch continuously to make sure the glaze does not burn.
5   Tip into a warmed serving bowl and garnish with the rosemary.
SERVING SUGGESTION
These onions make a sweet and spicy accompaniment to roasted and grilled red meats.

NUTRIENTS PER SERVING, WHEN SERVING 4: kilojoules 462, protein 2 g, carbohydrate 14 g (sugar 11 g), fat 6 g (saturated fat 3 g), good source of vitamins B group and E.

VEGETABLES ON THE SIDE: *(top)* CELERY AND APPLE; *(centre)* GLAZED ONIONS; *(bottom)* SKIRLIE TOMATOES.

DESSERTS

Nothing rounds off a good meal like a great dessert.
Choose from wonderful hot soufflés, cool whips, tempting
crumbles or flambéed fruits, or make a fast and fabulous
sweet sauce for a favourite sorbet or ice cream.

POACHED FRUIT WITH CHOCOLATE SAUCE

*Peaches and figs, poached in brandy and apple juice, are partnered by a lavish white chocolate sauce,
enriched with crème fraîche to give it smoothness and orange zest for a tangy citrus flavour.*

TIME: 20 MINUTES SERVES: 4

90 g white chocolate drops or solid white chocolate
1 cup apple juice
1 teaspoon caster sugar
1 tablespoon brandy
8 small or 4 large figs
2 large peaches or nectarines
150 g crème fraîche
1 orange

1 Put some hot water into a small pan. Set a bowl over it, making sure the bottom is clear of the water. Put the chocolate into the bowl (if you are using a bar, break it into pieces first); bring the water to simmering point. Stir the chocolate a little as it melts. Do not allow the water to boil as the chocolate will overheat. When it has melted, put the bowl aside, leaving the pan of hot water for later.

2 Meanwhile, pour the apple juice into a shallow saucepan or a frying pan with a lid. Add the caster sugar and brandy, bring the mixture to the boil, then reduce the heat.

3 Rinse the figs and cut large ones into quarters lengthways, small ones into halves. Halve and stone the peaches or nectarines, then cut each half into four slices. Add the fruit to the apple juice, cover and poach gently for 4 minutes. If the skins come off the peaches or nectarines, remove them.

4 While the fruit is cooking, stir the crème fraîche into the melted chocolate gradually with a balloon whisk, then beat until smooth. Put the bowl back on the pan of hot water while you finish off the fruit.

5 Transfer the poached fruit to a serving dish with a slotted spoon. Boil the juice for 5 minutes, or until reduced to a slightly heavy syrup, then pour it over the fruit.

6 While the syrup reduces, grate half the rind from the orange into the chocolate mixture, then add 2 tablespoons juice. Stir the sauce and serve with the fruit.

NUTRIENTS PER SERVING: *kilojoules 1544, protein 5 g, carbohydrate 36 g (sugar 36 g), fat 22 g (saturated fat 14 g), good source of vitamins B group, C and E.*

EASY DOES IT!

Melt the white chocolate quickly in a microwave oven. Put the chocolate pieces into a bowl, heat on low power for 30 seconds, then stir. If lumps remain, cook and stir in further ten-second bursts until smooth.

WAFFLES WITH FRUIT AND CARAMEL

Orange segments and banana slices soaked in orange juice make a luscious partner to hot, freshly toasted waffles, especially when served with a warm caramel sauce.

TIME: 20 MINUTES SERVES: 4

| 2 large oranges |
| 1 large banana |
| 2 tablespoons unsalted butter |
| ⅓ cup brown sugar |
| 3 tablespoons cream |
| 8 bought waffles |

To serve: 4 tablespoons natural yoghurt, optional

1 Remove the peel and white pith from the oranges with a sharp knife. Holding each orange over a bowl to catch the juice, remove the segments by cutting between the connecting white tissue, letting each segment fall into the bowl. Squeeze the remaining tissue to extract the rest of the juice.

2 Peel the banana, slice into the oranges, and mix gently together. Preheat the griller.

3 Melt the butter slowly in a small pan over moderate heat. Add the sugar and stir for about 2 minutes, until it has dissolved. Then add the cream and simmer the mixture gently for about 3 minutes, stirring frequently, until it turns a caramel colour. Remove from the heat.

4 Toast the waffles according to the instructions on the packet and place on four serving plates. Spoon a quarter of the orange and banana mixture onto each, and pour on the caramel sauce. Add a spoonful of yoghurt, if using, and serve.

NUTRIENTS PER SERVING: kilojoules 2235, protein 7 g, carbohydrate 50 g (sugar 26 g), fat 36 g (saturated fat 16 g), good source of vitamins A, B group, C and E, and calcium.

COOK'S SUGGESTION

If you toast the waffles while you are still simmering the cream mixture, make sure that you keep an eye on them, as they burn very easily.

283

BAKED APPLE WITH BRIOCHE

Sweet dessert apples in a spicy orange sauce can be left to bake in the oven while you enjoy your main course, then quickly finished off and served on toasted brioche for a really satisfying finale.

TIME: 30 MINUTES SERVES: 4

4 sweet dessert apples,
about 150 g each

3 teaspoons butter

1 large orange

½ teaspoon ground cinnamon

2 tablespoons brown sugar

4 brioche rolls

150 g natural yoghurt or 150 ml
thickened cream

1   Preheat the oven to 220°C and put an ovenproof dish in to heat.
2   Core the apples, then cut in half lengthways. Score the skins deeply several times with a sharp knife.
3   Place the apples, cut side down, in the heated dish, and dot over the top with the butter.
4   Finely grate the rind from the orange and squeeze the juice into a bowl. Stir in the cinnamon and half

the brown sugar. Pour the mixture over the apples.
5   Cover the dish with a lid or foil and bake for 10–15 minutes, or until the apples are tender.
6   Meanwhile, cut the brioche rolls in half widthways, then cut off the top and bottom crusts. Preheat the griller to high if you need it for toasting the brioche, and whip the cream, if using.

7 Two minutes before the apples are cooked, toast the brioche slices for about 1 minute each side, or until just lightly browned. Put two slices on each warmed serving plate and carefully place an apple half on each slice.

8 Spoon the cooking juices over the apples, sprinkle with the remaining brown sugar, and serve immediately with the yoghurt or whipped cream.

NUTRIENTS PER SERVING: kilojoules 1800, protein 6 g, carbohydrate 52 g (sugar 28 g), fat 23 g (saturated fat 11 g), good source of vitamins A, B group, C and E.

CINNAMON APPLE FRITTERS

Served piping hot, these slices of crisp apple in fluffy, light-as-air batter will fill the house with an irresistible aroma.

TIME: 15 MINUTES SERVES: 2

Vegetable oil for deep-frying
1 egg
Salt
4 tablespoons sparkling mineral water
3 tablespoons plain flour
2 tablespoons caster sugar
1 teaspoon ground cinnamon
2 crisp dessert apples

1 Half-fill a large wok or deep fryer with oil and put on to heat. Break the egg into a bowl, add a pinch of salt and whisk until frothy. Quickly whisk in the mineral water, then the flour – you are not aiming for a smooth batter.

2 Mix the sugar and cinnamon together on a saucer and put aside.

Peel, core and slice the apples into rings about 5 mm thick.

3 When the oil has reached a temperature of 190°C, and a few drops of the batter sizzle as soon as they are dropped in, dip each of the apple slices into the batter with a fork and drop into the oil. Deep-fry the fritters in two or three batches for 1–2 minutes each, or until puffed and golden, turning carefully with a slotted spoon halfway through cooking.

4 Drain on paper towels and serve immediately, sprinkled with the spiced sugar.

NUTRIENTS PER SERVING: kilojoules 1729, protein 5 g, carbohydrate 45 g (sugar 29 g), fat 25 g (saturated fat 4 g), good source of vitamins B group and E.

HOT CHOCOLATE SOUFFLÉS WITH RUM

These little chocolate soufflés are a breeze to make. You can start preparing them before you begin your meal and finish them off while the main course is being cleared away.

TIME: 30 MINUTES SERVES: 4–6

3 teaspoons unsalted butter, at room temperature
⅓ cup caster sugar
1 cup milk
100 g dark chocolate
5 eggs
2 tablespoons cornflour
2 tablespoons thick cream
2 tablespoons rum
1 tablespoon icing sugar, for sifting

1 Carefully butter the insides and rims of four 200-ml or six 150-ml soufflé dishes, then coat evenly with 1 tablespoon caster sugar.

2 Pour the milk into a small saucepan and put over moderate heat. Break the chocolate into small pieces and stir it into the milk. As soon as the milk reaches scalding point, remove from the heat, cover and leave to stand for 2–3 minutes, until the chocolate has melted.

3 Meanwhile, separate the eggs, put the whites into a large, clean bowl and put aside. Put 3 egg yolks into a small bowl – the other two are not needed and can be kept for another purpose.

4 Add 2 tablespoons caster sugar to the cornflour in a large pan, and over low heat gradually whisk in the chocolate milk to form a smooth paste. Then increase the heat, beating continuously, until the sauce boils and becomes stiff.

5 Remove from the heat and beat in the cream, rum and egg yolks. Scrape the mixture from the sides of the pan with a spatula and cover with the lid to prevent a skin forming, then put aside.

6 Before you begin your meal, preheat the oven to 230°C. Put a baking tray with a raised edge into the oven to heat.

7 When the main course is over, whisk the egg whites until they form soft peaks (an electric beater is quickest). Add the remaining caster sugar and whisk again until the whites are stiff and shiny.

8 Fold a large spoonful of the egg white into the chocolate sauce, then gently fold in all the remaining egg white. Spoon the mixture into the soufflé dishes and put on the baking tray in the oven.

9 Bake for 8–10 minutes, or until well-risen and lightly set, with soft centres. Remove from the oven, sift over the icing sugar, and serve immediately.

VARIATION
For a non-alcoholic soufflé, omit the rum and beat some finely grated orange zest into the sauce.

NUTRIENTS PER SERVING, WHEN SERVING 4:
kilojoules 1988, protein 9g, carbohydrate 53g (sugar 46g), fat 24g (saturated fat 13g), good source of vitamins A, B group and E.

COOK'S SUGGESTION

For successful soufflés, the oven must be very hot and the egg whites must always be beaten in a clean, dry bowl with a clean, dry whisk or electric beaters.

HOT RASPBERRY SOUFFLÉS

Raspberries give these individual desserts a beautiful colour and a delectable flavour. They must be eaten straight from the oven to capture the deliciously light, melt-in-the-mouth texture.

TIME: 25 MINUTES SERVES: 4

2 teaspoons unsalted butter, at room temperature
½ cup caster sugar
250 g raspberries
1 tablespoon kirsch, optional
4 large egg whites
1 tablespoon icing sugar, for sifting
To serve: thick pouring cream

1 Before you sit down to your main course, preheat the oven to 190°C. Grease the insides of four 200-ml soufflé dishes, or ovenproof cereal bowls, with the butter, then coat evenly with some of the caster sugar, tipping out any surplus. Place the dishes on a baking tray.

2 Purée the raspberries by pressing the fruit through a nylon or stainless steel sieve, using the back of a spoon. Stir the kirsch, if using, into the purée.

3 When you have finished the main course, whisk the egg whites with an electric beater until stiff but not dry, then gradually whisk in the remaining caster sugar. Beat until the mixture is shiny.

4 Carefully fold the raspberry purée into the egg whites, then spoon the mixture into the dishes and make a swirl on top of each. Leaving space above for the soufflés to rise, cook in the centre of the oven for 12–14 minutes, or until well risen and lightly set.

5 Remove the soufflés from the oven, sift icing sugar evenly over the top of each and serve with cream.

NUTRIENTS PER SERVING: kilojoules 1678, protein 5 g, carbohydrate 38 g (sugar 38 g), fat 26 g (saturated fat 16 g), good source of vitamins A, B group, C and E.

THREE FAST YOGHURT DESSERTS

MANGO BRÛLÉE

Voluptuous mangoes soaked in rum and cinnamon snuggle beneath a golden sugar topping.

TIME: 20 MINUTES SERVES: 4

2 large mangoes, about 400 g each
2 tablespoons rum
½ teaspoon ground cinnamon
350 g natural yoghurt
½ cup brown sugar

1 Preheat the griller to high.
2 Peel the mangoes (see box, below), cut off the two fat cheeks and dice, then cut off and dice the remaining flesh. Half fill four deep, flameproof ramekin dishes with the fruit.
3 Drizzle the rum over the fruit and sprinkle with cinnamon. Spoon in the yoghurt, smooth it level, then sprinkle the brown sugar evenly over the top.
4 Put the ramekins under the griller, about 10 cm from the heat, and cook for 4–5 minutes, until the sugar melts and turns golden brown. Serve hot or cold.

VARIATION
Fresh sliced peaches or bananas, or raspberries or strawberries, could be used instead of mangoes.

NUTRIENTS PER SERVING: kilojoules 1318, protein 7 g, carbohydrate 52 g (sugar 52 g), fat 8 g (saturated fat 5 g), good source of vitamins A, B group, C and E.

RASPBERRY CRUNCH

Muesli with raisins and almonds makes a substantial partner for soft juicy raspberries.

TIME: 10 MINUTES SERVES: 4

350 g raspberries
2 tablespoons caster sugar
500 g natural yoghurt
1½ cups muesli, or crunchy oat breakfast cereal with honey, raisins and almonds
1 tablespoon honey

To decorate: **a few extra raspberries, a little extra honey and muesli or breakfast cereal**

1 Put the raspberries and sugar into a bowl; mix and put aside.
2 In another bowl, mix the yoghurt with the muesli or breakfast cereal. Add the honey, stirring lightly, so the mixture is streaky.
3 Divide two-thirds of the mixture among four wide 250-ml glasses. Top with the sweetened raspberries, then add the remaining mixture. Drizzle a little honey over the top, sprinkle with muesli or cereal, and decorate with extra raspberries.
4 If it is served immediately, this dessert has a crunchy texture; if you prefer a softer, creamier texture, chill for 3–4 hours before serving.

NUTRIENTS PER SERVING: kilojoules 1331, protein 14 g, carbohydrate 52 g (sugar 37 g), fat 7 g (saturated fat 3 g), good source of vitamins B group, C and E.

STRAWBERRY CLOUDS

Crushed strawberries mixed into a yoghurt and vanilla meringue are transformed into a light-as-air treat.

TIME: 20 MINUTES SERVES: 4

250 g strawberries
¼ cup plus 1 tablespoon caster sugar
2 large egg whites
250 g natural yoghurt, chilled
½ teaspoon vanilla essence
To serve: almond bread

1 Hull the strawberries. Halve two large ones for a decoration and put the rest into a bowl. Sprinkle with 1 tablespoon caster sugar and crush with a fork.
2 In a large mixing bowl, whisk the egg whites until they form a soft peak, then gradually add the remaining caster sugar, whisking well after each addition, to make a stiff meringue.
3 Add the yoghurt and the vanilla essence to the meringue and gently fold in with a metal spoon.
4 Fold the mashed strawberries and their juice into the yoghurt mixture. Be careful not to mix too vigorously, or the light, airy texture will be lost.
5 Spoon the meringue into four 200-ml glasses and decorate with the reserved strawberry halves. Serve immediately with the almond bread, or chill for 2–3 hours.

VARIATION
Omit the almond bread and decorate the top of each strawberry cloud with a sprinkling of chopped, toasted almonds or pecans.

NUTRIENTS PER SERVING: kilojoules 691, protein 6 g, carbohydrate 23 g (sugar 23 g), fat 6 g (saturated fat 3 g), good source of vitamins B group, C and E.

YOGHURT DELIGHTS: *(top left)* RASPBERRY CRUNCH; *(centre right)* STRAWBERRY CLOUDS; *(bottom)* MANGO BRÛLÉE.

EASY DOES IT!

To peel a mango, score through the skin lengthways, dividing it into four equal sections, being careful not to cut into the flesh. Then insert a fork into the stalk end to hold the fruit steady, lift up the end corner of each section of skin with a knife and your thumb and gently peel back.

APRICOT AND SOUR CREAM CLAFOUTIS

*Canned apricots make a warming and substantial dessert when buried beneath an unusual batter
made with fruit juice and sour cream and topped with butter and sugar.*

TIME: 30 MINUTES SERVES: 4–6

Butter for greasing

**825 g canned apricot halves in
natural juice**

To serve: **crème fraîche or
thick cream**

For the batter:
150 ml sour cream
1 cup plain flour
2 large eggs
½ cup brown sugar
A few drops vanilla essence

For the topping:
3 teaspoons butter
2 tablespoons brown sugar

1 Preheat the oven to 200°C and
grease a shallow, ovenproof dish,
25–30 cm in diameter.

2 Drain the canned apricots,
reserving 100 ml juice, and arrange
them, cut side down, in the bottom
of the dish.
3 To make the batter, stir the sour
cream into the reserved apricot
juice. Place the flour in a separate
bowl and make a well in the centre.
Add the eggs, sugar and vanilla
essence, quickly whisk into the
flour to make a smooth paste, then
gradually whisk in the apricot juice
and sour cream mixture.
4 Pour the batter over the apricots
and bake the clafoutis in the oven
for 20 minutes.
5 Meanwhile, make the topping
by blending the butter and sugar
together with a fork in a small bowl.
6 Remove the clafoutis from
the oven after 15 minutes and dot
the butter and sugar mixture evenly

over the top. Return to the oven for
the remaining 5 minutes, or until
the batter is golden and puffed up.
7 Serve hot, with crème fraîche or
thick cream.
VARIATION
Canned peaches, plums or cherries
can be used instead of the apricots.

*NUTRIENTS PER SERVING, WHEN SERVING 4:
kilojoules 2323, protein 10 g, carbohydrate
65 g (sugar 46 g), fat 31 g (saturated fat 18 g),
good source of vitamins A, B group, C and E.*

COOK'S SUGGESTION

*Instead of the topping, sprinkle the
clafoutis with icing sugar before serving.
Alternatively, sprinkle it with brandy –
an apricot-flavoured brandy would
be particularly good*

PEAR MERINGUE

*Spicy poached pears are given a feather-light topping of meringue and
flaked almonds and served with a glittering red wine sauce.*

TIME: 30 MINUTES SERVES: 4

Butter for greasing
1 lemon
2 cups red wine
1 cup caster sugar
½ cinnamon stick or ¼ teaspoon ground cinnamon
4 large pears, firm but ripe
2 large egg whites
¼ teaspoon vanilla essence
¼ cup flaked almonds
2 tablespoons icing sugar

1 Preheat the oven to 220°C.
Lightly butter a shallow baking dish
just large enough to hold the pears
when they are halved.

2 Squeeze the lemon and pour the
juice into a saucepan, or a large
frying pan with a lid, wide enough
to hold the pear halves in a single
layer. Add the red wine, ½ cup
caster sugar and the cinnamon.
Bring to the boil, then reduce the
heat to a simmer.

3 Peel, halve and core the pears.
Lower into the simmering syrup
and cook gently for 10 minutes,
until just softened, basting with the
syrup from time to time.

4 Meanwhile, make the meringue.
Put the egg whites into a clean bowl
and whisk until stiff but not dry
(this is quickest and easiest with an
electric beater). Sprinkle in the
remaining caster sugar, one
tablespoon at a time, beating well
after each addition. Then add the
vanilla essence and beat until the
meringue is stiff and shiny.

5 Lift out the pear halves with a
slotted spoon, draining the juice,
and place in the baking dish,
hollow side up. Spoon the meringue
over each half, sprinkle some flaked
almonds over the meringue, and sift
the icing sugar over the top. Bake on
the middle shelf of the oven for
5 minutes or until the meringue is
lightly browned.

6 Meanwhile, boil the wine sauce
until reduced to a heavy syrup.
Discard the cinnamon stick, if used,
and pour the syrup into a jug.

7 Lift the dish of pears from the
oven very carefully, to make sure
the meringue does not slip off, and
serve with the wine sauce.

VARIATION

Sweet dessert apples or firm ripe
peaches or nectarines, peeled and
cut in half, or thick rings of peeled
fresh pineapple, can be used in
place of the pears. If you prefer a
non-alcoholic sauce, water or an
unsweetened fruit juice may be
substituted for the red wine.

*NUTRIENTS PER SERVING: kilojoules 1888,
protein 4 g, carbohydrate 90 g (sugar 89 g),
fat 4 g (saturated fat 0.3 g), good source of
vitamins B group and E.*

BAKED ALMOND PEARS

This luscious pear dessert is baked in a fruit syrup and topped with almond flavoured biscuits or crisp roasted almonds, to add a crunchy texture.

TIME: 30 MINUTES SERVES: 4

2 ½ tablespoons butter, at room temperature	
1 tablespoon caster sugar	
4 large pears, firm but ripe	
3 tablespoons white wine or orange juice	
¼ cup apricot jam or 2 tablespoons honey	
6 Amaretti biscuits or ½ cup blanched almonds	

To serve: cream or natural yoghurt

1 Preheat the oven to 200°C. Grease a shallow, round ovenproof dish with half the butter and sprinkle the caster sugar evenly over the top to coat the butter.
2 Peel and halve the pears, then cut lengthways into slices about 1 cm thick. Arrange the slices in a single, overlapping layer in the bottom of the dish.
3 Mix the wine or orange juice with the apricot jam or honey and pour the mixture over the pears.
4 Coarsely crush the Amaretti biscuits with a rolling pin or finely chop the almonds. Sprinkle over the pears. Dot the remaining butter evenly over the pears. Bake in the oven for 15–20 minutes, until the pears have softened and the biscuits or almonds are lightly browned. Serve with cream or yoghurt.

VARIATION
For a faster dessert, substitute eight canned pear halves for the fresh pears, sliced or left whole, and mix 2 tablespoons juice from the can with 2 tablespoons orange juice to replace the white wine. Bake for about 10 minutes to heat through and lightly brown the top.

NUTRIENTS PER SERVING: kilojoules 2058, protein 2 g, carbohydrate 42 g (sugar 36 g), fat 35 g (saturated fat 22 g), good source of vitamins A, B group and E.

SPICED PEACHES WITH MASCARPONE

The heat of a whole fresh chilli brings out the exquisite sweetness of the peaches in this spicy dessert, while sweetened mascarpone makes a refreshingly different alternative to cream.

TIME: 25 MINUTES SERVES: 4

½ cup plus 1 tablespoon caster sugar
2 star anise
1-cm length cinnamon stick
1 red chilli
2 thin slices fresh root ginger
1 lemon
1 kg peaches, firm but ripe
200 g mascarpone cheese

1 Put a kettle of water on to boil. Pour 150 ml water into a large saucepan and add ½ cup caster sugar, star anise, cinnamon, chilli and ginger. Stir over moderate heat until the sugar has dissolved, then bring to the boil.

2 Pare off 3 strips lemon rind, add to the sugar syrup, reduce the heat and simmer.

3 Halve the peaches and discard the stones. Put the halves into a bowl, cover with boiling water, leave for 1–2 minutes, then drain and peel. Cut each half into 4–6 slices and add to the syrup.

4 Bring to the boil, reduce the heat and simmer for 4–5 minutes, or until just softened. Meanwhile, squeeze the juice from the lemon.

5 Stir the remaining caster sugar into the mascarpone.

6 Remove the spiced peaches from the heat and add the lemon juice. Transfer to individual dishes and serve, warm or cold, with a little syrup and the mascarpone.

VARIATION

When served warm, this dessert makes an excellent accompaniment to pancakes, waffles or ice cream.

NUTRIENTS PER SERVING: kilojoules 1687, protein 4 g, carbohydrate 54 g (sugar 54 g), fat 21 g (saturated fat 13 g), good source of vitamins B group and C.

ICE CREAM WITH A TWIST

With good ice cream or sorbet in the freezer you are halfway to a great dessert. Add a special garnish (see page 22) or make one of these scrumptious transformations.

EACH MAKES ENOUGH TO SERVE 4

CHOC-CARAMEL SAUCE

The simplest, richest sauce for ice cream, easily made in minutes.

Cut a large Mars bar into slices, put into a bowl and add 150 ml milk or cream. Place the bowl over a saucepan of hot water and stir until melted. Pour immediately over vanilla ice cream.

MARSHMALLOW SAUCE

A sauce that tastes great served with chocolate ice cream.

Put 125 g large white marshmallows and 2 tablespoons cream into a bowl over a pan of hot water. Stir gently until completely melted and pour immediately over the ice cream.

RED WINE AND BUTTER SAUCE

A sophisticated sauce to pour over citrus or tropical fruit sorbets.

Put 2 tablespoons unsalted butter, 2 tablespoons caster sugar and 3 tablespoons red wine into a pan and whisk gently while heating. Cool slightly, then whisk again and serve.

BLACK CHERRY SPECIAL

Cheer up vanilla ice cream with a hot cherry sauce and a chocolate brownie.

Put 425 g canned pitted black cherries and about half their juice into a pan and heat gently. Stir in 1 tablespoon kirsch. Place 1 scoop ice cream in a tall glass, top with half a chocolate brownie and then another scoop of ice cream. Pour over the cherries; serve with the remaining half brownie.

LEMON BUTTER SAUCE

The perfect topping for vanilla and passionfruit ice cream.

Allow 2 cups vanilla ice cream to soften slightly. Stir in the pulp of one or two passionfruit and return to the freezer. Warm ½ cup lemon butter very gently and thin to pouring consistency with cream. Serve sauce at room temperature over the ice cream.

ROCKY ROAD ICE CREAM

A mixture of fruit and nuts, miniature marshmallows and chocolate turns ice cream into a crunchy treat.

Stir ¼ cup lightly toasted chopped almonds, ¼ cup seedless raisins and 50 g miniature marshmallows into a tub of slightly softened chocolate or chocolate chip ice cream. Return to the freezer for 10 minutes to firm before serving with whipped cream, chocolate sauce and a few chocolate shavings to decorate.

RASPBERRY COULIS

Soft berries make a juicy sauce for many ice creams and sorbets.

Purée 350 g fresh or frozen raspberries in a food processor. Pass through a sieve to remove the seeds and sweeten to taste with icing sugar. Add lemon juice, if you like, to enhance the flavour. Serve the coulis immediately, layered in a glass with ice cream or sorbet, or chill in the refrigerator until needed.

THREE FABULOUS DESSERTS: (*left*) ROCKY ROAD ICE CREAM; (*centre*) BLACK CHERRY SPECIAL; (*right*) RASPBERRY COULIS WITH VANILLA ICE CREAM.

HONEYED FRUIT KEBABS

A mix of fruits marinated in scented honey and nut oil and grilled on skewers make an unusual dessert; to serve, they are sprinkled with toasted hazelnuts and accompanied by cream.

TIME: 30 MINUTES   SERVES: 4

| 8 large strawberries |
| 2 canned or fresh pineapple rings |
| 1 small banana, slightly under-ripe |
| 1 firm pear, preferably Williams |
| 1 small starfruit |
| ¼ cup chopped hazelnuts |
| *To serve:* 150 ml thick cream |

For the marinade:

| 1 lime |
| 2 tablespoons honey, preferably acacia |
| 2 tablespoons hazelnut or walnut oil |

1 For the marinade, finely grate the lemon rind into a large, shallow dish. Squeeze the juice and add to the rind along with the honey and the nut oil. Mix and put aside.

2 As you prepare the fruits, add them to the marinade. Hull the strawberries. Halve the pineapple rings. Peel the banana and cut into four. Quarter and core the pear, then slice each quarter into two. Slice off and discard each end of the starfruit, trim along the ridges with a potato peeler, then cut into four thick slices. Put all the fruit aside for 10 minutes. Meanwhile, heat the griller to medium.

3 Thread the marinated fruit onto four metal skewers about 25 cm long. Begin with a piece of pineapple, then a strawberry, some pear, banana, strawberry then pear, and finish with a slice of starfruit, threaded on horizontally so that the star shape lies flat.

4 Place the skewers on the rack of the griller tray and brush with the marinade. Grill for 3 minutes, baste with the marinade and grill for a further 2 minutes. Turn the kebabs and repeat until the fruit is golden, with some crunchy dark patches.

5 While the fruit is under the griller, toast the chopped hazelnuts.

6 Transfer the cooked fruit kebabs very carefully onto a serving dish and sprinkle the toasted hazelnuts evenly over the top. Serve with the thick cream.

VARIATION

In summer, these kebabs can be cooked very successfully outdoors on the griller rack of a barbecue.

NUTRIENTS PER SERVING: kilojoules 1381, protein 2 g, carbohydrate 30 g (sugar 28 g), fat 24 g (saturated fat 12 g), good source of vitamins B group, C and E.

COOK'S SUGGESTION

Fruit softens considerably when grilled, so make sure you cut it into quite generous pieces and skewer each piece centrally so that nothing falls off during cooking or when serving.

GRILLED FIGS

This gorgeous dessert features plump ripe figs scented with rosewater and oozing with beautiful pink juices.

TIME: 20 MINUTES SERVES: 4

3 teaspoons butter, at room temperature
8 large figs
1 lemon
A few drops of rosewater
4 tablespoons caster sugar
4 tablespoons crème fraîche

1 Preheat the griller to its highest setting for 10 minutes. Lightly butter a small flameproof dish.
2 Remove the stalks from the figs, then cut in half.
3 Squeeze the juice from the lemon into a small bowl and add the rosewater. Toss the figs in the scented juice then arrange, cut side down, in one layer in the buttered dish. Sprinkle the skins liberally with 2 tablespoons sugar.
4 Place the figs under the hot griller and cook for 3–4 minutes. Turn, sprinkle the cut sides with the remaining sugar, and grill for a further 2–3 minutes. Serve piping hot, bathed in their pink juices, with the crème fraîche.

NUTRIENTS PER SERVING: kilojoules 1302, protein 2 g, carbohydrate 36 g (sugar 36 g), fat 18 g (saturated fat 12 g), good source of vitamin B group.

OATY PLUM CRUMBLE

Poached fresh plums are given a golden topping of crunchy oats, chopped nuts, mixed spices and brown sugar, then baked in the oven to make a comforting family treat.

TIME: 30 MINUTES SERVES: 4

1 kg plums, firm but ripe
½ cup caster sugar
3 tablespoons unsalted butter
1 teaspoon mixed spice
¾ cup rolled oats
⅓ cup brown sugar
½ cup mixed chopped nuts
To serve: whipped cream or ice cream

1 Preheat the oven to 230°C. Halve the plums and remove the stones. If the plums are large, cut into quarters.

2 Put the plums into a flameproof casserole, about 20 cm in diameter and 5 cm deep. Add the caster sugar and 2–3 tablespoons water. Cover and poach over moderate heat for 8–10 minutes, stirring occasionally, until the plums begin to soften.

3 Meanwhile, melt the butter in a frying pan, then stir in the mixed spice, rolled oats, brown sugar and chopped nuts.

4 Spoon the mixture evenly over the top of the plums. Put the casserole into the oven and bake for 12–15 minutes, checking regularly, until the oats are golden brown.

5 Serve the crumble straight from the casserole, hot or warm, with whipped cream or ice cream.

NUTRIENTS PER SERVING: kilojoules 2842, protein 9 g, carbohydrate 87 g (sugar 66 g), fat 35 g (saturated fat 17 g), good source of vitamins A, B group and E.

COOK'S SUGGESTION

If you do not have a flameproof casserole, poach the plums in an ordinary saucepan and then transfer to an ovenproof dish to bake.

FRUITY BREAD AND BUTTER PUDDING

Sweet summer fruits make a luxurious addition to an everyday favourite – a great classic that makes a warming and original finish to a dinner party.

TIME: 30 MINUTES SERVES: 4

1½ cups full-cream milk
300 g fresh or frozen mixed summer fruits, such as berries and stone fruits
2 tablespoons butter
8 slices wholemeal bread
2 tablespoons brown sugar
2 large eggs
½ teaspoon vanilla essence
Nutmeg for grating
1 teaspoon icing sugar
To serve: thick cream or natural yoghurt

1 Preheat the oven to 220°C. Heat the milk gently in a pan; do not let it boil. Meanwhile, if you are using frozen fruit, spread out on a plate to thaw a little.

2 Grease four 300-ml ovenproof dishes with a little butter.

3 Remove the crusts from the bread, spread the remaining butter over the slices and cut each one into four triangles.

4 Arrange a few pieces of bread in the bottom of each dish. Add a spoonful of fruit and a sprinkling of sugar, then repeat the layers, ending with a layer of bread.

5 Break the eggs into a bowl, whisk lightly, then stir in the warm milk and the vanilla. Whisk again, then carefully pour the mixture evenly over each dish.

6 Grate a little nutmeg over the puddings, transfer the dishes to a baking tray and bake the puddings for 15 minutes, or until just set and golden brown on top.

7 Sift icing sugar over the tops and serve warm with cream or yoghurt.
VARIATION
Use two 500-ml pudding basins and turn the puddings out on to a platter to serve.

NUTRIENTS PER SERVING: kilojoules 2708, protein 15 g, carbohydrate 52 g (sugar 23 g), fat 44 g (saturated fat 25 g), good source of vitamins A, B group, C, E and folate, and calcium, selenium and zinc.

COOK'S SUGGESTION
You can prepare the puddings some hours ahead of serving and keep refrigerated. Return to room temperature 30 minutes before you are ready to bake them.

WHIPPED DELIGHTS

GINGER AND CHOCOLATE MASCARPONE

A wickedly rich confection of dark chocolate, rum and creamy Italian cheese, studded with ginger.

TIME: 10 MINUTES SERVES: 4

3 pieces stem ginger in syrup
2 tablespoons ginger syrup from the jar
2 tablespoons dark rum
100 g dark chocolate
250 g mascarpone cheese
To serve: 4 brandy-snap baskets

1 Finely slice 1 piece ginger and put aside. Dice the remaining ginger finely and put into a bowl with the ginger syrup and the rum. Grate in the chocolate and stir to combine.
2 Add the mascarpone, mix well, then cover and chill for as long as you can. It will stiffen as it chills.
3 Scoop the mixture into the brandy-snap baskets, top with the reserved sliced ginger, and serve.

VARIATION
Try brandy, sweet sherry or coffee liqueur as a substitute for the rum.

NUTRIENTS PER SERVING: kilojoules 1611, protein 3 g, carbohydrate 34 g (sugar 32 g), fat 24 g (saturated fat 15 g), good source of vitamin E.

ZABAGLIONE

This mixture of eggs, sugar and Marsala fluffed-up over a gentle heat tastes wonderful eaten warm.

TIME: 15 MINUTES SERVES: 4

4 large egg yolks
2 tablespoons caster sugar
½ cup Marsala
To serve: 2 strawberries, halved, and 4 savoiardi biscuits

1 Choose a heatproof mixing bowl and a saucepan on which it will sit firmly. Fill the saucepan with about 7–8 cm water and heat until it starts to simmer.
2 Put the egg yolks into the mixing bowl, add the sugar and whisk until the mixture is light and creamy.
3 Place the mixing bowl over the pan of simmering water, then add the Marsala and continue to beat with a whisk until the mixture becomes thick and forms soft peaks.
4 Spoon the zabaglione into long-stemmed glasses, top with half a strawberry, and serve with a biscuit.

VARIATION
For a non-alcoholic zabaglione, you can use fresh orange juice instead of the Marsala. Just before serving, whisk in 1 teaspoon orange zest or very finely grated rind.

NUTRIENTS PER SERVING: kilojoules 741, protein 3 g, carbohydrate 12 g (sugar 12 g), fat 6 g (saturated fat 2 g), good source of vitamins B group and E.

CHESTNUT BRANDY CREAM

Chestnut purée fortified with brandy is whipped into a treat with thick cream and chocolate.

TIME: 20 MINUTES SERVES: 4

250 g canned, sweetened chestnut purée
2 tablespoons brandy
1 cup thick cream
50 g dark chocolate

1 Empty the can of chestnut purée into a large mixing bowl, pour in the brandy, then beat thoroughly, until the mixture is smooth, using either an electric beater or a hand-held balloon whisk.
2 Whip the cream until it holds soft peaks, then fold into the chestnut mixture.
3 Grate the dark chocolate and add half to the mixture.

4 Spoon the chestnut cream into four glasses, sprinkle the rest of the chocolate over the top and chill for 15 minutes before serving.

VARIATION
You may omit the brandy from the chestnut cream, if preferred, or use a chocolate or coffee liqueur.

NUTRIENTS PER SERVING: kilojoules 2034, protein 4 g, carbohydrate 42 g (sugar 17 g), fat 32 g (saturated fat 19 g), good source of vitamins A, B group and E.

CREAMY LEMON PUDDING

A little fresh cream transforms simple lemon butter into a delicious, mousse-like dessert.

TIME: 12 MINUTES SERVES: 4

200 g good quality lemon butter
1 cup thick cream
2 large egg whites
Salt
To serve: a few strips of lemon rind, 4–8 slices almond bread

1 Spoon the lemon butter into a bowl. Whip the cream until it will hold a soft peak, then fold into the lemon butter
2 Add a pinch of salt to the egg whites and whisk until they form soft peaks, then carefully fold into the lemon mixture.
3 Spoon into four serving dishes and chill for as long as possible.
4 Top with the lemon rind and serve with the almond bread.

NUTRIENTS PER SERVING: kilojoules 1310, protein 2 g, carbohydrate 31 g (sugar 19 g), fat 21 g (saturated fat 12 g), good source of vitamins A, B group and E.

EXQUISITELY RICH DESSERTS: *(top)* ZABAGLIONE; *(centre left)* CHESTNUT BRANDY CREAM; *(centre right)* CREAMY LEMON PUDDING; *(bottom)* GINGER AND CHOCOLATE MASCARPONE.

FLAMBÉED PINEAPPLE AND BANANAS

The sunny flavour of two of the best-loved tropical fruits is enhanced by the potent sweetness of hot rum and cooled with whipped cream or ice cream.

TIME: 30 MINUTES SERVES: 4

1 pineapple, about 800 g
1 tablespoon unsalted butter
⅓ cup brown sugar
3 large bananas, firm but ripe
3 tablespoons rum
To serve: whipped cream or vanilla ice cream

1 Peel the pineapple, cut in half lengthways and remove and discard the centre core. Cut each half across into eight slices, reserving any juice.

2 Melt the butter and brown sugar in a large, stainless-steel or enamel frying pan over moderate heat.

3 Peel the bananas, cut in half widthways, then lengthways.

4 Add the pineapple to the hot butter and sugar in the pan and cook over fairly high heat for 1–2 minutes, then add the bananas and cook for another 2–3 minutes, until heated through.

5 Pour the rum into the frying pan, heat for a few seconds, then stand well back and set alight with a match. Allow the rum to burn, shaking the pan very gently, until the flames die down. Pour any reserved pineapple juice into the pan and continue to heat the fruit for 1 minute.

6 Transfer the flambéed fruit to individual dishes and serve with whipped cream or ice cream.

NUTRIENTS PER SERVING: *kilojoules 1904, protein 3 g, carbohydrate 49 g (sugar 47 g), fat 25 g (saturated fat 16 g), good source of vitamins A, B group, C and E.*

RHUBARB AND STRAWBERRY COMPOTE

Tart rhubarb and sweet strawberries, simmered in orange juice, make a surprisingly successful combination of flavours, and are a refreshing way to use up a glut of summer fruits.

TIME: 20 MINUTES SERVES: 4

650 g rhubarb
¼ cup caster sugar
100 ml fresh orange juice
250 g strawberries
To serve: 200 ml thick cream

1 Trim and rinse the rhubarb, cut into 2.5-cm lengths and put into a large saucepan with the sugar and the orange juice. Cover the pan, bring the mixture to the boil, reduce the heat and simmer gently, uncovered, for 5–6 minutes, stirring occasionally.

2 While the rhubarb is cooking, hull the strawberries, then halve or quarter any large ones. Add to the rhubarb and simmer gently for 4–5 minutes, or until slightly softened. They should maintain their shape and still have some bite.

3 Taste and add a little more sugar if necessary. Transfer the compote to a serving dish and serve while still warm with the cream.

VARIATION

If you prefer, you can refrigerate the compote and serve it chilled, accompanied by ice cream or a little cold pouring custard.

NUTRIENTS PER SERVING: kilojoules 1327, protein 3 g, carbohydrate 24 g (sugar 24 g), fat 24 g (saturated fat 15 g), good source of vitamins A, B group, C and E.

COOK'S SUGGESTION

When buying rhubarb, choose a fresh-looking bunch with firm red stalks; any stalks with green tinges will be too sour. When cooking rhubarb, always use a stainless steel or enamel saucepan. And if you have no fresh orange juice for this recipe, squeeze the juice from 2 large oranges.

PEACH AND RASPBERRY CROUSTADES

Golden peaches, nestling among rich red raspberries on a bed of featherlight pastry, bring the sweetness of summer to the table.

TIME: 30 MINUTES SERVES: 4

4 medium-sized peaches, firm but ripe
2 tablespoons good-quality raspberry jam
3 tablespoons unsalted butter
150 g ready-to-use filo pastry
100 g raspberries
2 tablespoons icing sugar
To serve: cream or crème fraîche

1 Preheat the oven to 200°C and halve, stone and slice the peaches.
2 Melt the jam over low heat and sieve into a cup or ramekin. Put some hot water from the tap into a small bowl and stand the container of jam in the water to keep warm; put aside.
3 Gently melt the butter, then cut the filo pastry into 12 rectangles, each about 25 × 12 cm. The exact size of the rectangles does not matter too much, as the pastry will be crumpled into pleats.
4 Lightly brush a baking tray with some of the melted butter. Place one filo strip on the baking tray and brush with butter. Place another filo strip on top and brush with butter, then repeat with the third strip to make the base of one croustade. Repeat the process, to make three more bases.
5 Place your hands at the short ends of each of the pastry rectangles and gently push the ends together, pleating and scrunching until you have made a 'corrugated' croustade about 15 × 12 cm.
6 Carefully arrange the peach slices inside the folds on top of the pastry. Scatter the raspberries over the top. Brush with the jam and bake for 15–20 minutes, or until the pastry is crisp and golden.
7 Transfer the croustades to individual dishes and serve hot or warm, dredged with icing sugar and accompanied by the cream or crème fraîche.

NUTRIENTS PER SERVING: kilojoules 2302, protein 5 g, carbohydrate 49 g (sugar 29 g), fat 38 g (saturated fat 23 g), good source of vitamins A, B group, C and E.

FRESH BERRIES WITH SABAYON SAUCE

A French adaptation of the classic Italian dessert, zabaglione, sabayon is always served as a sauce and here it elevates strawberries and raspberries to sensational heights.

TIME: 20 MINUTES SERVES: 4

| 1 punnet strawberries or blueberries |
| 1 punnet raspberries |
| 3 egg yolks |
| ⅓ cup caster sugar |
| ½ cup brandy, rum or orange-flavoured liqueur |

1 Hull the berries, if needed, and divide between four dessert glasses.
2 Beat the egg yolks and caster sugar in the top half of a double boiler, over gently simmering water, for 2–3 minutes, until creamy.
3 Beating continuously, add the brandy, rum or liqueur in a thin steady stream. Continue to beat for 10–12 minutes, until the sauce is thick. Remove from the heat.
4 Spoon the sauce over the berries and serve immediately.

SERVING SUGGESTION
You can serve this dessert on its own, or accompany it with crisp dessert biscuits

NUTRIENTS PER SERVING: kilojoules 1043, protein 3 g, carbohydrate 36 g (sugar 36 g), fat 4 g (saturated fat 1.3 g), good source of vitamins A, B group and C.

COOK'S SUGGESTION
If you do not have a double boiler, the sabayon can be made in a heatproof bowl placed over a saucepan of gently simmering water. Make sure no water splashes into the bowl.

FAMILY MEALS

Delicious meals need not take forever to cook. These menus mingle wonderful tastes with clever contrasts of colour and texture, yet the preparation and cooking time is cut to the minimum. There are meals for all occasions, packed with healthy goodness, with a selection for vegetarians. Meal planning has never been so easy.

DINNERS FOR FOUR

SPICY PORK BURGERS WITH GUACAMOLE, *page 164*

BAKED ALMOND PEARS, *page 292*

The spicy burgers are a good contrast to the buttery fruit dessert.

IN ADVANCE
• Make the burger mixture, then shape and chill.
• Prepare the pears, then place in a baking dish with the white wine mixture and chill. Prepare the almond topping and put aside. Put the cream or yoghurt into a serving bowl and chill.

BEFORE DINNER
• Preheat the oven for the pears.

• Cook the pork burgers and make the guacamole.
• Add the almond topping to the chilled pears and syrup and put the dessert in the oven to bake while you eat the main course.

CHICKEN WITH MUSHROOM SAUCE, *page 176*
BOILED NEW POTATOES
STEAMED BROCCOLI

OATY PLUM CRUMBLE, *page 298*

The main course with its creamy mushroom sauce is well balanced by a crunchy, lightly spiced crumble.

IN ADVANCE
• Prepare the potatoes and broccoli.
• Prepare and cook the plums, then prepare the crumble topping and chill, separately.

BEFORE DINNER
• Spoon the crumble over the plums. Whip the cream and chill.
• Boil the potatoes. Fry the chicken; put in a low oven to keep warm, then steam the broccoli over the potatoes. Make the sauce; drain the vegetables. Remove the chicken from the oven, increase the heat and

bake the crumble while you eat the main course: chilled crumble takes an extra 5–10 minutes to bake.

QUICK CASSOULET, *page 170*
CRUSTY BREAD
GREEN SALAD

MANGO BRÛLÉE, *page 288*

This sophisticated version of sausages and beans is followed by fruit and creamy yoghurt with a crunchy toffee top.

IN ADVANCE
• Prepare a green leaf salad and a vinaigrette dressing; chill separately.
• Make the mango brûlée and chill.

BEFORE DINNER
• Make the cassoulet. (If you prefer, the main course can be made in advance and then reheated.)
• Toss salad in dressing.

GEMFISH BAKED WITH PESTO, WITH CRUSHED GARLIC POTATOES, *page 114*

STEAMED GREEN BEANS

FLAMBÉED PINEAPPLE AND BANANAS, *page 302*

Firm white fish with a tasty topping, served with a rich mash and simple steamed beans, is followed by a luscious hot dessert.

IN ADVANCE
• Peel and slice the pineapple and whip the cream for the dessert; cover and chill, separately.
• Peel the potatoes; cover with cold water. Prepare some green beans. Skin the gemfish, if necessary.

BEFORE DINNER
• Preheat the oven for the fish. Put the potatoes on to boil. Prepare the fish and put it in the oven to bake. Steam the beans over the potatoes.
• While they are cooking, put the butter and sugar into a large frying pan ready for the dessert. Place the pineapple slices, bananas, rum and matches nearby.
• Drain and mash the potatoes with the garlic, butter and cream, then drain the green beans and serve the main course.

AFTER THE MAIN COURSE
• Peel and dice the bananas and flambé with the pineapple.

PASTA WITH RUSTIC SAUCE, *page 209*

RASPBERRY CRUNCH, *page 288*

The simple sausage sauce is always welcome, while layers of yoghurt, fruit and crunchy oats form the dessert.

IN ADVANCE
• Make the dessert and chill.
• The pasta sauce can be made in advance and reheated, if you prefer.

BEFORE DINNER
• Cook the pasta, and cook or reheat the sauce

GAZPACHO, *page 29*

LAMB NOISETTES WITH SPINACH, *page 162*

FRUITY BREAD AND BUTTER PUDDING, *page 299*

Chilled gazpacho provides a chunky contrast to the tender lamb, while a brilliant pudding rounds off the meal.

IN ADVANCE
• Make the soup and chill.

• Assemble the puddings; chill.

BEFORE DINNER
• Preheat the oven to low. Make the main course and keep warm in the oven while you serve the soup.

AFTER THE FIRST COURSE
• Take the lamb noisettes out of the oven, increase the heat and put the puddings in to bake.

WATERMELON AND FETA CHEESE, *page 58*

COUSCOUS WITH PRAWNS AND MINT, *page 219*

ICE CREAM WITH LEMON BUTTER SAUCE, *page 288*

Juicy melon and salty cheese makes a vivid starter to a main course of shellfish and zucchini followed by a cool dessert.

IN ADVANCE
• Prepare the watermelon and salad leaves and chill, separately.
• Prepare the zucchini and chill.
• Add the passionfruit to the vanilla ice cream and refreeze.

BEFORE DINNER
• Drain the feta cheese and assemble the first course.
• Make the main course and keep warm while you eat the starter.

AFTER THE MAIN COURSE
• Make the lemon butter sauce.

FAMILY MEALS

LUNCHES FOR FOUR

SPANISH-STYLE CHICKEN, *page 179*
CRUSTY BREAD

ZABAGLIONE, *page 300*

The brightly coloured, well-flavoured chicken casserole contrasts well with the frothy texture of the zabaglione.

BEFORE LUNCH
• Make the chicken casserole.
• While the casserole is cooking, assemble the egg yolks and sugar for the zabaglione and put aside.
AFTER THE MAIN COURSE
• Make and serve the zabaglione.

COOL CUCUMBER SOUP, PAGE 28

BAKED FISH PLAKI, *page 113*
RICE
GREEN SALAD WITH OLIVES AND FETA CHEESE

This summery cucumber and yoghurt soup, served cold, makes an easy appetiser to the hot main course .

IN ADVANCE
• Make the soup, cover and chill.
• Prepare some salad leaves and put into a salad bowl; drain and chop the feta cheese; make a salad dressing, then chill, separately.
BEFORE LUNCH
• Preheat the oven to low and boil a kettle of water for the rice. Make the plaki. While the fish is cooking, put some rice on to cook. When both are cooked, keep warm in the oven while you serve the soup.
AFTER THE FIRST COURSE
• Add the feta cheese, some black olives and the dressing to the green salad leaves and toss.

SPICED CARROT AND CHICK PEA FRITTERS, *page 248*

CREAMY LEMON PUDDING, *page 300*

These colourful fritters can be served on focaccia as a change from buns, while the dessert is simple and delicious.

IN ADVANCE
• Make the dessert and chill.
• Prepare the salad leaves and chill.
BEFORE LUNCH
• Make the fritters and serve on buns or in foccaccia with the salad.

YABBY PÂTÉ, *page 52*

BLACKENED WHITE FISH, *page 134*
CAJUN POTATO SALAD, *page 104*

The tasty pâté has enough power to stand up to the strong flavours of the fish and the Cajun-style salad.

IN ADVANCE
• Make the pâté and chill.
• Make the potato salad and chill.
• Crumb the fish and chill.

BEFORE LUNCH
• Preheat the oven; fry the fish and keep warm in the oven while you serve the first course.

VEGETABLE PRIMAVERA, *page 232*

APRICOT AND SOUR CREAM CLAFOUTIS, *page 290*

The sweet batter pudding adds weight to the light main course of fresh vegetables with spinach and ricotta pasta.

IN ADVANCE
• Assemble the apricots in their ovenproof dish, make the batter and the butter topping; put aside.
BEFORE LUNCH
• Preheat the oven to low and put both a large saucepan and a kettle of water on to boil.
• Prepare and cook the vegetables and cook the pasta.
• Pour the batter over the apricots. Bake the dessert while you are enjoying the main course.

BARBECUES FOR FOUR

WARM CHEESE AND TOMATO DIP,
page 74

**SPICED LAMB KEBABS WITH PITA
BREAD,** *page 160*

HONEYED FRUIT KEBABS,
page 296

*The spicy starter prepares the
tastebuds for the kebabs, and can be eaten
while they are cooking. The fruit dessert
ends the meal on a refreshing note.*

IN ADVANCE
• Make the dip up to Step 4.
• Assemble the lamb kebabs, make
the yoghurt dressing, prepare the
salad and chill, separately.
• Make the marinade for the fruit,
assemble the kebabs, pour over the
marinade, then cover and chill.
• Toast the hazelnuts.

BEFORE LUNCH
• Cook the dip and serve.
• Start cooking the lamb kebabs.
Loosely wrap the cut pita breads in
foil and place on the side of the
barbecue to warm. Toss the salad.

AFTER THE MAIN COURSE
• Barbecue the fruit kebabs.

AVOCADO AND WATERCRESS CREAM,
page 74

BEAN AND MUSHROOM BURGERS, *page 248*

*The luscious spread can be enjoyed
with melba toast as the intensely
flavoured burgers are cooking*

IN ADVANCE
• Make the avocado cream and cover
the surface closely; chill. Make the
melba toast and put aside.
• Mix the burger ingredients and
shape; make the relish and chill.

BEFORE LUNCH
• Serve the entrée while you
barbecue the burgers, reheat the
relish and warm the pitta breads.

THAI CHILLI CHICKEN BROCHETTES,
page 72
STEAMED RICE

**FRESH FRUIT SORBET WITH RASPBERRY
COULIS,** *page 294*

*The tangy skewered chicken needs only a
cool and simple dessert to follow.*

IN ADVANCE
• Prepare the chicken and put aside
to marinate for as long as possible.

BEFORE LUNCH
• Put the rice on to cook and
preheat the barbecue.
• Thread the chicken pieces onto
skewers and heat the marinade
while the brochettes are cooking.

AFTER THE MAIN COURSE
• Serve out the sorbet and top with
the coulis.

BRUNCH FOR FOUR

**SALMON PIZZAS WITH YOGHURT
AND DILL,** *page 110*
LOCKET'S SAVOURY, *page 58*
MIXED BEANS WITH PANCETTA, *page 269*

RHUBARB AND STRAWBERRY COMPOTE,
page 303

*Serve this menu buffet-style for a lazy
Sunday meal. The mixed bean dish makes
a refreshing contrast to the two other
savoury dishes, and the clean-flavoured
compote provides a sweet balance.*

IN ADVANCE
• Assemble the salmon pizzas.
• Make the compote and chill.

BEFORE BRUNCH
• Make the mixed beans with
pancetta; this dish can be served at
room temperature.
• Bake the salmon pizzas.
• Make the Locket's savoury.

SPECIAL OCCASIONS

DINNER PARTIES FOR FOUR

GOAT'S CHEESE SOUFFLÉS, *page 50*
SALAD

TUNA WITH WASABI BUTTER, *page 116*
STEAMED NEW POTATOES

SPICED PEACHES WITH
MASCARPONE, *page 293*

*The goat's cheese soufflés, served chilled,
make a strong prelude to the grilled tuna
with its hot butter dressing. The spicy
peaches, served chilled, cut through the
richness of the first two courses.*

IN ADVANCE

• Cook the soufflés, prepare the
salad leaves, fry the bacon then
make the dressing; chill separately.
• Prepare the wasabi butter for the
tuna and freeze.
• Poach the peaches, sweeten the
mascarpone and chill, separately.

BEFORE DINNER

• Preheat the oven and griller. Steam
the potatoes and grill the fish. Take
the wasabi butter out of the freezer
and slice it. Keep the potatoes and
tuna warm in the oven.
• Assemble the salads and carefully
turn out the cheese soufflés on top.

TROPICAL SALAD WITH LIME
DRESSING, *page 49*

DUCK BREASTS WITH BLACKBERRY
SAUCE, *page 191*
NEW POTATOES WITH
CRÈME FRAÎCHE

HOT CHOCOLATE SOUFFLÉS WITH
RUM, *page 286*

*The peppery starter makes a colourful
contrast to duck breasts with a berry
sauce, and the rich chocolate
soufflé is surprisingly filling.*

IN ADVANCE

• Prepare the watercress, pawpaws
and the lime salad dressing and
chill, separately.
• Scrub the new potatoes, put in a
saucepan and cover with cold water.
• Prepare the chocolate soufflé
mixture up to Step 5.

BEFORE DINNER

• Preheat the oven to low.
• Add salt to the potatoes and bring
to the boil. Cook the duck and
blackberry sauce. Drain the cooked
potatoes and keep the main course
warm in the oven.
• Prepare the avocados, arrange the
salad on serving plates and pour
over the lime dressing.

AFTER THE FIRST COURSE

• When you remove the main course
from the oven, raise the heat for the
hot chocolate soufflés.
• Stir the crème fraîche through the
new potatoes.

AFTER THE MAIN COURSE

• Finish making the soufflés and
put in the oven to bake while you
clear away the main course.

SMOKED TROUT WITH PEAR
AND ROCKET, *page 56*

STEAK AND ONION KEBABS, *page 147*
MASHED POTATOES
ORANGE AND SESAME CARROTS,
page 262

STRAWBERRY CLOUDS, *page 288*

*A light salad prepares the way for beef
kebabs with a red wine sauce, served with
sweet carrots, followed by an airy dessert.*

IN ADVANCE

• Make the dessert and chill.

• Prepare the smoked trout and the rocket salad, make the salad dressing and horseradish sauce and chill, separately.

• Prepare and assemble the steak and onion kebabs.

• Prepare the carrots, peel and dice the potatoes, then cover both with cold water.

• Dry fry the sesame seeds ready for the carrots.

BEFORE DINNER

• Preheat the griller to high and the oven to low.

• Prepare the pears, then assemble the smoked trout salad and chill until ready to serve.

• Put the potatoes on to boil. Make the orange sauce for the carrots, then cook the carrots. Grill the steak kebabs.

• Put the kebabs and cooked carrots in the oven while you make the red wine sauce and drain and mash the potatoes

• Put them in the oven while you serve and eat the first course.

A THAI FEAST FOR EIGHT

(use double quantities of each recipe)

VEGETABLES WITH COCONUT DRESSING, *page 88*
THAI NOODLE SALAD, *page 85*
SCALLOPS WITH THAI FLAVOURINGS, *page 133*
THAI BEEF SALAD, *page 86*

A chunky salad contrasts with the creamy scallops and spicy beef, while the noodle dish provides a filling element.

IN ADVANCE

• Prepare the vegetables and make the dressing; chill separately.

• Make the noodle salad, preparing extra snow peas and lemon grass for the scallop dish, then chill.

• Prepare the beef and its salad and chill, separately.

BEFORE DINNER

• Preheat the oven to low. Toss the vegetable salad in its dressing.

• Cook the scallops and keep warm.

• Stir-fry the beef and lemon grass, make the hot dressing and add to its salad ingredients.

AN INDIAN FEAST FOR EIGHT

(use double quantities of each recipe)

PUNJABI POTATO PATTIES, *page 277*
BEEF BALTI, *page 146*
CHICKEN AND SPINACH CURRY, *page 185*
PRAWNS MASALA, *page 137*
RICE

Crisp potato cakes complement the sweet coconut sauce of the prawns, which contrasts with the strong beefy flavour of the balti dish and the light chicken curry.

IN ADVANCE

• Make the potato cakes and chill.

• Prepare the vegetables and beef for the balti; chill. Prepare the chicken and vegetables for the curry; chill.

• Prepare the prawns masala; chill.

• Measure out the spices for each dish onto separate saucers.

BEFORE DINNER

• Put a kettle of water on to boil for the rice, then preheat the oven to low.

• Make the beef balti and the chicken curry; keep warm.

• Meanwhile, put the rice on to cook with the water from the kettle and make the prawns masala.

• Drain the rice and keep warm in the oven, with the masala, while you serve the potato patties.

SPECIAL OCCASIONS

ROMANTIC DINNERS FOR TWO

(use half quantities of each recipe where necessary)

GRILLED OYSTERS, *page 60*

GINGERED PORK ON WILTED WATERCRESS, *page 165*

FRESH BERRIES WITH SABAYON SAUCE, *page 305*

The grilled oysters introduce an impressive presentation of gingered pork, while the sabayon sauce makes an adult-only addition to the luscious summer berries.

IN ADVANCE
• Make the breadcrumb topping and add it to the oysters, then chill.
• Peel the potatoes and cover with cold water. Prepare the pork, mix with the grated ginger, cover and chill. Prepare the watercress; chill. Toast the sesame seeds, then make the omelette and chill.
• Make the sabayon sauce and put aside.
• Prepare the berries.

BEFORE DINNER
• Preheat the griller and the oven.
• Put the sesame omelette in the oven to warm. Cook the pork and its sauce, then keep warm in the oven. Bring the potatoes to the boil and let them cook on a low heat while you prepare and eat the first course.
• Grill the oysters.

AFTER THE FIRST COURSE
• Drain the potatoes, slice the omelette into strips and assemble the main course.

AFTER THE MAIN COURSE
• Gently reheat the sabayon sauce and pour it over the berries.

FRUIT WITH PROSCIUTTO, *page 58*

PAN-FRIED STEAK WITH SHALLOTS IN RED WINE SAUCE, *page 142*
CURRIED PARSNIP PURÉE, *page 262*

GINGER AND CHOCOLATE MASCARPONE, *page 300*

This menu allows you to spend plenty of time with your loved one: the starter merely requires good shopping; the dessert can be made well ahead; and the tempting main course is served with a simple side dish of well-flavoured vegetable purée.

IN ADVANCE
• Arrange your choice of fruit with slices of prosciutto on serving plates and chill.
• Make the mascarpone dessert and chill.
• Make the parsnip purée and chill.

BEFORE DINNER
• Put the curried parsnip purée in a covered dish in a low oven to reheat while you serve the first course.

AFTER THE FIRST COURSE
• Fry the steaks and keep warm while you make the shallots in red wine sauce.

INDEX

ACKNOWLEDGMENTS

Photographs and illustrations in this book are the copyright of Reader's Digest and the photographer and illustrator for each is listed below.

PHOTOGRAPHY

Martin Brigdale 28, 38, 39, 67, 76, 82, 83, 91, 99, 104, 105, 113, 124, 132, 133, 146, 147, 165, 173, 178, 179, 190, 191, 212, 216, 227, 232, 233, 242–243, 258, 259, 263, 266, 267, 274–275, 282, 296, 297
Gus Filgate 11 (*top right, bottom right*), 12–13, 16, 18 (*bottom right*), 37, 40, 45, 51, 56, 62, 63, 94, 95, 102, 103, 114, 127, 136, 137, 140, 154, 155, 176, 177, 184, 185, 200, 201, 208, 209, 211, 218, 219, 228, 229, 237, 239, 245, 246, 249, 251, 256, 257, 260, 261, 264, 283, 285, 290, 291, 292, 299, 304
John Hollingshead 2, 3, 6, 7, 9, 13 (*centre right*), 20 (*bottom right*), 23 (*bottom*), 26–27, 29, 31, 36, 41, 44, 46–47, 48, 52, 57, 58, 59, 66, 69, 71, 72, 75, 77, 78, 79, 80–81, 84, 87, 92–93, 98, 101, 106–107, 108, 111, 112, 115, 118, 119, 123, 125, 126, 128–129, 130, 131, 138–139, 143,
150, 151, 152–153, 157, 161, 162, 166, 174–175, 181, 193, 194, 195, 196, 197, 199, 204–205, 207, 213, 214–15, 221, 225, 230–231, 235, 253, 254–255, 265, 270–271, 279, 280–281, 284–285, 289, 294–295, 301, 305, 306–307, 308–309, 310–311, 312
James Murphy 34, 43, 53, 60, 61, 88, 89, 109, 117, 135, 141, 144, 145, 158, 159, 167, 168, 171, 223, 226, 240, 241, 276
Peter Myers 4-5, 32, 33, 35, 49, 54, 64–65, 70, 73, 85, 86, 96, 97, 110, 120, 121, 148–149, 156, 163, 164, 169, 170, 182, 183, 186–187, 188, 189, 202, 203, 206, 217, 222, 236, 244, 247, 250, 268, 269, 272, 273, 277, 286, 287, 293, 298, 302
Jon Stewart 10, 11 (*top left, bottom left*), 13 (*bottom right*), 14, 15, 17, 18 (*left, top right*), 19, 20 (*left, top right*), 21, 23 (*top right*), 25

ILLUSTRATIONS

Diane Broadley 1, 6, 8, 10, 12, 16, 19, 22, 24, 39, 42, 62, 92, 94, 103, 109, 128, 149 (*bottom*), 207, 214, 237, 243, 262, 270 (*top*)
Stan North 50, 53, 96, 149 (*top*), 179, 186, 188, 210, 220, 252, 268, 270 (*bottom*), 282, 288